W0010505

Funding
Special
Education

NINETEENTH ANNUAL YEARBOOK
OF THE AMERICAN EDUCATION FINANCE ASSOCIATION
1998

Funding Special Education

Edited by:

Thomas B. Parrish
Jay G. Chambers
Cassandra M. Guarino

CORWIN PRESS, INC.
A Sage Publications Company
Thousand Oaks, California

For information:

Corwin Press, Inc.
A Sage Publications Company
2455 Teller Road
Thousand Oaks, California 91320
E-mail: order@corwinpress.com

SAGE Publications Ltd.
6 Bonhill Street
London EC2A 4PU
United Kingdom

SAGE Publications India Pvt. Ltd.
M-32 Market
Greater Kailash I
New Delhi 110 048 India

Printed in the United States of America

Library of Congress Cataloging-in-Publication Data

Main entry under title:
Funding special education / edited by Thomas B. Parrish, Jay G. Chambers, Cassandra M. Guarino.
    p. cm. — (Yearbook of the American Education Finance Association; v. 19)
    Includes bibliographical references and index.
    ISBN 0-8039-6624-5 (cloth : acid-free paper)
    1. Handicapped children—Education—Finance. 2. Special education—United States—Finance. 3. Special education—Finance. 4. Handicapped children—Education—United States—Finance. 5. Handicapped children—Education—Finance. I. Parrish, Thomas. II. Chambers, Jay G. III. Guarino, Cassandra M. IV. Series: Annual yearbook of the American Education Finance Association; 19th.
    LC3981 .F87 1998
    379.1'216'0973—dc21   98-40250

This book is printed on acid-free paper.

99 00 01 02 03 04 05 10 9 8 7 6 5 4 3 2 1

Corwin Editorial Assistant: Kristen L. Gibson
Production Editor: Astrid Virding
Designer/Typesetter: Danielle Dillahunt
Indexer: Teri Greenberg
Cover Designer: Tracy E. Miller

Contents

Foreword

With the passage of the Education for All Handicapped Children Act (Pub. L. 94-142) in 1975, programs and related services for students with disabilities became a major component of public education in the United States. This landmark legislation—renamed the Individuals with Disabilities Education Act (IDEA) in 1990—enshrined into law and practice the right to a free and appropriate public education for all children and youth with disabilities. The IDEA Amendments of 1997 (Pub L. 105-17) reauthorized this legislation, with significant new mandates, including changes in the law's fiscal provisions. Collectively, these statutes represent bold and significant milestones in the implementation and development of federal special education policy and finance.

Whereas the federal government has provided leadership and funding support under the IDEA, the provision of special education services in this country has been jointly funded by local and state education agencies, along with federal appropriations. Although many children with disabilities were unserved or underserved prior to the passage of Pub. L. 94-142, many states and localities had a strong history of providing education and support services for children with disabilities long before passage of the IDEA. In fact, the majority of funding for special education services in this country continues to come from states and local school districts.

This rich history and the prominence that special education has assumed as a major component of the overall education enterprise render this American Education Finance Association Yearbook on special education finance an important addition to the literature on education funding. Despite the fact that the national expenditure on special education programs and services is estimated to be over $32 billion per year, much of the traditional scholarly work relating to education finance has tended to disregard issues unique to special education. At the same time, unprecedented levels of interest in these topics have surfaced in the national media over the past few years. For example, feature articles on special education spending have appeared in *U.S. News & World Report*, *The New York Times*, and the *Wall Street Journal*. A segment on this topic was also featured in a recent edition of television's *60 Minutes*.

Several reasons may account for the high level of interest. Whereas much of this publicity has focused on concerns about rising costs associated with special education, a recent *Phi Delta Kappan-Gallup Poll of the Public's Attitudes Toward the Public Schools* showed 47% of the respondents saying that *too little* of the total education budgets is being spent on students with special needs, whereas 41% said that current levels of spending are about right (Elam, Rose, & Gallup, 1996).

There is also increased attention to the relationship between special education funding and special education services. Special education policy makers are increasingly aware that the nature of the provisions underlying special education funding has had an impact on the ways in which special education programming is designed and provided. Indeed, special education funding policy has the potential to create incentives that may foster "best practices" or clash with the letter or spirit of federal and state law. Other important considerations relate to special education effectiveness. It is vitally important that special education dollars be spent well—especially for the children who receive these services, for whom the stakes are high. Issues such as these have, in fact, prompted the federal government and over two thirds of the states to actively reexamine or change the ways in which they fund special education programs.

This Yearbook represents a significant contribution to the description and analysis of special education funding issues that are challenging the states, the nation, and our neighbors abroad as we approach the 21st century. The U.S. Department of Education is pleased to support this volume, which is coedited by researchers from the Center for Special Education Finance, a national research center funded by the Department's Office of Special Education Programs.

LOU DANIELSON

OFFICE OF SPECIAL EDUCATION PROGRAMS (OSEP)

Reference

Elam, S. M., Rose, L. C., & Gallup, A. M. (1996, September). The 29th annual Phi Delta Kappa/Gallup poll of the public's attitudes toward the public schools. *Phi Delta Kappan, 78*(1), 41-59.

Preface

THOMAS B. PARRISH

CASSANDRA M. GUARINO

Special education occupies an increasingly prominent position in the world of education and school finance. Although the extent to which this continued expansion is a positive development is debatable, the national expenditure on special education is currently estimated to be about $35 billion per year with over 10% of U.S. school children in special education programs. If it was ever possible or appropriate to divorce special education programming from larger education finance concerns, that era has long passed.

The question of how special education programs are best incorporated and considered within the context of traditional education finance concerns, however, is complex. The vast majority of special education children spend most of their time in general education programs and have education needs that are quite similar to those of the general population. At the same time, a minority of these students were once excluded from the right to a free and public education and have needs that are very specialized. Given this history of exclusion and the very specialized education requirements of some of these children, the additional procedural safeguards and entitlements they receive clearly seem warranted.

As an example, it has long been documented that, on average, about twice as much is spent on special education students than on their general education counterparts (Kakalik, Furry, Thomas, & Carney, 1981; Moore, Walker, & Holland, 1982; Rossmiller, Hale, & Frohreich, 1970). How great the disparity in program funding *should* be between general and special education children, however, is still a matter of controversy. Such concerns are at the heart of the equity, adequacy, accountability, and productivity debates that have long engaged policy makers and scholars of education finance.

These concepts are difficult to define and operationalize in the world of policy formation without the additional issues associated with special education programs. This may be why the analogy of special education programs being conducted in portable classrooms in school parking lots seems to pertain to discussions of general education program and fiscal reform. Often, perhaps because special education is seen as "special," the implications of proposed education program and fiscal reforms are not fully considered for these programs. Too often, special education is excluded from the mainstream literature and not invited to the forums in which policy reforms are being discussed and decided. It is hoped that this volume will contribute to a fuller incorporation of special education fiscal policy concerns into the mainstream of the education finance literature and fiscal policy discussions at all levels of governance.

The first group of chapters in this book discusses fiscal and program policy pertaining to special education funding in the United States and in Europe. In the opening chapter, Deborah A. Verstegen traces the history of federal special education legislation, contextualizing it within the civil rights movement. Inspired by minority rights advocates, proponents for children with disabilities began in the 1960s to formulate their claims in terms of "rights." As a result of their efforts, a new title devoted specifically to children with disabilities, Title VI, was included in the Elementary and Secondary Education Act in 1966. The subsequent transformations of this initial legislation into the Education of the Handicapped Act, the Education for All Handicapped Children Act, the Individuals with Disabilities Education Act, various amendments, and the recent IDEA Reauthorization are described in the chapter.

The chapter titled "Consolidating Categorical Educational Programs at the Local Level," by Margaret J. McLaughlin, discusses efforts to pool resources normally earmarked for separate programs, such as special education, bilingual education, and Title I, in order to optimize educational quality for all students. Based on data obtained from interviews with school administrators, McLaughlin finds that a culture of collaboration, a significant degree of local autonomy, and a focus on systemic reform are needed as contextual preconditions for consolidation. Although a movement towards consolidation is slowly gathering force, most school systems still have a long way to go before they achieve the flexibility currently being promoted at the federal and state level.

Margaret E. Goertz et al. describe current efforts to incorporate special education reform into the larger scheme of standards-based reform. Currently, standards-based reform has been characterized by the introduction of challenging performance standards, an accountability system based on student assessments, and a restructuring of the governance system in favor of decentralization and community involvement. At present, many members of the special education community are promoting the development of performance indicators, parental involvement, and links to accountability for special education students. Such efforts, however, are often fraught with technical and political problems. More unity and public support are needed to ensure that this population of students gains full access to the benefits of the reform process.

The link between special education funding systems and the integration of special education students into regular education in Europe is described by Meijer et al. The authors present research on the integration and funding status in four countries: Austria, England, Denmark, and the Netherlands. These particular countries present a notable amount of variation in their funding policies and, thus, in the resulting structure of incentives and disincentives with regard to integration practices. The authors synthesize their findings and then present an analytical framework to guide further research on the impact of funding on integration.

The second section of this book presents methodological and policy profiles from the states. In "The Patterns of Expenditures on Students with Disabilities: A Methodological and Empirical Analysis," Jay G. Chambers uses data from a sample of individual special education students to examine the factors affecting variations in expenditures for students with disabilities. The chapter is based largely upon a study conducted by the Center for Special Education Finance (CSEF) for the Commonwealth of Massachusetts following the Education Reform Act passed by the state's legislature in 1993. The study uses a resource cost model approach to explain expenditure patterns for students with disabilities. Chambers finds that cost is affected by primary disability, placement, and levels of need for adaptation of curricular materials, behavioral supports, and physical/medical supports. Perceptions of student needs and the relationship to inclusionary practices as factors in cost variations are also discussed.

Robert E. Feir reports on the effects of reforms to Pennsylvania's special education system in 1990 and 1991. Before 1990, Pennsylvania had the distinction of being the only state to have a statutory requirement to pay 100% of the "excess costs" of educating special education students. A rapid increase in the proportion of students targeted for special education during the 1980s and a corresponding growth in the educational budget deficit prompted the legislature to shift fiscal responsibility for special education expenditures from the state to the districts. Feir quantifies the effects on patterns of expenditure and service delivery during the four years following reform and compares these to the stated intentions of the policy. The state succeeded in capping its growing debt and in changing service delivery patterns, but the desired changes in expenditure allocations to special education met with mixed success at the district level.

Lankford and Wyckoff discuss the causes and effects of the large increase in the percentage of school district allocations to special education that occurred between 1980 and 1993 in New York State. They apply descriptive analysis and econometric modeling to state-level data in order to identify the factors generating the change and to determine whether or not it has reduced resources going to general education students. They find that the growth in special education expenditures over the 13-year period under consideration resulted from a combination of increased expenditures per disabled student and an increased number of students with disabilities.

Fruchter, Parrish, and Berne focus on proposed special education finance reforms for New York City. The authors point out that despite improvements in special education services over the past twenty years, such factors as inadequate accountability, over-reliance on separate settings, over-representation of students of color in special education, inappropriate referrals to special education, and siphoning resources to students who are not disabled have continued to produce limited outcomes. Proposed reforms center around a school-based model that restructures schools and classrooms, deploys personnel in new ways, and reconceptualizes instruction and assessment. Fiscal reforms are proposed that are shaped by the desired education initiatives, rather than the reverse which often occurs in many settings. Financial incentives and disincentives are used to encourage improved educational outcomes.

The final group of chapters discusses trends and new developments in special education funding. First, Parrish and Wolman summarize results from a survey of the states conducted by the national Center for Special Education Finance (CSEF). Despite commonly cited concerns that special education costs are rising out of control, Parrish and Wolman note that much less is known than may be expected about these costs. Only half the states are able to report what is spent on special education programming, and many of those cannot do so with high levels of confidence. This chapter provides the best data available about special education revenues, costs, enrollments, and expenditures across the states and for the nation. The authors conclude that interest in restructuring education is likely to grow and focus increasingly on programs for children with disabilities. Various state systems for funding special education and corresponding reform initiatives are described.

The next chapter, by Verstegen, discusses recent developments in the state high court treatment of issues of equity and adequacy in school funding systems. Whereas early state court decisions were forced to rely upon the equal rights protection clause of the U.S. Constitution in addressing allegations of unjust financial disparity within the educational system, most of the fifty states have, over time, incorporated guarantees of equity and adequacy directly into their own constitutions and education articles. A recent spate of claims that these state provisions have been violated has ushered in a "new wave" of school finance litigation. The new cases have enabled the judicial branch of state government to exert a direct and powerful influence on the reform of education finance systems. Verstegen provides detailed descriptions of three high profile cases from Alabama, Wyoming, and Ohio.

Considerable challenges face the school finance community relating to the operationalization of such concepts as equity, adequacy, accountability, and efficiency within a policy environment. Although each of these concepts focuses on a specific aspect of public education, in practice, they are often linked. Each requires a more complete consideration of what is being produced through the provision of public education services and how it can be measured. Although more work is needed to clarify these standards, it is already evident, as is pointed out throughout the chapters in this volume, that the kinds of dual service systems that have been created for general and special education students can be better integrated in order to improve outcomes related to all four of these important concepts. Special education has become a vital component of the nation's overall education system. It is essential that future work to address fiscal policy challenges include the special needs of children with disabilities along with those of all children.

References

Kakalik, J. S., Furry, W. S., Thomas, M. A., & Carney, M. F. (1981). *The cost of special education* (A Rand Note). Santa Monica, CA: RAND.

Moore, M. T., Walker, L. J., & Holland, R. P. (1982). *Fine tuning special education finance: A guide for state policy makers.* Princeton, NJ: Education Testing Service.

Rossmiller, R. A., Hale, J. A., & Frohreich, L. E. (1970). *Education programs for exceptional children: Resource configuration and costs.* Madison: University of Wisconsin, Department of Educational Administration.

About the Contributors

Robert Berne is the Vice President for Academic Development at New York University (NYU). Previously, he was Dean of NYU's Robert F. Wagner Graduate School of Public Service, where he has been on the faculty since 1976. He is an active researcher in educational policy and school finance, focusing on the area of equity. He has written and edited numerous books and articles on education policy and government finance, including *Hard Lessons: Public Schools and Privatization* (with Carol Ascher and Norm Fruchter), *The Measurement of Equity in School Finance* (with Leanna Stiefel), and *The Relationships Between Financial Reporting and the Measurement of Financial Condition.* He was Director of Policy Research for the New York State Temporary Commission on State Aid to Local School Districts (Salerno Commission) and Executive Director of the Temporary State Commission on New York City School Governance (Marchi Commission). He chaired The Outcome Equity Study Group for the New York State Commissioner of Education, Thomas Sobol, and is the coeditor of *Outcome Equity in Education.*

Jay G. Chambers is the Co-Director and Senior Research Fellow of the Education and Public Sector Finance Center at the American Institutes for Research (AIR). He is also codirects the Center for Special Education Finance (CSEF), which is currently housed at AIR. He is a nationally recognized expert in school finance and educational cost analysis.

Over the past 24 years, he has directed and been involved in many national and state-level studies related to programmatic and resource costs in education and has published numerous articles in professional journals and books on this subject. His research and writing has covered virtually every major educational or related service program, from early intervention to vocational education for children, from birth through secondary education. He has also written and conducted projects working directly with local school districts, state departments of education, and the National Center for Education Statistics to improve the quality of fiscal and cost information for school decision making. Prior to his current position at AIR, he was president of the Associates for Education Finance and Planning in California, 1981 to 1990; from 1978 to 1985, he served as the Associate Director of the Institute for Research on Educational Finance and Governance located at Stanford University; and he has been a faculty member at the Universities of Rochester and Chicago. He has been a consultant to state legislatures and served as an expert witness on issues related to school finance. He holds a PhD in economics from Stanford University.

Robert E. Feir is President of EdStrat21, an education strategies and project management consulting group. He also is CEO and Managing Partner of the Learning Resources Group, Inc., providing consultation, training, and technical assistance to help employers lead education transformation efforts in their local communities. He has been executive director of the Pennsylvania State Board of Education, the Pennsylvania Senate Education Committee, and the Pennsylvania Business-Education Partnership. Prior to his state-level work, he was a teacher, curriculum coordinator, school superintendent, and assistant director of an intermediate unit (regional education service agency). He holds a PhD in political science from Pennsylvania State University and master's degrees in political science from the State University of New York at Albany and in education administration from Bucknell University.

Norm Fruchter helped found the Institute for Education and Social Policy at New York University and currently serves as director. From

1987 to 1996, he was Program Advisor for Education at the Aaron Diamond Foundation and helped develop the New Visions Project that produced almost 20 new, small New York City public secondary schools. During the 1980s, he conducted school change studies for Advocates for Children of New York and evaluations of national school improvement programs for the Academy for Educational Development (AED). With several AED colleagues, he coauthored *New Directions in Parent Involvement*. From 1983 to 1993, he served as an elected member of the Brooklyn district school board—the last 4 years, he served as president. He coauthored *Hard Lessons: Public Schools and Privatization* in 1996 and *Choosing Equality: The Case for Democratic Schooling*, which won the 1988 American Library Association's Oboler Prize for Intellectual Freedom. During the 1970s, he helped organize and direct an alternative high school for dropouts in Newark, New Jersey, a bachelor's degree program for public sector workers at Saint Peter's College in Jersey City, and a program to train parents to work for school improvement in a dozen New Jersey cities. He wrote the novels *Coat Upon a Stick* (1962) and *Single File* (1970) and edited *New Left Review* from 1960 to 1962 and *Studies on the Left* from 1965 to 1970. He made the films *Troublemakers,* an award-winning documentary about Students for a Democratic Society's Newark organizing project in 1966; *Summer '68,* which was about the movements that coalesced at the 1968 Democratic Convention in Chicago; and *People's War,* a documentary shot in North Vietnam in 1969. He is also a founding member of NEWSREEL, chronicler of the civil rights, antiwar, and student movements.

Margaret E. Goertz is Professor in the Graduate School of Education at the University of Pennsylvania, a codirector of the Consortium for Policy Research in Education and a codirector of the Center for Policy Research on the Impact of General and Special Education Reform. Previously, she was Executive Director of the Education Policy Research Division of Educational Testing Service. Her research focuses on issues of education finance, state education reform policies, and state and federal programs for special needs students. Her current research activities include studies of standards-based reform in education and the allocation of school-level resources.

Cassandra M. Guarino, MA, is a Research Scientist at American Institutes for Research. She holds advanced degrees in economics and education policy analysis from Stanford University and is currently working toward a doctorate in the economics of education. Her research interests include education finance, returns to education, human capital investment choices, and medical education. Her background includes teaching, corporate management, advanced statistical skills, and both qualitative and quantitative research in labor economics and medical education.

Hamilton Lankford is Associate Professor of Economics and Public Policy at the State University of New York at Albany. He received his PhD in Economics from the University of North Carolina at Chapel Hill and was a dissertation fellow at the Brookings Institution. His current research focuses on the economics of education. He has collaborated with Jim Wyckoff on a series of projects examining public and private school choice and the allocation of school expenditures. He was awarded an NSF-ASSA-Census Fellowship to examine the effects of school choice and residential location choice on the racial composition of urban schools. He is also engaged in research examining the implicit subsidy to school districts from the property tax deduction on federal and state income taxes.

Margaret J. McLaughlin has been involved in special education all of her professional career, beginning as a teacher of students with serious emotional and behavior disorders. She earned her PhD at the University of Virginia and has held positions at the former U.S. Office of Education and the University of Washington. Currently, she directs a research institute within the College of Education at the University of Maryland, where she directs several national projects investigating educational reforms and students with disabilities. She recently co-chaired the National Academy of Sciences Committee on Goals 2000 and Students with Disabilities. She teaches graduate courses in disability policy and has written extensively in this area.

Cor J. W. Meijer earned his PhD at the University of Groningen, the Netherlands. He is currently a staff member of the European Agency for Development in Special Needs Education, located in Middelfart, Denmark. His main task is to gather and analyze data on special provision and on financing of special needs education in Europe. He also coordinates a nationwide evaluation of the current integration policy in the Netherlands. He has conducted several studies on special and regular education and is mainly involved in comparative research on special education and integration. He has acted as consultant on special needs issues to the Organization for Economic Cooperation and Development and various other national and international bodies. He is the coeditor of *New Perspectives on Special Education* and of *Inclusive Education: A Global Agenda* and serves on different editorial boards, one of which is the *International Journal of Inclusive Education.*

Thomas B. Parrish is Principal Research Scientist at the American Institutes for Research in Palo Alto, California, where he codirects the Education and Public Sector Finance Group. He also codirects the national Center for Special Education Finance funded by the Office of Special Education Programs at the U.S. Department of Education. Currently, he also directs the national Targeting and Resource Allocation Study of Title 1 and other federal programs. He has become a national expert in the area of the costs of, and fiscal policies for, special education programs. He has directed and participated in numerous cost analysis, fiscal policy, and evaluation projects conducted for federal, state, and local agencies over the past 15 years. He has appeared before numerous legislative bodies and written extensively on issues relating to special education finance and state funding formulas. He coedited the most recent edition of the *Journal of Education Finance,* which was dedicated to issues pertaining to special education.

Sip Jan Pijl, PhD, is Senior Researcher at the Groningen Institute for Educational Research, University of Groningen, the Netherlands. He is involved in studies on the integration of students with special needs into regular education and has conducted international comparative research on integration. He currently works part-time for the European Agency for Development in Special Needs Education.

Suzanne M. Raber is an educational researcher who specializes in program evaluation and policy analysis in such diverse areas within kindergarten through 12th-grade education as reform and restructuring, special education, school-to-work, mathematics and science enrichment, and school finance. She has conducted research at local, state, and national levels for a large metropolitan school district, a social science consulting firm, and a national association representing state boards of education. She holds an MS from Cornell University in developmental psychology. Currently, she is serving as a senior research associate for a school district in the Washington, DC, metropolitan area.

Virginia Roach is the Deputy Executive Director of the National Association of State Boards of Education. There, she is the principal investigator for the Center for Policy Research on the Impact of General and Special Education Reform. She is nationally known for her work in special education policy, particularly the inclusion of students with disabilities in general education programs and reform. In addition to authoring several articles and papers, she has reviewed numerous documents and policies for states and local districts, advised state and local policy makers and administrators on creating inclusive schools, and provided workshops to teachers and paraprofessionals on adapting instruction for students with disabilities. She also works on teacher development and has provided extensive technical assistance to states that wish to revise their teacher licensure and certification policies. She earned her EdD at Teachers College, Columbia University.

Deborah A. Verstegen is Professor of Education Policy and Finance at the University of Virginia, Curry School of Education. She has served on the American Education Finance Association Board of Directors, has been editor of the *Journal of Education Finance* and is currently its education policy editor, and is a member of the University Council for Education Administration Finance Center advisory board as well as numerous editorial boards and panels. Her research focus is equal opportunity in state and federal policy. She has written over 130 articles, reviews, and books in this and related areas. She was fellow at Oxford University (UK) and received an Alumni Achievement Award from the University of Wisconsin in 1997.

Sietske Waslander is Sociologist and Researcher at the University of Groningen, the Netherlands. She coordinates an international Organisation for Economic Cooperation and Development project aimed at developing indicators for cross-curriculum competencies. Other work reflects her wide interest, with publications on topics such as curriculum effects in the labor market, school choice, funding of special education, and downward mobility. She is currently preparing a PhD on markets and democracy in education.

Jean Wolman is Research Scientist at the American Institutes for Research, where she has directed or participated in a variety of projects related to special education finance, assessment, transition, and self-determination. As Manager of Dissemination for the Center for Special Education Finance for the past 5 years, she has produced, edited, and disseminated newsletters, policy papers, and briefs, and Web pages for educators, policy makers, and researchers across the country. She holds an MA in Education from the University of Chicago.

James Wyckoff is Associate Professor of Public Administration and Policy and Economics at the State University of New York at Albany. He received his PhD in Economics from the University of North Carolina at Chapel Hill. His research is focused largely on the economics of education. Over the past several years, in collaboration with Hamilton Lankford, he has pursued two lines of research. The first addresses issues of public and private school choice, examining factors relevant to these choices and how these choices affect the racial and economic characteristics and the academic quality of students in public and private schools. The second examines how public schools allocate resources. This work explores changing resource allocations over time, with particular focus on teacher compensation and special education.

PART I

Fiscal Program And Policy

ONE

Civil Rights and Disability Policy
A HISTORICAL PERSPECTIVE

DEBORAH A. VERSTEGEN

Early History and Background[1]

Prior to the 1960s, public education for exceptional children and youth depended on the "generosity of private charity and the largesse of state and local governments" (Tweedie, 1983, p. 49). Some states authorized special education programs, but they remained discretionary; in other states, compulsory attendance laws excluded children with disabilities; and in still others, where special education programs did exist, they remained largely a caretaking venture. Children with disabilities who were fortunate enough to gain entry into public schools often faced "isolation and minimal services," and a disproportionate number of racial minorities were classified as handicapped and segregated into special programs and classrooms (p. 49).

During the 1960s, spurred by the claims of other minorities, advocates for children with disabilities began to speak in terms of rights, drawing their inspiration from economically disadvantaged groups and the civil rights movements at the time. Like racial, ethnic, and linguistic minorities and the poor, children with disabilities were a "minority excluded from participation in politics and their share of society's affluence" (Tweedie, 1983, p. 51). Reformers recognized the political powerlessness of individuals with disabilities, similar to that of individuals who were the focus of the civil rights and poverty movements; therefore, a similar judicial strategy was pursued.

The key legal precedents for judicial reform were based on the right to equal educational opportunity established in *Brown v. Board of Education*, the 1954 Supreme Court decision that found that racially separate schools were unconstitutional, and *Goldberg v. Kelly*, a case involving public assistance (Tweedie, 1983, p. 54). The legal strategy for children with disabilities would rely on similar constitutionally required guarantees for equal opportunity but focus on state, not federal, constitutions.

Right to education litigation for children with disabilities proliferated across the country during the last half of the 1960s and into the 1970s as activists escalated pressure on schools and the judiciary for reform. These suits threatened school districts with expensive litigation, disruption, and the complexity of implementing subsequent court-ordered programs while providing reformers a viable bargaining tool to use in securing changes in school policies and legislation. However, constraints on school resources posed a major barrier to reform, and "afraid that litigation and court-ordered programs would cut into existing programs, and unable to provide needed reforms on their own, schools sought financial assistance from Congress" (Tweedie, 1983, p. 50).

Title VI and the Elementary and Secondary Education Act

In 1966, Congressional hearings before an ad hoc Subcommittee on the Education and Labor Committee revealed that only about one third of the 5.5 million children with disabilities in the country were being provided appropriate special education services. According to a House Committee report issued at the time, the remaining two thirds were either totally excluded from public schools or "sitting idly in regular classrooms awaiting the time when they were old enough to 'drop out.' "[2] Federal programs directed at children with disabilities, the Committee reported, were "minimal, fractionated, uncoordinated, and frequently given a low priority in the education community."[3]

In response to this situation, in 1966, Congress added a new Title VI to the Elementary and Secondary Education Act (Pub. L. 89-750). Under this new authority, a program of grants to the states was established to assist with the education of children with disabilities. The legislation also created a national Advisory Committee on Handicapped Children and mandated the creation of a Bureau of Education for the Handicapped within the U.S. Office of Education. The Bureau was to be responsible for administering programs and projects relating to the education and training of children and youth with disabilities, including programs and projects for training teachers and for conducting research in the field of special education.

Education of the Handicapped Act

In 1970, the Elementary and Secondary Education Amendments repealed Title VI (as of July, 1971) and created a separate act, titled the Education of the Handicapped Act (EHA; 1971), which consolidated a number of previously separate federal grant authorities relating to children with disabilities. This new authority, the precursor of the current Individuals with Disabilities Education Act, was the first freestanding statute for children with disabilities.

The EHA was divided into 7 parts. Part A set forth the title of the bill and the definitions and provided for the Bureau of Education for the Handicapped and the National Advisory Committee on Handicapped Children, the acquisition of equipment, and the construction of necessary facilities. Part B authorized grants to the states and outlying areas to assist them in initiating, expanding, and improving programs for the education of children with disabilities. Part C authorized grants for regional resource centers; centers for deaf-blind children; experimental preschool and early education programs; and research, innovation, training, and dissemination activities in connection with these centers. Part D authorized grants to institutions of higher education to assist in recruiting and training special education and physical education personnel. Part E authorized grants for research relating to education and recreation for exceptional children and youth. Part F authorized the National Center on Educational Media and Materials for the Handicapped to provide for the Bureau of Education for the Handicapped, a centralized agency to coordinate the communication system between various aspects of comprehensive media and materials development, and a delivery system for making instructional media and technology available to all programs in education for children with disabilities. Part G authorized special programs for children with specific learning disabilities.

The Education Amendments of 1974

To help states faced with meeting court- or legislatively imposed "right to education" mandates, the Education Amendments of 1974 (Pub. L. 93-380) significantly expanded the authority and appropriations of the basic grant-to-states program (Part B) for the education of children with disabilities. According to a Senate Committee report on the legislation, "Increased awareness of the educational needs of handicapped children and landmark court decisions establishing the right to education for handicapped children pointed to the necessity of an expanded Federal fiscal role."[4]

The 1974 amendments enhanced provisions for the protection of exceptional children's rights by due process procedures and the assurance of confidentiality, laid the basis for comprehensive planning, and authorized a sharp increase in funds to assist states in educating children with disabilities in the public schools. Pub. L. 93-380 also required the states to establish a goal of providing full educational opportunities for all children with disabilities and submit detailed plans and timetables for achieving this goal. In addition, the Act provided procedural safeguards for use in identifying, evaluating, and placing children with disabilities into programs and mandated that such youngsters be integrated into regular classes whenever possible. It also required the states to provide assurances that testing and evaluation materials would be selected and administered on a nondiscriminatory basis and placed a priority on the use of EHA funds for children not receiving an education program. Last, Pub. L. 93-380 elevated the head of the Bureau of Education for the Handicapped to the status of Deputy Commissioner of Education.

A series of landmark court cases established in law the right to education for all children with disabilities. In 1971, the Federal Eastern District Court of Pennsylvania approved a consent agreement establishing that every school-age mentally challenged child in the Commonwealth of Pennsylvania had a right to a public education (*Pennsylvania Association for Retarded Children [PARC] v. Commonwealth of Pennsylvania.*)[5] The PARC strategy included extensive professional and expert testimony indicating that all children can learn and that education benefits all children, including children with disabilities. They "insisted that education be seen as individuals learning to cope and function within their environments" (Tweedie, 1983, p. 53). PARC was followed by a court order from the U.S. District Court in the District of Columbia, *Mills v. Board of Education of the District of Columbia*,[6] restating the same principle but extending it to all exceptional children. The court also established procedural safeguards for children with disabilities and addressed the issue of funding directly:

> The defendants are required by the Constitution of the United States, the District of Columbia Code, and their own regulations to provide a publicly-supported education for these "exceptional" children. Their failure to fulfill this clear duty to include and retain these children in the public school system, or otherwise provide them with publicly-supported education, and their failure to afford them due process hearings and periodical review, cannot be excused by the claim that there are insufficient funds.[7]

PARC and *Mills* served as models for the movement's litigation strategy. Following these initial decisions in 1971 and 1972 and with similar decisions in 27 states by 1974, the Senate Committee on Labor and Public Welfare concluded, "it is clear today that this 'right to education' is no longer in question."

Education for All Handicapped Children Act

In 1975, extensive hearings to extend and amend the Education of the Handicapped Act, held by the House Subcommittee on Select Education and the Senate Subcommittee on the Handicapped, revealed the dire need to provide financial assistance to states to assist them in providing a free and appropriate education to all children and, thus, to substantially extend the law.

Testimony indicated that a large percentage of children with disabilities remained unserved or underserved across the United States, often due to state financial constraints. Statistics provided by the Bureau of Education for the Handicapped estimated that of the more than 8 million children (between birth and 21 years) with disabilities requiring special education and related services, only half (3.9 million) were receiving an appropriate education; 1.75 million children with disabilities—usually those with the most severe disabilities—were receiving no education at all, and 2.5 million children with disabilities were receiving an inappropriate education.[8] According to the Committee,

> The long-range implications of these statistics are that public agencies and taxpayers will spend billions of dollars over the lifetimes of these individuals to maintain such persons as dependents and in a minimally acceptable lifestyle. With proper education services, many would be able to become productive citizens, contributing to society instead of being forced to remain burdens. Others, through such services, would increase their independence, thus reducing their dependence on society.[9]

The Committee on Education and Labor in the U.S. House of Representatives, reporting the bill from Committee, found that financial constraints were impinging on a disabled child's right to an education across the states, stating, "state financial resources are frequently inadequate to the task of providing an education for all handicapped children."[10]

The Committee on Labor and Public Welfare in the U.S. Senate concurred: "States have made substantial efforts to comply; however, lack of financial resources have prevented the implementation of the various decisions which have been rendered."[11] The Committee summed up the situation thusly:

> It is this Committee's belief that the Congress must take a more active role under its responsibility for equal protection of the laws

to guarantee that handicapped children are provided equal educational opportunity. It can no longer be the policy of the Government to merely establish an unenforceable goal requiring all children to be in school.[12]

Subsequently, passage of the Education for All Handicapped Children Act (Pub. L. 94-142) in 1975 amended the provisions for state assistance under Part B of the EHA and marked a significant milestone in the nation's efforts to educate exceptional children and youth. The Act so expanded the Part B program into a multi-billion-dollar federal commitment to assisting state and local education agencies in providing appropriate education services for children with disabilities.

As signed into law, Pub. L. 94-142 included several major provisions, such as providing a new state funding formula based on need rather than population, providing a new intrastate funding formula that required 75% of funds to be distributed to localities according to need, and providing a limit on the number of students the federal government would support in each state at 12% of the population. The 12% limitation was intended to discourage "over-labeling" of children.[13] The Senate Committee stipulated that the funding provided under Pub. L. 94-142 was to assist states in carrying out their responsibilities under state laws rather than to provide full federal funding for all special education costs, stating,

The Committee rejects the argument that the Federal Government should only mandate services to handicapped children if, in fact, funds are appropriated in sufficient amounts to cover the full cost of this education. The Committee recognizes the States' primary responsibility to uphold the Constitution of the United States and their own State Constitutions and State laws as well as the Congress' own responsibility under the 14th Amendment to assure equal protection of the law.[14]

The Act required that children with disabilities be provided a free and appropriate education, mandated an individual education plan for each child with a disability, and created incentives for providing services to preschool children ages 3 to 5 years.

Pub. L. 94-142 also included new or expanded definitions for, for example, free and appropriate public education, related services, and special education. The term *special education* in the Act was defined as "specially designed instruction, at no cost to parents or guardians to meet the unique needs of a child with disabilities, including classroom instruction, instruction in physical education, home instruction, and instruction in hospitals and institutions."[15] In addition, the Committee encouraged the combination of local educational agencies or the creation of special school districts to meet the special needs of children with disabilities.[16]

The Education of All Handicapped Children Act established a new entitlement formula, to go into effect at the close of September 31, 1977, and remain in effect permanently thereafter.[17] The maximum amount of the grant that a state was entitled to receive was equal to the number of children with disabilities, ages 3 through 21 years, receiving special education and related services, multiplied by a specified percentage of the national average per pupil expenditure (APPE) for public elementary and secondary schools in the United States. The Act called for a gradually increasing percentage of federal aid, beginning with 5% of the APPE in fiscal year (FY) 1978, to 10% of the APPE in FY 1979, to 20% in FY 1980, to 30% in FY 1981, and to 40% in FY 1982 and succeeding fiscal years. A hold-harmless provision was added that stipulated that no state would receive an amount in any fiscal year that was less than the amount the state received in the fiscal year ending September 30, 1977, the final year of the previous population-based formula.

Beginning in 1979 and thereafter, 25% of the funds allocated to states could be used by the state educational agency (SEA); of this, 5% or $200,000 could be used for administration of the Act. The remainder (20%) could be used by the SEA for support and direct services but was to be matched on a program basis from nonfederal funds. Of the funds allocated to states, 75% were required to be distributed to local educational agencies and intermediate educational units in the state in an amount that bears the same ratio of 3-to-21-aged children receiving services in a local education agency or intermediate unit to the aggregate number of such children in the state. To receive funds, the local education agency or intermediate unit had to be eligible to receive at least $7,500 and submit an application that met the requirements of the Act.

Children with disabilities, placed in a private school or educational agency by a local education agency, were also entitled to receive special education and related services at no cost to their parents or guardians. A ratable adjustment was applied if sums appropriated were insufficient to meet the full obligations under the Act.

The new formula enacted under Pub. L. 94-142 was a significant shift from the way funds had previously been distributed to a state under the EHA, which based allocations (a) to states on the number of all children (i.e., population) aged 3 to 21 years within a state times $8.75 per child and (b) within states to local educational agencies on a discretionary (competitive) project basis.

Related to the finance formula change under Pub. L. 94-142, from a census-based system to a special education child count, the Senate Committee on Labor and Public Welfare explained,

> The Committee wished to develop a formula that would target funding and eligibility for funding on the population of handicapped children for whom services would be provided. The Committee adopted this formula in order to provide an incentive to states to serve all handicapped children and to assure that the entitlement is based on the number of children actually receiving special education and related services within the State and for whom the State or the local educational agency is paying for such education. The formula in existing law, the Education of the Handicapped Act, distributes Federal funds to the States on the number of all children, aged three to twenty-one within such State.[18]

Related to the distribution of funds within a state, which shifted under Pub. L. 94-142 from a discretionary project grant to a formula allotment based on a local educational agency's special education-eligible children, the House Committee reporting the bill explained,

> It is the Committee's view that a program of this scope must distribute Federal funds on a local allocation basis . . . especially in light of the requirement that each local educational agency must participate in individualized educational planning for each

handicapped child. The local allocation approach ensures that the amount that any local educational agency receives will bear some relationship to the cost of educating the children involved.[19]

The new within-state distribution formula generated under Pub. L. 94-142 allowed funds to flow to areas of need with relatively higher rates of special-education-eligible students and to create an incentive to locate and serve those students. In this regard and as related to the shift in the interstate formulae from a population (census) to a need-based system driven by identified children with disabilities, the Committee on Labor and Public Welfare stated,

> [It] believes the simple "pass-through" of funds based solely on the population of the local educational agency fails to provide an adequate incentive for serving all children . . . [and] reduces the ability of a State to target funds in such a way as will assure all handicapped children a free and appropriate education.[20]

In addition, the level of funding per pupil was significantly altered under the Act. Previously, as discussed, $8.75 per student was provided, based on a state's 3-to-21-year-old population. Under Pub. L. 94-142, a uniform amount of funding was provided on an eligible-child basis. The funding level per child was determined by a "reasonable dollar amount that relate[d] to actual dollars spent on children" with disabilities.[21]

The Senate Committee on Labor and Public Welfare and the House of Representatives Committee on Education and Labor based the recommended funding level on research studies done in 1970 by the National Education Finance Project (NEFP). The NEFP estimated the actual cost of educating a child with disabilities was, on the average, double the cost of educating a nondisabled child.[22]

The Committee noted, however, that other sources of federal aid existed at the time that could assist states in providing education and related services to children with disabilities, including Titles I, III, and IV of the Elementary and Secondary Education Act of 1966 (ESEA), funding available under Part A of ESEA for Handicapped Children (Pub. L. 89-313), the Vocational Education Act, the Rehabilitation Act, the Head Start Program, social services, and the Developmental Disabilities Act.[23] This indicated the intent that federal funding streams could be integrated on behalf of children with disabilities.

The intent of the Congress was that federal funds expended for programs under Part B of the EHA should be used to pay only the excess costs directly attributable to the education of children with disabilities.[24] *Excess costs,* as defined in the Act, were

those costs that are in excess of the average annual per student expenditure in a local educational agency during the preceding school year for an elementary or secondary school student . . . and which shall be computed after deducting amounts received under the Act or under Title I [remedial education] or VII [bilingual education] of the Elementary and Secondary Education Act of 1965, and any State or local funds expended under Part B or such titles.[25]

This provision was underscored by a maintenance-of-effort provision and requirements that funds supplement and not supplant state and local funding. Under the Act, a limitation on the number of children counted for allocation purposes was established at 12% of the number of all children aged 5 to 17 within a state, to limit overclassification and mislabeling, and a new category was added for children with specific learning disabilities.

The Education for All Handicapped Children Act of 1975 (Pub. L. 94-142) also included a separate authority to encourage states to serve preschool children between the ages of 3 and 5. States were entitled to receive up to $300 per year in federal aid for each child with a disability in that age range receiving appropriate education services. However, per capita grants were to be ratably reduced during any fiscal year in which appropriations were insufficient to cover the states' full entitlement.

Education of the Handicapped Amendments of 1983 (Pub. L. 98-199)

In 1983, Congress amended EHA to expand incentives for preschool special education programs from birth to 5 years of age and to provide early intervention and transition programs. In addition, Congress vested administrative authority for all programs under EHA with the Office of Special Education Programs. Language impairment was added as an eligible disability category. Section 6 of Pub. L. 98-199 also required changes in the Part B, State Grant, program to allow a 90-day review period, thus replacing the 30-day review period otherwise required for education programs authorized by the General Education Provisions Act. In addition, provisions related to data collection, annual reporting, and evaluations were added, with a focus on evaluation, program impact, and effectiveness.

Education of the Handicapped Amendments of 1986

In the 1986 amendments to the Act (Pub. L. 99-457), Congress sharply increased the annual per capita allowance a state was eligible to receive on behalf of each pre-school-aged child with a disability. To qualify for additional aid, a state was required to take steps to ensure that all children with disabilities between 3 and 5 years of age were receiving appropriate special education services no later than the beginning of FY 1990 or, under certain circumstances, FY 1991.

During FY 1987 through FY 1989, if the annual appropriation exceeded the amount necessary to make such payments to all participating states, the excess amount was to be distributed among the states based on their estimated increase in enrollment compared to the preceding fiscal year; however, the additional amount received by any given state could not exceed $3,800 per student.

In addition to authorizing a sharp expansion in preschool grants, a new program of early-intervention grants to the states was enacted for infants and toddlers, under Part H. The amendments of 1986 also expanded the early-education project grant program. The previous authority for planning, development, and implementation grants was eliminated and, instead, the Secretary was authorized to fund (a) demonstration and outreach programs as well as experimental projects and training related to exemplary early education models and practices, (b) a technical assistance program to aid states and other public and private agencies to expand early education services for children from birth to 8 years of age, and (c) early childhood research institutes, plus other research activities. Early intervention and preschool services were also added as a fundable activity under nearly all of the other discretionary training, research, and demonstration authorities of the Act.

1990 Amendments:
The Individuals With Disabilities Education Act

Among the noteworthy features of the 1990 amendments (Pub. L. 101-476) were the following: (a) changing the name of the EHA to the Individuals with Disabilities Education Act (IDEA), (b) revising the definition of the term *children with disabilities* to add "children with autism" and "children with traumatic brain injury" to the previously noted disabilities that qualify a student for special education and related services under the IDEA, (c) substituting the term *disabilities* for the term *handicapped* throughout the Act, (d) clarifying the settings in which special education services could be delivered to include instruction in settings other than schools and traditional classrooms, (e) allowing suits in federal courts against the states to enforce IDEA, (f) adding administrative provisions, and (g) requiring the Secretary of Education to award grants to minority higher education institutions to help them compete in IDEA discretionary grant competitions (Aleman, 1991).

1991 Amendments to the Individuals
with Disabilities Education Act

The chief purpose of the Individuals With Disabilities Education Act Amendments of 1991 (Pub. L. 102-119) was to reauthorize Part H programs. Additional changes included allowing states to include "developmental delay" as an eligibility category for preschoolers, requiring Part B state plans to include policies and procedures for the smooth transition from Part H to preschool services, providing for the flexible use of Part B and Part H funds during the transition, increasing the maximum allocation under Section 619 (preschool programs for ages 3-5 years) from $1,000 to $1,500 per child, and providing for the improvement of services to Indian children with disabilities by clarifying the role of the Bureau of Indian Affairs. Also, minimum funding for State administration increased from $350,000 to $450,000.

The reauthorization of the Elementary and Secondary Education Act in 1994 also provided changes in the IDEA, including the repeal of the Chapter 1 Handicapped Act that was merged into IDEA; and under ESEA, Title III, the Jeffords amendments were enacted, which provided the authority to remove children with disabilities from the classroom to another setting if they brought firearms to school.

Reauthorization of the IDEA, 1996-1997

In 1997, the 105th Congress completed a revision and extension of the IDEA that the 104th Congress had undertaken but did not conclude. Fiscal, legal, and programmatic issues were highlighted in the reauthorization and included changing the funding formula under that Act and improving educational results for children with disabilities, which became a new focus of the struggle for reform and improvement of education for children with disabilities (see Aleman & Jones, 1997a).

The 1997 amendments (Pub. L. 105-17) to the IDEA, signed into law on June 4, 1997, by President Clinton, has been the largest restructuring of federal aid for children with disabilities since enactment of Pub. L. 94-142 in 1975.[26] Under the 1997 amendments, the IDEA continues to authorize three formula grant programs and several discretionary programs. It contains four parts. Part A includes definitions, findings, and purposes. Part B includes the grants-to-states program (section 611) and preschool program (section 619). Part C includes the infants and toddlers program, formerly Part H. Part D includes discretionary grants, formerly section 618 and Parts C through G. The centerpiece of the IDEA is the grant-to-states program, Part B. Over 70% of all appropriations are devoted to it, and over 5 million children with disabilities are reached by it.[27]

Key features of the IDEA reauthorization include changes in funding:[28]

New state and substate funding formulas. Under the Part B, Grants to States Program, enactment of appropriations above $4.9 billion triggers a new state formula that distributes a base amount to states equal to their allocations in the year before the trigger was reached. New money is based on the total school-age population (weighted 85%) and the total school-age population in poverty (weighted 15%). Minimum and maximum grant provisions ensure that there would be a floor and ceiling on the amount of aid going to states. Within-state allocations are distributed in the same way grants to states are distributed, with certain changes in the definitions of school-aged children and children in poverty.

Fiscal relief to local school districts. When federal appropriations for the grants-to-states program exceed $4.1 billion and a school district gets a larger award, the district is permitted to reduce local spending on special education. Certain exclusions are also provided to the maintenance-of-effort provision, and funds can be used more flexibly in certain cases. Benefits from special education grants can accrue to children without disabilities, as long as the IEPs are being met for exceptional children and youths, and funding can be used for school-wide projects based on the number of participating children with disabilities to total district counts.

Placement neutral formula. If the state funding formula is based on the type of setting in which a child is served, the state must ensure that the funding mechanism does not encourage segregated placements or that the formula will be revised.

State administration. Effective immediately on enactment of the reauthorization, states could retain 25% of the total award under Part B for 1997, multiplied by the lesser of the growth of inflation or appropriations over the prior year. Of this, 20% or $500,000 (whichever is greater) may be used for administration of the state grant program and preschool program.[29] When annual appropriation increases are larger than inflation increases, each state must reserve funds for local education agencies for capacity building and improvement.

Preschool program. Effective immediately on passage of the reauthorization, 1997 awards for preschoolers would be based on the child count (old) formula. In 1998 and thereafter, funding above the 1997 amount would be based on a new formula that is distributed on total school-aged population (85%) and school-aged population in poverty (15%; see also, Aleman, 1997).

Other changes include a focus on discipline and education results.

Emphasis on educational results. Each IEP for children with disabilities must relate programming for the child to achievement in the general education curriculum. Furthermore, states must establish performance goals and indicators for exceptional children and youth and must include children with disabilities in statewide assessments and alternative assessments.

Expanded procedures for the discipline of children with disabilities. Schools have specific statutory authority to remove certain misbehaving students with disabilities from classrooms and place them in alternative settings for up to 45 days. Also, new, but limited, authority is provided to hearing officers to change the placement of exceptional children.

No cessation of educational services. No cessation of educational services is permitted regardless of whether a child with a disability is expelled from school for disciplinary reasons that do not pertain to the disability.

Limits are provided on the recovery of attorneys' fees. Parents who prevail in due process disputes with school districts may not recover attorneys' fees connected to meetings on the IEP of their exceptional child.

Increased reliance placed on mediation. Before parents can request a formal due process hearing over a dispute about the schooling of their child, they must be offered mediation and encouraged through counseling to try mediation first to resolve the problem.

Restructured and streamlined special purpose programs. There are three broad special purpose programs: state program improvement grants; coordinated research and personnel preparation; and coordinated technical assistance, support, and dissemination.

Summary

The IDEA has had a long history intertwined with the struggle for civil rights in the United States and is marked by bold Congressional action to enshrine in law and practice the right to a free and appropriate education for all children with disabilities. Today, the IDEA, formerly known as the EHA, is the primary source of federal aid to state and local school systems for instructional and support services for infants, toddlers, children, and youth with disabilities, from birth through age 21. Judged by any standard, the legislation has been successful in promoting the access of children with disabilities into public schooling and ensuring them a free and appropriate education designed to meet their unique needs and requirements.

This is not to say that the goal of access has been completely attained, however, and reformers should be cautioned to maintain a dual focus in future disability policy aimed at both equity of access and enhanced results. At the same time, it is essential that the struggle for disability rights be kept in mind and hard-won rights to education, due process procedures, and other successes obtained during the past two decades be maintained and strengthened.

Statistics of disproportionality continue to raise serious questions about the delivery of services to racial minorities and children in poverty. Facilities access in schools for children with disabilities is far from complete, and stringent federal budgets and heightened competition continue to threaten the funds that are available for children with disabilities in attempts to redistribute them across entire schools for all children regardless of need. At the same time, the rate of child poverty in the United States, unparalleled in industrial nations, has propelled new questions to the fore as related to disability policy, questions that no doubt will be joined by others (see Verstegen, in press) as the quest for disability rights and results continues and moves into the new millennium.

Notes

1. For a history of special education prior to the 1960s, see Lazerson (1983).

2. U.S. House of Representatives, Committee on Education and Labor. Education for All Handicapped Children Act of 1975 (94th Congress, 1st Session, Report No. 94-332). Washington, DC: U.S. House of Representatives. In U.S. Senate, Committee on Labor and Public Welfare, Subcommittee on the Handicapped. (1976). *Education for the Handicapped Act as Amended Through December 31, 1975* (Report No. 72-611). Washington, DC: Government Printing Office.

3. U.S. Senate, *The Education of the Handicapped Act*, p. 2.

4. U.S. Senate, *The Education of the Handicapped Act*, p. 193.

5. *Pennsylvania Association for Retarded Children v. Commonwealth of Pennsylvania*, 334 F. Supp. 1257 (E.D. Pa. 1971) and 343 F. Supp. 279 (E.D. Pa. 1972).

6. *Mills v. Board of Education of the District of Colombia*, 348 F. Supp. 866 (D.D.C. 1972).

7. *Mills* at 876.

8. U.S. Senate, *The Education of the Handicapped Act*, pp. 131, 198.

9. U.S. Senate, Committee on Labor and Public Welfare (Report No. 92-168) 94th Congress, 1st Session. In U.S. Senate, *The Education of the Handicapped Act*, p. 199.

10. U.S. Senate, *The Education of the Handicapped Act*, p. 131.

11. U.S. Senate, *The Education of the Handicapped Act*, p. 197.

12. U.S. Senate, *The Education of the Handicapped Act*, p. 199.

13. U.S. Senate, *The Education of the Handicapped Act*, p. 136.

14. Committee on Labor and Public Welfare. In U.S. Senate, *The Education of the Handicapped Act*, p. 213.

15. Pub. L. 94-142, Sec. 602 (16)(A)(B).

16. Committee on Labor and Public Welfare. In U.S. Senate, *The Education of the Handicapped Act*, p. 206.

17. Joint Explanatory Statement of the Committee of Conference. In U.S. Senate, *The Education of the Handicapped Act*, p. 101.

18. Committee on Labor and Public Welfare. In U.S. Senate, *The Education of the Handicapped Act*, pp. 204-205.

19. Committee on Education and Labor. In U.S. Senate, *The Education of the Handicapped Act*, p. 16.

20. U.S. Senate, *The Education of the Handicapped Act*, p. 206.

21. U.S. Senate, *The Education of the Handicapped Act*, p. 205.

22. Committee on Labor and Public Welfare. In U.S. Senate, *The Education of the Handicapped Act*, p. 205.

23. Committee on Labor and Public Welfare. In U.S. Senate, *The Education of the Handicapped Act*, p. 213.

24. Committee on Education and Labor. In U.S. Senate, *The Education of the Handicapped Act*, p. 143.

25. Pub. L. 94-142, Sec. 602(21)(A)(B).

26. For a discussion of issues related to the reauthorization, see Parrish and Verstegen (1994a, 1994b) and Verstegen (1996).

27. For a review, see Aleman (1996).

28. This section is taken, in part, from Aleman and Jones (1997b, pp. 4-5).

29. If the state is the lead agency under Part C (Infants and Toddlers), administration funds may also be used for this program.

References

Aleman, S. R. (1991, March 28). *EHA amendments of 1990, Pub. L. 101-476: A summary* (91-297 EPW). Washington, DC: Library of Congress, Congressional Research Service.

Aleman, S. R. (1996, December 9). *Special education: Programmatic issues in the Individuals With Disabilities Education Act* (97-6 EPW). Washington, DC: Library of Congress, Congressional Research Service.

Aleman, S. R. (1997, May 7). *Memorandum: Estimated state allocations under preschool formula contained in H.R. 5 and S. 216.* Library of Congress, Congressional Research Service.

Aleman, S. R., & Jones, N. L. (1997a, February 14). *Individuals With Disabilities Education Act: Reauthorization issues* (97-114 EPW). Washington, DC: Library of Congress, Congressional Research Services.

Aleman, S. R., & Jones, N. L. (1997b, June 4). *Individuals With Disabilities Education Act reauthorization legislation: An overview.* Washington, DC: Library of Congress, Congressional Research Services.

Lazerson, M. (1983). The origins of special education. In J. G. Chambers & W. T. Hartman (Eds.), *Special education policies: Their history, implementation, and finance* (pp. 15-47). Philadelphia: Temple University Press.

Parrish, T. B., & Verstegen, D. A. (1994a, June). *Fiscal provisions of the Individuals with Disabilities Education Act: Policy issues and alternatives* (Policy Paper No. 3). Palo Alto, CA: American Institutes for Research, Center for Special Education Finance.

Parrish, T. B., & Verstegen, D. A. (1994b). The current federal role in special education funding. *Educational Considerations, 22*(1), 36-39.

Tweedie, J. (1983). The politics of legalization in special education reform. In J. G. Chambers & W. T. Hartman (Eds.), *Special education policies: Their history, implementation and finance* (pp. 48-73). Philadelphia, PA: Temple University Press.

Verstegen, D. A. (1996). Integrating services and resources for children under the Individuals With Disabilities Education Act: Federal perspectives and issues. *Journal of Education Finance, 21*(4), 477-505.

Verstegen, D. A. (in press). *New directions in special education finance litigation.* Palo Alto, CA: American Institutes for Research, Center for Special Education Finance.

T W O

Consolidating Categorical Educational Programs at the Local Level

MARGARET J. McLAUGHLIN

The current climate of educational reform in the United States is challenging fiscal policies on two fronts. Calls for increased regulatory flexibility and local control over resources are creating pressures to create greater fiscal flexibility. In addition, pressures to fund educational reforms, such as new curricula and assessments, technologies, and professional development, are causing states and local districts to seek ways to use existing dollars to support new reforms. A possible response to both needs is to consolidate a number of existing categorical educational program resources that are currently targeted at special populations, such as low-income underachievers, students with disabilities, bilingual students, or migrant students.

Program consolidation, including blending funds as well as human and other resources, is viewed as one way to create greater flexibility in the educational system and decrease regulatory burden. The term *program consolidation*, as used in this chapter, refers to strategies that merge or blur distinctions among personnel, services, or funding streams that have been targeted through statute and regulation for specific populations of students. These include the federal programs of Title I and Title VII of Improving America's Schools Act and the Individuals with Disabilities Education Act (IDEA), and various state compensatory, special, and bilingual education programs. Collectively, these education initiatives are sometimes referred to as *categorical programs.* Creating more fluid programs permits greater autonomy at the school site and may lead to the development of programs that are more innovative and responsive to individual communities. In addition to promoting innovation and increasing program options, consolidation may lead to greater efficiency through reducing costs associated with redundant services, overlapping or duplicate staff roles and functions, the extraordinary costs that can be associated with determining which students are eligible for a special program, and the need to maintain burdensome fiscal audit procedures. However, one of the great dilemmas for all categorical programs is how to move toward a more flexible service system that is more integrated with general education without losing program identity or jeopardizing the resources allocated to specific students.

This chapter presents data obtained from two separate studies that examined the extent to which special education programs and resources are being consolidated with other targeted educational programs, specifically Title I and bilingual education. Both studies were qualitative and involved extensive interviews and document reviews. The findings from these studies point to specific factors that can promote more flexible or consolidated programs. Knowledge of these factors can contribute to changes in policies as well as administration of programs.

Increasing Regulatory Flexibility as a Reform Strategy

Federal strategies to increase regulatory flexibility within educational programs represent a shift away from the traditional assistance programs that target funds to specific groups of children, such as economically disadvantaged pupils (Title I, Elementary and Secondary Education Act [ESEA]), or students with disabilities (IDEA). These programs were enacted to supplement the basic education being provided by schools. Over time, these federal programs for children with special learning needs have evolved into separate, and often isolated, programs within schools. In addition, state programs have been created that supplement or support the targeted federal assistance. Some researchers have found that the regulations governing these programs have resulted in extensive paperwork and, to a large extent, have defined where and how supplemental services were delivered and who was to deliver them (Moore, Walker, & Holland, 1982; Tsang & Levin, 1983). In addition, they argue that this fragmentation is encouraged by the federal and state regulations that govern fiscal accountability, such as the "supplement not supplant" and "non-co-mingling of funds" provisions.

In contrast, the Goals 2000: Educate America Act (1994) calls for "simultaneous top-down and bottom-up education reform [as] necessary to spur creative and innovative approaches by individual schools to help all students achieve internationally competitive standards" (Sec. 20. 301; 1994). To encourage greater flexibility and innovation, the Act provides two mechanisms. Section 311 provides opportunity for states, local education agencies, or schools to waive certain statutory or regulatory requirements of certain federal educational programs (including programs such as Title I and Title II of ESEA, and the Carl D. Perkins Vocational and Applied Technology Act [311(a)(1)]). In addition, the Act authorizes and extends the Educational Flexibility Partnership Demonstration Act, which was designed to stimulate the development of models of state-level consolidated policy and program frameworks. Similar waiver authority is granted under Improving America's Schools Act and the School-to-Work Opportunities Act. The IDEA has been excluded from these federal waiver provisions.

These strategies signal the interest on the part of federal policy makers to limit and redefine the federal role in education to one that supports local innovation and school improvement strategies within the broad parameters defined by a system of standards and assessments. Provisions within the recently reauthorized IDEA seek to align special education policy with the basic concepts of standards-based reform. For instance, students with disabilities are required to be included in existing state or local assessments or appropriate alternatives, and states must develop performance goals and indicators. Funding formulas have also been modified to eliminate incentives for overidentification of students as disabled through a census-based formula that applies after certain levels of federal funding. The new law permits educators to provide incidental benefits to nondisabled students when serving an identified student according to his or her individual education plan (IEP). IDEA funds may also be applied to schoolwide programs.

Another reason why school administrators are exploring greater resource consolidation is for cost efficiency and the desire to increase resources available to support reform initiatives. It is generally acknowledged that if school systems are to implement many of the new education reforms, including higher standards, new assessments, and more rigorous results-based accountability, they will need to increase knowledge and skills of teachers and the quantity of resources, including time, class size, technology, and instructional materials.

Consolidating or blending resources currently allocated under the various educational categorical programs is one of the options for increasing educational expenditures for systemic reform. Consolidation can result in more efficient use of funds, such as pooling professional development resources to support a common agenda. Reducing redundancy in services to students as well as in materials and supports can also free up dollars for additional activities. The consolidation of programs can also alter the social organization of the schools by removing artificial barriers between teachers, classrooms, and students. Therefore, it is no surprise that recent federal statutes have included provisions for regulatory waivers and other fiscal mechanisms to create greater flexibility within programs and encourage greater resource consolidation. Although some special education policy makers and advocates have resisted consolidation of IDEA with other targeted assistance programs, local schools and districts are implementing more flexible services. The findings of the studies reported in this chapter provide some perspective on how program consolidation, particularly involving special education, is conceptualized at the school and district levels and the perceptions of various program administrators regarding the implementation of consolidated programs.

Descriptions of the Studies

Two separate studies were conducted that explored issues of consolidation of categorical programs. The first study (McLaughlin, 1996) examined state and local responses to increasing regulatory flexibility among three federal-state programs: state compensatory education (Title I), bilingual education programs (Title VII), and special education programs (Part B of IDEA). This study involved interviews with 22 state and local administrators of each of the categorical programs in California, Maryland, and Massachusetts. The three to four local districts selected in each state were chosen on the basis of their current program efforts to consolidate programs. Open-ended interviews focused on descriptions of actual programs, perceived barriers, and facilitators. Information obtained from the interviews was categorized into four issues: features of consolidated programs, program administration, challenges to consolidation, and human factors that affect change.

A second investigation using case study methodology was conducted in five local school districts that were engaged in major reform initiatives. The districts were selected on the basis of their reform agendas and their geographic and demographic characteristics. The districts included a large urban district with a predominantly African-American student population; two suburban districts, one relatively small and stable, the other a large and fast-growing district; and two rural districts, one county district and one in a small town. Two districts had implemented major state-mandated reform initiatives and were among the earliest recipients of Goals 2000 planning and implementation grants. The other three districts were in states that were in the process of implementing newly developed state or local standards or assessments and other reforms such as governance changes. Each district was visited by a team of researchers, including the author, and an average of 41 interviews per district were conducted with central office administrators, principals, teachers, parents, and other staff or community members. Interviews were conducted using structured protocols. Questions were organized under the broad reform topics of standard setting, assessment, accountability, governance, teacher policy, and special education. Questions about program consolidation were embedded in interview questions related to governance changes, inclusion, and professional development. All interviews were taped, transcribed, and coded. Ethnograph 4.0 was used to assist analyses of transcripts.

Findings

Findings from the two studies were examined and common themes identified. Because the two studies were conducted for different purposes at different points in time, the states and districts selected for investigation and specific interview questions differ. As a result, findings from each study serve as a source for triangulating the conclusions drawn from each investigation. The crosscutting themes identified from the studies suggest specific factors that should be considered in consolidating program resources.

The findings from the two studies suggest that there are a number of factors that promote greater program consolidation. Some of these are organizational features of schools that can exist irrespective of whether a school is attempting to consolidate or blend programs. Interviews noted that when certain conditions existed in schools, program consolidation was facilitated. When these conditions are absent, consolidated efforts may be thwarted. Other factors identified specifically relate to efforts to promote more flexible programs. In other words, when a district attempts to implement consolidation models, what are the factors that impede or enable the changes?

The factors that promote program consolidation are (a) a culture of collaboration, (b) increased school site autonomy, (c) a focus on systemic reform, (d) leadership and knowledge, (e) advocacy for specific programs and students, (f) personnel, and (g) competing program regulations and the power of special education.

Promoting Program Consolidation

There are several conditions that exist within schools that appear to promote program consolidation. Changes in how schools are governed provide greater flexibility for teachers and principals at a school site to organize curriculum and instruction in ways that respond to their students' needs or to their own pedagogical orientation or preferences. In addition, larger state or local system initiatives, such as standards and assessments, are designed to focus schools on very specific goals and create the targets for schoolwide improvement and resource allocation. This larger context can support other innovations, and the first three factors in the following discussion—culture of collaboration, increased school site autonomy, and systemic reform— are critical elements of that context.

Culture of Collaboration

A major impetus for consolidation of targeted fiscal and human resources at the school level is the current emphasis on creating collaborative professional cultures within schools. The emphasis on collaboration is motivated by several factors. Current research related to high-performing restructuring schools points to the importance of creating professional communities within schools and encouraging sharing and support among teachers (Apple, Hargreaves, & Fullan, 1992). The emphasis on practitioner as researcher and the desire to promote educational development from the bottom up are also creating an ethos of collaboration, sharing, and collegiality in some schools (Cochran-Smith & Lytle, 1990, 1993; Hollingsworth & Sockett, 1994). In addition, new curriculum and pedagogy as well as assessments that accentuate integration of subject matter and a less fragmented curriculum are also motivating teachers to collaborate and communicate. In fact, in districts that are implementing new standards and assessments and requiring that all students participate, special and general education teachers can be particularly motivated toward greater instructional collaboration.

For categorical programs, the focus on increased instructional collaboration has additional significance. Title I administrators have long been concerned about the fragmented and redundant instruction that students received in pullout programs. Lack of efficacy of these traditional service models prompted Title I administrators and teachers to examine how to provide instruction to Title-I-eligible students that is linked to the general curriculum and classroom instruction (Allington & McGill-Franzen, 1989; Anderson & Pelicer, 1980; Myers, Gelzheiser, Yelich, & Gallagher, 1990). Among special educators, the strong force for increasing collaboration has come from the movement to create inclusive schools and classrooms. Recent changes to IDEA requiring that these students participate in assessment and access the general education curriculum are also becoming powerful catalysts for collaboration in the schools.

Generally, all five case study districts are actively promoting greater inclusion of students with disabilities, and most are seeking ways to spread the special education and Title I resources more broadly across the school as part of overall school improvement efforts targeted at raising student achievement levels. Faced with increased numbers of students coming to school with challenging behaviors and academic problems, some principals and program administrators hope that collaborative instructional models will help them achieve better outcomes with all students.

The prevalent instructional collaboration models being implemented in schools include (a) collaboration and consultation in planning instruction and (b) collaboration in instruction through team teaching or coteaching. Collaboration also occurs at the central office levels when program administrators meet as part of teams for planning and ongoing program administration. However, almost all administrators who were interviewed suggested that school-based instructional collaboration was the most effective in creating true program consolidation. In fact, as evidenced throughout the two studies, even when central office administrators or principals supported collaboration, it did not occur without teacher support. Administrators viewed their roles as giving permission and creating opportunities for teachers to experiment, but collaboration was implemented teacher by teacher.

Increasing School Site Autonomy

A second major factor contributing to program consolidation is the decentralization of decision making and authority from central office to local school sites. This includes both formal changes in governance, such as site-based management (SBM), as well as informal district cultures that promote building independence. Site-based decision making requires local site councils and participation of staff and parents in key decisions as well as formal school improvement plans. Regardless of whether the schools included in these investigations conformed to specific procedures, such as SBM, the individual school determined whether there would be any program consolidation.

When principals supported blending resources or breaking down barriers between teachers and classrooms, consolidation tended to occur, at least among a few teachers. This consolidation would occur even in districts where it was not a priority. A common statement made by several principals who were initiating more flexible service models was, "It's better to ask forgiveness than permission." In other districts, principals would say that they told the central office what they wanted to do, and they got support to go ahead. Central office staff said that they would sort out the administrative and fiscal details, but the design of the innovation was the school's responsibility. With respect to special education, the major concerns were to make sure that students received what their IEPs required and that parents of these students were notified of changes (even if they did not constitute formal changes in goals or placements).

When principals did not support or value the consolidation, it did not occur. Some principals had very strict notions of what Title I, bilingual, and special education programs should do. Some of the principals might best be described as traditionalists who were accustomed to audits and strict fiscal accounting and having central office dictate programs. They expressed difficulty with the transition to more power and budgetary control. In the case of both bilingual and special education, few principals appeared to have strong knowledge of what these programs were supposed to be and were willing to relinquish responsibility for administration to central office or to a special education teacher or psychologist that they trusted. In some of these schools, individual teachers collaborated in a limited way, but the overall organization of the school maintained separation of programs.

The impact of school autonomy increased when school site councils controlled decisions about budgets. In those instances, schools received funds in specific categories and allocated resources more or less as the council deemed appropriate. This could include allocating positions, choosing textbooks and materials, and designing professional development activities. The degree to which resources from targeted programs, such as Title I, special education, and bilingual education, were considered by site teams varied. If a team had knowledge of the programs and a general vision for what the program should achieve, they would make decisions to use those resources in more fluid ways. Across the case study sites, there were examples of school improvement teams making decisions to dedicate a portion of a special-education-funded position to provide consultation and direct student support to general education students. However, unless teams had explicit permission to blend categorical funds or positions, they rarely did. Just as a principal's knowledge influences decisions, a team that does not include advocates for program consolidation or that believes that there is something inviolable about the special programs in the school will not tackle program consolidation.

Interviews from the five case studies indicated that the move to site-based decision making frustrated some central office administrators. In one district, a special education administrator was concerned that a particular school site team had decided to group all special education students in particular classes at each grade level. This was done at the request of both the classroom teachers and special educators to solve logistical problems. The district administrator would have preferred a more proportional distribution of students but had to accept the decision of the team. In another school district, some schools had adopted a particular model for teaching reading that used all general and special education teachers in the building. Two of the central office categorical-program administrators opposed this idea but could not prohibit its implementation.

Focus on Systemic Reform

A systemic approach to education reform emerged in the 1990s as a way to address policy and resource fragmentation. The core of systemic reform is a set of standards and student performance targets that serve to focus individual school and system planning and budgeting. Thus, at the school level, a participatory planning process should occur that considers all programs and resources and focuses them on the central target of improving student achievement. In sites where strong local or state standards and assessments were being implemented, there was definite indication that school-level planning was focused more on improving student performance. There was also evidence that, to varying degrees, principals and school improvement teams were looking at every available resource, most typically Title I, to use in the effort. For example, a junior high school principal in one of the case study sites spoke of how he was using his Title I teacher to support curricular development in his feeder elementary schools so that the students would be ready to take the state assessments when they reached his school. A similar example in a middle school in a second district involved special education. That principal designated a special education teacher to help feeder schools implement curricular changes for special education students.

Similar focused planning was not as evident for special education or bilingual programs unless those students participated in the assessments and the schools were held accountable for their performance. Yet, when these students did participate in standards assessments, the two programs could still be separated from schoolwide planning and school improvement plans. In particular, teachers and principals perceived that the purpose of special education programs was to provide what individual students needed and that resources were driven by those needs as opposed to schoolwide goals. Many special education teachers supported greater instructional collaboration with other teachers and were willing to teach students other than those identified as disabled. However, they were rarely involved in larger schoolwide systemic reform initiatives. This lack of involvement occurred at the district and the state levels. This separation is attributed in part to the purpose and individual focus of special education services and in part to the perception among many general educators that special education students are in some ways qualitatively different from the general education population and not a part of the total school. However, as some special education administrators noted, the specific exclusion of IDEA from recent federal waiver provisions provided in both Goals 2000 (311(a)(1)) and Improving America's Schools Act (1994) reinforces existing beliefs that special education must be considered separately.

The three major contextual or organizational factors just discussed are important in establishing a climate for program reform. However, as noted, they are insufficient or countermanded by a number of factors that specifically support or preclude the development of more flexible programs.

The following factors—leadership and program knowledge, program advocacy, personnel, and competing regulations and the power of special education—were identified as being specifically related to a school's or system's ability to consolidate categorical programs. The four factors were identified specifically as they related to resource blending across Title I, special education, and bilingual programs.

Leadership and Program Knowledge

Many interviewees across studies cited the importance of program leadership and having an advocate for collaboration and program consolidation at the top. Local-level administrators consider state leadership critical to ensuring that their initiatives are not only legal but endorsed by the state. State-level administrators acknowledge that local administrators hold the keys to making collaboration a reality. One of the significant challenges is that many local administrators of categorical programs are not moving to endorse the concept of program consolidation at the pace state administrators would like to see.

As discussed, principals appeared to have complex and diverse perceptions of what program consolidation means. The same held true for local administrators. Leadership appeared to need a clear state-level edict regarding how programs were to be blended or what collaborative models should look like. However, in general, the state-level perspective was to move away from being prescriptive and toward supporting local problem solving and model building. Without knowledge of program policies, local administrators relied on the state program leaders and their own finance officers to prescribe what was allowable or how budgets were to be constructed. Fear of audits was seen as a major factor blocking greater consolidation. Traditionally, program heads have known that these resources may be used in certain ways that conformed to some legal standard. There was fear, as well as a degree of inertia, among many local district and building administrators when it came to implementing new ways of providing educational services.

Knowledge of regulatory requirements is particularly important for categorical program administrators. A number of Title I directors perceived special education as a barrier to greater collaboration because of the federal guarantee of individualized services. However, these directors admitted that they knew little or nothing of the specific state or federal program regulations and did not know where the barriers were. Conversely, special education administrators considered special education to be flexible compared to Title I, which they perceived as overly concerned with audits and nonsupplanting requirements. However, as several state administrators noted, many program directors either did not understand their own program regulations or, when they were informed, chose to ignore that knowledge.

Clearly, the key to making collaboration work is knowledge of effective models, commitment, communication, and a systemic plan that is designed collaboratively. What seemed to work best was local program administrators meeting together regularly to share knowledge and develop a common vision for how educational programs should be configured. In districts with such leadership, a can-do attitude seemed to propel everyone to look beyond current procedures and unresolved issues to provide better education for all students.

Program Advocacy

Generally, state and local program administrators voiced a strong need to protect resources and programs for their respective students. Some special education administrators were concerned about commingling funds and other human resources for fear that special educational services would be diluted. At the same time, they supported increasing the inclusion of students with disabilities into regular classrooms and reducing the numbers of referrals to special education. These administrators also wanted to increase collaboration among teachers in a school and to use specialists in ways that can support both students with disabilities and other students at risk of school failure.

Bilingual program administrators tended to be less optimistic about consolidated programs. They endorsed the concept but were concerned about the tremendous shortages of bilingual teachers and the resulting lack of potential for bilingual students to be supported in regular classrooms. Also, because of the limited state and federal funds available, these administrators felt the need to ensure that every dollar they do have be provided to the eligible bilingual students.

All categorical program administrators expressed a desire to protect the identity of their programs. Administrators of bilingual programs spoke of how bilingual students are the least empowered in the educational system. These students frequently come from families with little or no education, no knowledge of how to advocate for their children, and no status in the community at large. These administrators believed that they, along with the bilingual teachers, serve an important role as advocates for the students and families in the school system. These administrators were also convinced that their students would be the first to have their services diluted or lost.

Turf guarding was mentioned a number of times under the auspices of advocacy for programs. Two specific attempts to foster collaboration between Title I and special education in two separate school districts were reportedly actively sabotaged by the local Title I director because both models were promoted by special education experts and considered to infringe on the carefully controlled Title I resources. Guarding program resources and information is a major challenge at the school level, as well. If special education or bilingual teachers or both do not want to give up their students or their status as specialists, efforts to promote program consolidation often fail. Implicit in these comments is the need to establish alternative accountability structures that do not rely on tracking dollars but instead, focus on learning. That is, some of the concerns about loss of resources may be mitigated if there are assurances that students with special needs are achieving appropriate educational outcomes.

Personnel

A number of personnel factors contribute to program consolidation, including teachers' attitudes, skills, and knowledge of how to collaborate. In fact, a major focus for professional development in several of the case study sites was teacher collaboration. Teacher certification policies and qualifications also affect the ability to enhance collaboration. As noted earlier, the lack of bilingual teachers in general education and bilingual classrooms has been a problem. Also, state regulations that govern who can deliver special education services have created barriers to using personnel more flexibly. In fact, special education is the only categorical program that has historically had rigorous and separate certification—although that is changing in some states for bilingual education. Certification requirements have also posed barriers to greater collaboration at the school level, where some personnel believed that only qualified special educators may actually deliver special education services to students with disabilities. In some cases, this means only individuals trained to teach students with particular disabilities. Careful documentation on the student's IEP of who would provide specific educational services could overcome these restrictive personnel requirements. However, lack of knowledge about what is permissible stymied some schools. Some special education teachers believed they would lose their status and position in coteaching arrangements with regular classroom teachers and would resist giving up their specialized classes or roles. Bilingual administrators were very concerned about what they perceived to be a lack of knowledge and competence among special educators in the area of bilingual education. They expressed the concern that special educators lacked professional development related to non-English-speaking students and were not able to participate effectively in the instruction of these students. Both bilingual and Title I teachers saw their own roles as those that supported typical students who just needed a little extra help. In contrast, they saw special education students as disabled and atypical.

Competing Program Regulations and the Power of Special Education

Among the more frequently expressed concerns of administrators of Title I and bilingual programs was that special education would take over in any consolidated or blended program and would usurp all available funding because of the special education entitlement of required services. Because students with disabilities have been protected by a very strong special education law, these students will get whatever is on their IEPs, regardless of the cost. Under these conditions, some non-special-education administrators felt that they needed to guard their resources and their staffs, as well as maintain the integrity of their service delivery systems. In addition, there was a perception among some administrators that special educators have more advanced degrees and would take over in any consolidated program model. Administrators noted several examples where special education directors assumed leadership for all categorical programs when local districts moved to more consolidated programs. Interviewees attributed this to two factors. First, the individual was perceived as pushing for more collaboration and instructional inclusion. However, those interviewed also believed that the district needed to make certain that the new administrator was knowledgeable about special education procedures. Given the concerns about legal issues, non-special-education administrators felt that they would not be likely first choices to administer consolidated programs. Despite the image of special education as a potential predator on other categorical programs, special educators also expressed some of these same insecurities under a more consolidated model. They believed that general education would attempt to access special education dollars to shore up their own programs and would totally neglect students with disabilities. Yet irrespective of administrators' concerns, a climate of trust and collaboration was fostered at the school level when teachers came together to support common learning goals in a school.

Summary and Conclusions

This research has attempted to provide a snapshot of some of the current practices and issues involved in consolidating certain categorical educational programs. As evident in this research, there is still a long way to go in creating the types of flexible educational systems being promoted in current federal and state restructuring initiatives. Despite the encouragement and some degree of regulatory flexibility provided by the federal and state governments, local districts continue to administer and offer separate programs. However, despite a longstanding culture of separatism and the fear of legal repercussions, some districts and individual schools are taking advantage of an emphasis on systemic reform and changes in governance to explore new collaborative educational models. In general, these models are designed to use school staff more flexibly and to provide a more coordinated and comprehensive education to students who need specialized services. Even within separate administrative structures, there is clearly a move to foster greater collaboration at the school building level with less segregation of staff and students within classrooms. The focus on inclusion of students with disabilities is having a significant influence on fostering that collaboration. In addition, rapidly changing demographics and increasing fiscal pressures in the nation's schools are creating pressures on local districts to use resources more efficiently and to look to new and more flexible ways of educating increasingly diverse student populations. Despite efforts to achieve greater consolidation and more flexible education programs, a deeply embedded culture of separation continues to support turf guarding and reinforces the belief that different types of students need very different educational experiences.

Federal and state laws and regulations governing categorical programs also continue to restrict the consolidation process. The original intent of these categorical programs to supplement and not supplant basic education continues to be the greatest challenge for changing program administration. Some administrators hope that recent changes to Title I and IDEA will offer opportunities for increased instructional collaboration and more opportunity to support at-risk students without formally identifying them as disabled. Yet most acknowledge that the federal regulatory changes are relatively modest and will not necessarily have an impact on the behavior of teachers. Moreover, teachers and principals can do a great deal of blending of services under present laws. Yet there has been only limited progress. Most administrators believe that the keys to success will be coordinated central office administration accompanied by some rigorous form of accountability for student learning. These strategies will also need to be supported by organizational changes, such as site-based decision making. A system of universal accountability creates ownership for all students at the local school level.

In summary, efforts to promote greater flexibility and coordination among programs are successful in a number of school districts, due in large part to a combination of strong local leadership, school site organization, and teacher skills. A significant barrier to consolidation is the very history of categorical programs and the myriad federal and state program regulations. Historically, school districts have been held closely accountable for ensuring that eligible students were indeed receiving extra educational services. Now, under the aegis of school reform, a more powerful type of accountability is emerging. This is accountability for improved student performance on critical educational outcomes. Although this new framework offers an opportunity for moving away from rigid categorical funding toward more flexible resource allocation, it is not yet a reality. For example, scores of students with disabilities are routinely exempted from statewide assessments. According to the National Center on Education Outcomes (1997), at least 30 states cannot report on the performance of students with disabilities on their statewide assessments. Nonetheless, the notion of increased accountability for student learning, pressures to use educational resources more efficiently to support schoolwide improvement efforts, and the push to create more collaborative and inclusive schools are fundamentally altering federal and state roles and the relationships between local districts and individual schools. The conditions exist for promoting greater program consolidation. The success of these efforts will rest on ensuring that all personnel have the knowledge and skills necessary to make these changes.

References

Allington, R., & McGill-Franzen, A. (1989). School response to reading failure: Instruction for Chapter I and special education students in grades two, four and eight. *Elementary School Journal, 89,* 529-582.

Anderson, L. W., & Pelicer, L. P. (1980). Synthesis of research on compensatory and remedial education. *Educational Leadership, 48*(1), 10-16.

Apple, M., Hargreaves, A., & Fullan, M. G. (1992). *Understanding teacher development.* New York: Teachers College Press.

Cochran-Smith, M., & Lytle, S. (1990). Research on teaching and teacher research: The issues that divide. *Educational Researcher, 19*(2), 2-11.

Cochran-Smith, M., & Lytle, S. (1993). *Inside outside: Teacher research and knowledge.* New York: Teachers College Press.

Goals 2000: Educate America Act 1994, Pub. L. 103-227, 103rd Congress, 108 Stat. 125 (1994).

Hollingsworth, S., & Sockett, H. (Eds.). (1994). *Teacher research and educational reform (NSSE Yearbook).* Chicago: University of Chicago Press.

Improving America's Schools Act of 1994, Pub. L. 103-382, 1994.

McLaughlin, M. J. (1996). Consolidating categorical resources to support local school improvement: Issues and perspectives. *Journal of Education Finance, 21,* 506-526.

Moore, M. T., Walker, L. J., & Holland, R. P. (1982). *Fine tuning special education finance: A guide for state policy makers.* Princeton, NJ: Education Testing Service.

Myers, J., Gelzheiser, L., Yelich, G., & Gallagher, M. (1990). Classroom, remedial, and resource teachers' views of pullout programs. *Elementary School Journal, 90*(5), 533-545.

National Center on Education Outcomes. (1997). *1997 state special educational outcomes: A report on state activities during educational reform.* Minneapolis, MN: Author.

Tsang, M., & Levin, H. M. (1983). The impact of intergovernmental grants on educational expenditures. *Review of Educational Research, 53*(3), 329-369.

THREE

What Will It Take?
INCLUDING STUDENTS WITH DISABILITIES IN STANDARDS-BASED EDUCATION REFORM

MARGARET E. GOERTZ

MARGARET J. McLAUGHLIN

VIRGINIA ROACH

SUZANNE M. RABER

State education policies have been in a state of flux for the past decade in response to increasing political and popular pressure to raise academic standards and increase achievement among *all* students in the United States. Almost no education policy, including curriculum, assessment, accountability, personnel development, finance, and governance, has remained untouched. Currently, states are creating wide-ranging and frequently controversial policies within a common policy framework. This framework, often referred to as *standards-based reform*, is characterized by a set of challenging content and student performance standards, a strong public accountability system that is based on student assessments, and a restructured governance system that calls for enhanced regulatory flexibility, greater autonomy at the school site, and increased parent and community involvement (Smith & O'Day, 1991). Individual state reform policies are shaped by a number of state characteristics, including demographics and wealth as well as the traditional balance of state versus local control. In turn, local school districts interpret and implement those policies and define their own directions. Within this context of reform, states and local districts also have been grappling with demands to examine and refine special education policies, programs, and practices. Issues related to inclusion, defining who is eligible for special education, costs, and the educational outcomes of students with disabilities are increasingly occupying special education policy makers and administrators. These special education issues and general educational reform initiatives are converging as policy makers endeavor to create a results-based system that offers challenging curriculum and demands high expectations of all students. With 70% of special education students spending at least 40% of the school day in the regular classroom (U.S. Department of Education, 1995), a majority of students with disabilities will be directly affected by instructional changes that take place in the regular education classroom. The 1997 reauthorization of the Individuals with Disabilities Education Act (IDEA)[1] includes provisions that are designed to bring students with disabilities into state assessment and accountability programs. States must establish goals for the performance of children with disabilities and develop indicators to judge children's progress. Students with disabilities must be included in general state and district assessment programs with appropriate accommodations, and states and districts must develop and implement alternative assessments for those students who cannot participate in regular testing programs.

This call for the inclusion of *all* students in standards-based reforms requires both special and general educators, as well as policy makers, to address the following kinds of issues:

- What types of standards are states setting, and will they be applicable to all students? What are the implications of these standards for curriculum and the instruction of students with disabilities, especially given the broad range of exceptionalities, functioning levels, and diversity of learners within special education?

- How will students with disabilities be assessed? How will schools and school districts be held accountable for the performance of students with disabilities on new standards?

- To what extent will competencies for new teachers and ongoing professional development enhance the ability of both special and general education teachers to help all students meet new standards?

- What are the resource and finance implications of moving toward a more inclusive educational system?

In this chapter, we use work we are conducting for the Center for Policy Research on the Impact of General and Special Education Reform (the Center)[2] to describe the status of state standards, state assessment and accountability systems, and state policies for the preparation and ongoing development of teachers, discuss steps that policy makers and educators are taking to include students with disabilities in these larger reforms, and identify fiscal issues and other issues of policy and practice that reformers face as they strive to include all students in standards-based reforms. Data are drawn from four studies: (a) a longitudinal study of general education policy reforms in 18 states; (b) in-depth case studies of state policy and local response to education reforms in four of these states; (c) in-depth case studies of five local school districts engaged in both general and special education reforms; and (d) a 50-state survey of how students with disabilities are considered within state policy, conducted jointly by the Council of Chief State School Officers (CCSSO) and the Center (the CCSSO-Center survey).[3]

State and Local Standard Setting

The Status of Standards

Perhaps the most prominent state-level activity in recent years has been the creation of content and student performance standards that are designed to guide local district and school curriculum and instruction. According to the 1996 CCSSO-Center survey, 40 states and federal jurisdictions have standards in one or more of the following content areas ready for implementation: mathematics, science, English-language arts, history, and social studies. A number of states are in the process of developing their standards. A total of 35 states indicated that their standards will apply to students with disabilities and 4 states indicated that, although their standards will apply to students with disabilities, local discretion is allowed.

State content standards vary in terms of how broad or generic versus specific they are as well as how they are incorporated into state policy. Some states have developed model curricular frameworks to guide local district curriculum goals; other states use assessments as the tool to define what students are expected to learn and be able to do. The 18 states in the Center's study reflect this variation. Some, like Vermont, have adopted broad learner outcomes that emphasize general knowledge, skills, and attitudes students should acquire by the time they graduate from high school. Vermont chose to define its initial set of student outcomes, *The Common Core of Learning,* (Vermont Department of Education, 1993) in terms of 21 generic student skills. This approach has allowed the state to stress the interdisciplinary aspects of the curriculum. Other states, such as Connecticut and New Mexico, have broad generic goal statements but are also developing student content standards or curriculum frameworks in separate disciplines. States such as Michigan and New Jersey have created only content-specific student outcomes. State standards also vary on whether they are primarily academic or comprehensive, that is, including affective domains and career standards as well as traditional academic disciplines. For example, Maryland's *High School Core Learning Goals* (Maryland State Department of Education, 1996) include a set of "Skills for Success," which cover learning, thinking, communication, technology, and interpersonal skills.

A more detailed review of standards documents belonging to 7 states was conducted by Margaret McLaughlin to describe requirements in the areas of mathematics, science, social science, and language arts-reading-writing. The descriptions suggest certain commonalities. For example, mathematics standards among the 7 states are very similar and reflect the influence of the National Council of Teachers of Mathematics Standards. Science standards may differ in terms of whether they are organized in specific fields of study (e.g., earth science, biology, etc.), but all stress experimentation, application, and concepts as opposed to literal or discrete knowledge of facts or terminology. Writing processes are heavily integrated throughout curricular areas and demand skills in writing for varied purposes and audiences. The emphasis on writing is strong and requires students to demonstrate basic writing conventions, such as grammar, spelling, and logical and persuasive communication (McDonnell, McLaughlin, & Morison, 1997). Although these are only a few examples, it is reasonable to conclude that current state standards are overwhelmingly academic, broaden the knowledge and skills required within a subject matter area, and are designed to require that students apply or use the knowledge to solve problems, construct projects, or engage in other complex tasks.

Local districts studied by the Center are incorporating their state's standards in local standards and curriculum. Like states, the districts are in different stages of developing standards, and these standards vary in content and coverage. But these local standards are similar in several ways to the state standards: They emphasize processes, application of specific facts or knowledge, subject matter integration, and communication skills, particularly writing. Teachers in some study districts report that the standards are shaping what they teach and how they teach it. There are more facts, concepts, and processes to teach. Subject matter content must be integrated; for instance, writing is required in mathematics and science. Student-directed learning is also emphasized through experimentation, projects, and other hands-on activities. As a result, teachers in these districts report greater demands on instructional time as well as their own knowledge of curriculum and instruction. In other study districts, school-to-work concepts and national curricular reform project seems to have strong influences on curriculum and instruction.

Including Students With Disabilities in the Standards

Standards-based reform calls for high standards for all students, and many states include statements to this effect in their standards documents. As a result, the critical policy issue in special education has changed from "how do students with disabilities get appropriate access to educational programs?" to "how do these students get appropriate access to the instruction and curriculum required by these higher standards?" Yet based on interviews with state special education directors and state directors of curriculum and instruction, it appears that special education has not played a major role in the development of either state content standards or specific curriculum frameworks in most states. Their chief role has been to review the documents and perhaps develop interpretations of how the standards can be accommodated or modified for students with disabilities.

Some states, however, are attempting to create opportunities for special educators and other teachers to gain knowledge about how to interpret the standards for their specific populations. For example, the Colorado Department of Education (1996) has a document, *Opportunities for Success*, that provides a guide to local school districts as they implement state and local standards with students with disabilities and other special populations, including language minority and Title I students. The document, which was developed with broad input from many special and other educators across the state, provides a comprehensive list of "essential learnings" for specific groups of students, classroom practices that assist particular students to meet standards, and possible assessment accommodations and adaptations. Examples of these essential learnings include social skills, communication expectations, and learning strategies. For students with disabilities, the document can be used by individual education plan (IEP) teams as they begin to examine how to ensure that each student will be included in state or local standards.

Special educators within some state departments of education and local school districts are attempting to align IEP forms and processes with newly developed standards. By doing so, it is hoped that IEPs will provide students with disabilities access to the standards and through them, broader educational experiences. The emphasis on experiential learning and more student-centered instructional practices evident in the standards and related curricular reforms was generally endorsed by both special and general education teachers as being better suited to students with disabilities. For example, using simple experiments to teach science concepts benefits students who may require more concrete instruction.

A major concern of special educators in several of our study districts, however, is how to incorporate individualized educational goals within a standards framework. Given a finite amount of instructional time, or an inflexible curriculum, or both, at the high school level, teachers are concerned about how to fit in more basic literacy skills or skills in other nonacademic domains. These concerns about competing priorities are also expressed by some parents of students with disabilities. Administrators wonder what resources will be required to move beyond rhetoric to actual applications that ensure students with disabilities and other low-achieving students will meet the new standards. General education teachers also express concerns about how to apply standards to students with disabilities and question how one set of standards could apply to all students, particularly those experiencing difficulties learning.

State Assessment and Accountability

The areas of assessment and increased accountability have been among the more controversial areas of policy development in recent years. The state role in student assessment dates to the mid-1970s when many states implemented minimum competency programs to measure and report student performance. By 1994-1995, 45 of the 50 states conducted some form of statewide assessment (CCSSO-North Central Regional Educational Laboratory [NCREL], 1996). According to more recent data from the National Center for Educational Outcomes (Elliott, Thurlow, & Ysseldyke, 1996), 43 of these states are developing new assessments, usually to bring them in line with new state content standards.

The states are at different stages of this alignment process. Assessments in a few states currently measure basic skills. Other states, such as Connecticut, Florida, Michigan, and New Jersey, are moving incrementally toward testing higher-order skills and are adding open-ended response and performance items to their multiple choice assessment formats. And a few, such as Vermont and Kentucky, have adopted statewide portfolio assessment systems. Some of the states have a mix of tests that assess different skill levels. For example, Maryland retained its Functional Test, which tests basic skills in four areas and is required for high school graduation. Yet it also implemented the Maryland School Performance Assessment Program (MSPAP), which measures student performance on the state's more demanding learning outcomes.

States use assessment programs for three major purposes. One use is what McLaughlin and Shepard (1995) call "certification of individual achievement." For example, 17 states currently require students to pass a proficiency test to receive a high school diploma (CCSSO, 1996). A second use is to identify students or school districts in need of special help, especially remediation. Connecticut uses data from the Connecticut Mastery Test to allocate compensatory education aid to school districts and to identify "priority school districts," which receive additional resources. Kentucky sends "distinguished educators" to assist schools whose students do not show adequate progress on the state assessment. Third, many of the states, such as New Mexico and Pennsylvania, use state assessments as more general indicators of student performance, with results published in school or district "report cards." These indicators are often used to hold schools and school districts accountable for their performance, through sanctions or incentive programs, state accreditation programs, public pressure, or some combination of these.

Educators and policy makers face three general sets of issues as they consider how to include students with disabilities in state and local assessment and accountability systems that are increasingly linked to more rigorous academic content standards:

1. Who should be included in the state and local assessments?
2. How should scores of students with disabilities be reported?
3. How will students with disabilities be included in state and local high school graduation standards?

Including Students With Disabilities in Assessments

Participation of students with disabilities in state and local mandated assessments is a major goal of special education policy makers and is a requirement under the 1997 reauthorization of IDEA. Yet at the time of the reauthorization, participation rates for these students varied widely from state to state, ranging from 0% to 100% (Erickson, Thurlow, Thor, & Seyfarth, 1996). In an effort to increase participation, states have been developing guidelines for exemption decisions and the differing assessment accommodations available to students with disabilities. A few states, such as Kentucky, require that all students be included in their state assessments. Most participate in the regular assessment with adaptations consistent with the normal delivery of instructional activities. Those students with the most severe disabilities, who are following a functional curriculum, may participate in an "alternative portfolio" assessment, but their scores are also to be considered in the accountability process. Most of the 43 states that have written guidelines about the participation of students with disabilities in state assessments, however, leave the decision up to the IEP teams; only about half of these states require that the decision be documented (Erickson, Thurlow, & Ysseldyke, 1996). The local districts in our study permitted students with disabilities to receive assessment accommodations. But regardless of the specificity of state guidelines, individual assessment accommodation decisions were made at the school level through the IEP process or by a building team. Some states, such as Maryland, are beginning to monitor local use of exclusions from state assessments, and the number of exemptions from state assessments are now published on the school report cards in that state.

Participation decisions may also differ by grade level tested or by type of test (when a state has multiple tests). In Maryland, for example, exemptions from the Maryland Functional Test, required for graduation, are made less frequently and documented more carefully than exemptions for MSPAP. Rules governing assessment accommodations can differ depending on whether the assessment is a nationally norm-referenced instrument or performance based or a portfolio assessment. One issue that is confronting special educators as they attempt to increase participation in state and local assessment reports is the unsystematic use of accommodations and the effects of those on test results.

Other issues are the resistance to including academically low-performing students in assessments used for school accountability and establishing the link between the IEP and what is being assessed to ensure that students with disabilities have the opportunity to learn the content. In our local district study, most teachers recognized the structure and focus that content standards provide, but the state or local assessments (or both) set the performance expectations, and teachers generally had doubts about how students with cognitively based disabilities would meet them. Including students with disabilities in accountability reporting, however, was perceived by many respondents to provide an impetus for increased instructional collaboration between general and special educators, both within schools and across schools and districts through statewide professional networks. And, as with state officials, local educators feel that the movement toward alternative forms of assessment, such as performance-based and portfolio assessment, is well-suited to students with disabilities because they are more easily accommodated and will perform better on such tests. This is an untested hypothesis, however.

Holding Schools and Districts Accountable

At the core of all of these efforts is the desire to ensure public accountability for each student. Yet most states do not require districts to report the number of students excluded from their assessments or to disaggregate data for students with disabilities who do participate in state assessments, although some states are moving in those directions. In some states, current student data systems do not include such disaggregation capabilities. This situation will change over the next few years, as the IDEA reauthorization requires states to track the academic progress of students with disabilities and the Improving America's Schools Act (IASA) of 1994[4] requires states to be able to compare the performance of students with disabilities on state assessments with that of nondisabled students.

Accountability means more than public reports of student test scores. School and district accreditation has been a primary tool by which states monitor the quality of their public schools. According to the CCSSO-Center survey, 32 states have an accreditation process that includes a review of programs or services for students with disabilities. A wide variety of indicators are used, including personnel audits, teacher certification, facility accessibility, and components of the instructional program. As part of this effort, states are looking for ways to reduce their reliance on these process indicators and move more toward program quality indicators. For example, California instituted a Program Quality Review (PQR) several years ago that is a school self-study process supplemented with periodic outside review. The PQR, which is part of the state's larger school improvement process, focuses on both classroom instruction and student work. Missouri is trying to pare down special education monitoring procedures to the bare bones required by federal law and focus more on applying quality indicators and student outcomes in their Missouri School Improvement Process to all students.

The dilemma for state special education authorities is how to balance the procedural demands of IDEA with the new emphasis on results or outputs. State-level interviews revealed an increase in the practice of conducting monitoring and accreditation visits of special and general education programs at the same time. But some state department of education staff feel that federally dictated procedural compliance monitoring gets in the way of truly integrating special education into state monitoring efforts that lead to improved performance. They fear that if they shift to a results-based system, they will do so at the risk of federal audits and compliance violations. The challenge of program consolidation at the school level can be compounded by layers of local and state program regulations, fiscal accountability provisions, and turf guarding among program administrators. Overall, there is confusion as well as incomplete knowledge on the part of state and local special education administrators about what is permissible under the various current federal and state educational laws (McLaughlin, 1996).

Higher Standards and High School Graduation

For individual students, high school graduation is a paramount concern. Students first want to know if they will graduate and, if so, with what type of diploma. Parents, teachers, and students alike are concerned with the impact of new graduation, grading, and diploma requirements on students with disabilities. The 1996 CCSSO-Center survey indicated that the graduation policies in 38 states will apply to students with disabilities. Among these states, 18 indicate that all students with "mild" disabilities will be expected to complete graduation requirements, and 12 states will permit local IEP determination. A total of 9 states will apply the requirements to students with "severe" disabilities and 16 states indicated that this would be an IEP decision.

Several of the districts we studied are first concentrating on defining new graduation and grading policies for the general student population before clarifying these policies with respect to students with disabilities. Some districts are grappling with the meaning of differentiated diplomas when certificates of attendance are routinely granted to students with disabilities as well as other students who have not met state or district graduation standards.

Teacher Policies

Teacher Licensure

Essential to full implementation of the new content standards will be teachers who have the knowledge and skill to teach the expanded content in new ways. The Center's research indicates state policy makers are attempting to create general education teacher certification requirements, including new appraisal procedures, that reflect state content standards. To meet these goals, states are beginning to move from licensure based on completion of required courses to performance-based licensure systems that focus on authentic documentation of what teachers know and can do. Many states are requiring prospective teachers to major in an academic area, rather than, or in addition to, education. And like student testing, teacher assessment systems are moving beyond basic skills and are incorporating more varied testing formats, such as portfolios, assessment centers, and mechanisms for evaluating the performance of beginning teachers in the classroom.

The trend in special education teacher licensure or certification is moving toward licenses in fewer and broader categories, but special education licensure remains separate from many of the general education certification changes. By and large, special education certification has remained outside of this discussion and maintains a separate set of competencies linked to disability type and not curricular focus. In addition, states differ in policies designed to prepare regular classroom teachers to work with a diverse group of learners. The 1996 CCSSO-Center survey inquired about the state certification requirements that address preparing all teachers to teach students with disabilities. At the elementary level, 26 states require all teachers to complete a course related to teaching students with disabilities. At the secondary level, 23 states require such a course.

Additional questions about teacher policy in the survey included approval of teacher preparation programs, competencies required for certification, teacher certification tests, and required practical experiences. The latter is particularly important as a measure of the extent to which teachers are being prepared to accommodate students with disabilities in general education classrooms. Only 10 states require general education teachers to have some practical experience with students with disabilities, and 1 state encourages but does not require such experience. Among these states, requirements vary in terms of specificity, including "inclusion of diverse populations in student teaching" and "competency with students with a full range of exceptionalities" (Rhim & McLaughlin, 1997, p. 16).

Whereas states are primarily focused on improving the quality of fully licensed teachers, many of our study districts were primarily concerned with improving the availability of fully licensed teachers. The reasons cited for teacher shortages varied across the states but included the rapid growth of a diverse student population in urban communities, the general isolation of rural districts, and low teacher pay. Other state policies designed to address poor student achievement, such as class size reduction, have also increased the demand for teachers in a tight labor market. These teacher shortages are exacerbated in special education.

Professional Development

States are generally recognizing the critical role of professional development in implementing new reforms. Yet they play a limited role in the design and financing of teacher professional development generally and in those linked to the new content standards in particu-lar. States may require districts to provide in-service opportunities, require educators to develop plans for continued professional growth, or establish guidelines for or approve in-service activities used for recertification. But these guidelines generally do not specify content, control quality, or link to the new student content standards.

Most districts must rely on local funds or federal categorical aid programs, such as Title I, the Eisenhower Mathematics and Science Education Program, and the Comprehensive System of Professional Development to support professional development activities. And even those states that fund professional development provide too few dollars to support the kind of extended, long-term professional devel-opment that the research shows to be most effective (see Corcoran, 1995; Little, 1993). Part of the problem is that professional develop-ment as an educational investment has limited political support and is vulnerable at times of fiscal crisis. Minnesota, for example, used to require that school districts set aside a fixed percentage of their general state aid payments for professional development, but this funding mechanism met resistance in the legislature and school districts.

Although financial support of professional development remains limited, some states are developing or supporting (or both) statewide structures to support professional development of teachers, especially as focused on new state policies in curriculum and assessment. These structures include teacher subject matter networks and teacher assess-ment networks, professional development centers, and state policies designed to change the structure and paradigm of local professional development.

Several trends in professional development show promise for greater coordination between special and general educators. First, some states are structuring opportunities for special and general education teach-ers to work together to develop tools that support the inclusion of students with disabilities in standards-based curriculum. Teachers in Kentucky, for example, are developing inclusive, thematic units of study aligned with standards and addressing the needs of diverse learners. The Maryland Assessment Consortium also brings together general and special education teachers to develop performance tasks aligned with that state's assessments that can be used as instructional tools and curriculum-embedded assessments. Second, some states, such as Missouri and Pennsylvania, are requiring general education teachers, as part of their ongoing professional development, to strengthen their skills in working with the diversity of children in their classrooms.

Last, some states are combining training funds (or requiring districts to create coordinated training with money from different sources) to help all teachers work more effectively with one another to better meet the needs of all students. For example, California's School-Based Program Coordination Act[5] allows school sites the flexibility to consolidate categorical funds for professional development, including special education, into a single schoolwide plan. That state has also reorganized all of its state department of education personnel into grade-level units to better coordinate professional development and its link with curriculum and instruction.

At the local level, decisions about the content of professional development are increasingly becoming the province of individual schools. And schools appear to be focusing their professional development on larger district goals, particularly around standards and assessments. This movement has the positive effect of providing special education teachers with the opportunity to learn about the district's general education curriculum at the same time as their colleagues in regular classrooms. Some district special education directors worry, however, that the specialized professional development needs of special educators will be secondary to those of other classroom teachers in their schools and hence not addressed in schoolwide programs. Alternatively, some study districts report an increased demand by general education teachers for training in behavior modification and curricular adaptation—traditionally special education topics—as ways to work with an increasingly diverse student population. Two of our study districts are taking steps to pool different sources of professional development funds to support more coordinated and comprehensive services.

Resource Issues for Standards-Based Reform

The preceding sections have highlighted some complex challenges that policy makers at all levels of the educational system will have to address to increase the participation of students with disabilities in standards-based reform. Some of these challenges, such as developing and administering assessments aligned with more challenging content standards, affect all students and teachers. Others are particularly associated with the involvement of students with disabilities, such as establishing systematic procedures for making decisions about assessment accommodations and score reporting. Many of the challenges relate to capacity building—for example, providing professional development to the regular and special education teachers who are implementing standards-based reform. Nearly all of the challenges will entail some additional costs.

Two major questions facing educators and policy makers are these:

1. What will it cost to reform education (including standards-based reform) and to serve a growing number of students (including an increasing number of students with special needs)?
2. How will we pay for these increased costs in an era of slower economic growth and competing demands on limited tax dollars?

Will Standards-Based Education Reform Cost More?

Research sheds little, if any, light on how much it will cost for all children to achieve higher standards. There are a few studies focused on specific education interventions (e.g., the cost of interventions such as the "Success for All" program [Slavin & Fashola, 1998]), but there are none that look systematically at what resources are required to bring all students to higher standards, what these resources cost, and where these resources come from (new dollars or the reallocation of existing dollars). Researchers have made some broad estimates, however, of how much should be spent in selected areas, such as professional development and assessment.

The National Commission on Teaching and America's Future (1996) has recommended that states allocate 1% of state and local funds for "more focused and effective professional development," in addition to matching grants to local school districts that increase their investments in professional development (p. 121). This investment would cost $2.75 billion a year. It is not clear, however, whether this cost entails new dollars or can be covered by reallocating existing professional development expenditures. Estimates of past expenditures on professional development include not only direct expenditures on formal professional development activities but administrative and teacher time used for the supervision process to improve instruction, opportunity costs associated with reduced instructional time when teachers are released from their classrooms, and the increases in teacher salaries that occur as a result of professional development. By these estimates, past expenditures ranged from 3.4% to 5.7% of district budgets (Corcoran, 1995).

The cost of developing and implementing large-scale performance assessments includes the development of test items, training teachers in how to administer and score new assessment formats as well as how to integrate performance-based tasks into their daily teaching, showing teachers how to make appropriate modifications and adaptations in assessments for students with special needs, and providing teachers with the time to score and then interpret the results of new assessments. Estimated costs of performance-based assessment programs range from less than $2 to over $100 per student tested, depending on which subjects and how many students are tested; how they are assessed (e.g., the mix of multiple-choice and open-ended questions, performance tasks, and portfolios); who is involved in the development, administration, and scoring of the test; the level and kind of training associated with these tasks; and the type and sources of materials used in the tasks.

These estimates do *not* include the potential costs of modifying or adapting the assessments for students with disabilities. Sometimes, these costs might be minimal, such as providing a student with a calculator or extended time. But often, the costs are more significant and involve additional personnel, equipment, or materials; examples include providing a reader or scribe, preparing a Braille or large-print edition of an assessment, or providing high-tech equipment.

How Will We Pay for Standards-Based Reform?

The resources needed to implement standards-based and other education reform, as well as to support continued growth in our student population, will undoubtedly be found through a combination of reallocating existing resources and searching for new dollars. Both alternatives raise a number of issues, however.

The reallocation of resources could be achieved in a number of ways. First, public schools could reallocate dollars spent on noninstructional activities, especially administration, into classroom instruction. The question, however, is what noninstructional functions should be cut? Although 40 cents of each education dollar is spent on nondirect instructional services, about three quarters of this amount is used for instructional support, such as student services, curriculum development and professional development, the operation and maintenance of school buildings, and transporting students to school and feeding them (Odden, Monk, Nakib, & Picus, 1995). Some would argue that it is just such services that are needed to ensure that all students meet the new standards.

Others argue that policy makers should look at how spending within certain categories, such as professional development, could be structured differently to support instructional reform. For example, teachers could receive salary increments for involvement in new forms of professional development, such as teacher networks, or teacher compensation systems could be revised to reward changes in teacher knowledge and skills rather than seat work.

A third approach is to systematically reallocate resources within schools and school districts. In the most basic form, the federal government and states have reduced fiscal and programmatic regulations so that schools have more flexibility in using categorical resources to serve their students. For example, the IASA (the reauthorization of the Elementary and Secondary Education Act) encourages states and districts to develop consolidated plans that promote cross-program coordination and integration of selected federal and state funds, including those for professional development, in support of school improvement. High-poverty schools may also use Title I and other federal funds and resources to upgrade the entire educational program of the school, rather than targeting resources only on students eligible for Title I services ("schoolwide" programs). Although funds from IDEA may not be included in either the federal consolidated planning process or schoolwide programs as defined in the IASA, the 1997 amendments to IDEA do allow special education funds to be used to carry out schoolwide programs as long as the amount of money does not exceed the district's per pupil allocation of IDEA funds for the students in that school. However, there is still resistance to mingling categorical funds, and, as mentioned earlier, fear of audits and regulations inherent in categorical programs constrains collaboration and consolidation efforts (see also McLaughlin, Chapter 2, in this volume).

Initiatives that allow schools and school districts to use existing resources more flexibly and that encourage innovative programming and new ways of allocating resources are necessary but not sufficient to ensure that all students, including students with disabilities, have the opportunity to meet higher standards. New dollars will have to be found. Yet the outlook for large increases in education revenues is not promising. State support for education, which provides nearly half of education revenues, will be limited by moderate economic growth, a need to offset cuts in federal aid for health and social welfare programs, conservative state tax policy, and continued strong competition for state tax dollars from corrections and health programs. This situation is aggravated by growing public dissatisfaction with the heavy reliance on property taxation to fund education.

Slow growth in education funding will also intensify competition for funds within the education sector, with a potentially negative impact on special education. In response to stagnant budgets or growing special education enrollments (and therefore costs), or both, some states have taken steps to limit spending on special education. New Jersey, for example, froze state special education funds for 3 years and recently limited the percentage of learning-disabled students in a district who would be eligible for state aid. Other states, such as Nebraska and Missouri, have capped the growth in state special education aid. Declining state support for both regular and special education has placed even greater fiscal and political pressure on local school districts, which cannot restrict the provision of special education services to eligible students. Some relief may be forthcoming from the federal government. Congress increased the appropriation for Part B of IDEA by 34% in fiscal year 1997, the first significant funding increase in many years, with the intent of expanding the dollars available for special education services. Congressional support of IDEA continues; proposed increases in Part B funding range from 11% to 24% for fiscal year 1998.

Summary

States across the country are in the process of creating more challenging content and performance standards for students and developing policies to hold students, teachers, schools, or school districts (or combinations of these) accountable for meeting these standards. Members of the special education community, bolstered by new requirements in the two largest federal education programs—Title I and IDEA—have called for states and local school systems to ensure that students with disabilities have full access to standards-based reform. To date, special educators have not been full partners in the design and implementation of new standards and assessments, but some states and districts are bringing general and special educators together to develop curriculum, assessments, and instructional approaches that address the needs of diverse learners.

Many challenges remain, however, before students with disabilities participate fully in standards-based reform. State and local standards should be reviewed to ensure that they are relevant to the full range of educational goals for students with disabilities. Educators and parents must take steps to align IEP forms and processes with new standards and find ways to incorporate expanded learning opportunities into a circumscribed school day. Policy makers must measure, report, and hold schools and school districts accountable for the performance of students with disabilities, activities fraught with technical and political problems. Special and general educators must transcend their own separateness and work together to ensure that standards-based reform does improve the outcomes for students with disabilities. Last, citizens and their elected officials must address the real costs of building the capacities of their schools and school systems to provide high quality education to *all* students.

Notes

1. 1997 Amendments to IDEA, Pub. L. No. 105-17 (1997).
2. The Center for Policy Research on the Impact of General and Special Education Reform was established in 1994 by the U.S. Department of Education's Office of Special Education Programs (Grant #H023H40002) to study the interaction between current general and special education policies and their impacts on students with disabilities. The Center is a joint endeavor of the National Association of State Boards of Education, the Institute for the Study of Exceptional Children and Youth at the University of Maryland, and the Consortium for Policy Research in Education at the University of Pennsylvania. The contents of this chapter are solely the responsibility of the authors and do not necessarily represent the views of the U.S. Department of Education. Portions of this chapter are drawn from McLaughlin (1997).
3. Since 1987, CCSSO has conducted a biannual survey of states to collect indicators for the development of state education policies. In the 1996 survey, CCSSO, in collaboration with the Center, added 10 specific questions related to how students with disabilities are considered within state policy. The survey findings are reported in Rhim and McLaughlin (1997).
4. Improving America's Schools Act of 1994, Pub. L.103-382, Title III, Sec. 331, 108 Stat. 3965 (1994).
5. School-Based Program Coordination Act, Cal. Educ. Code 52-800 to 52-890 (1981).

References

Colorado Department of Education. (1996). *Opportunities for success.* Denver, CO: Author.

Corcoran, T. C. (1995). *Transforming professional development for teachers: A guide for state policymakers.* Washington, DC: National Governors Association.

Council of Chief State School Officers. (1996). *Key state education policies on K-12 education: Content standards, graduation, teacher licensure, time and attendance.* Washington, DC: Author.

Council of Chief State School Officers & North Central Regional Educational Laboratory. (1996, May). *The status of state student assessment programs in the United States.* Washington, DC: Council of Chief State School Officers.

Elliott, J., Thurlow, M. L., & Ysseldyke, J. (1996, October). *Assessment guidelines that maximize participation of students with disabilities in large-scale assessments: Characteristics and considerations* (Synthesis Report 25). Minneapolis: University of Minnesota, National Center on Educational Outcomes.

Erickson, R., Thurlow, M. L., Thor, K., & Seyfarth, A. (1996). *1995 state special education outcomes.* Minneapolis: University of Minnesota, National Center on Educational Outcomes.

Erickson, R., Thurlow, M. L., & Ysseldyke, J. E. (1996). *Neglected numerators, drifting denominators, and fractured fractions: Determining participation rates for students with disabilities in statewide assessment programs*. Minneapolis: University of Minnesota, National Center on Educational Outcomes.

Little, J. W. (1993). Teachers' professional development and education reform. *Educational Evaluation and Policy Analysis, 15*, 129-151.

Maryland State Department of Education. (1996). *High school core learning goals*. Baltimore: Author.

McDonnell, L. M., McLaughlin, M. J., & Morison, P. (Eds.). (1997). *Educating one and all: Students with disabilities and standards-based reform* (a report by the National Research Council Committee on Goals 2000 and the Inclusion of Students With Disabilities). Washington, DC: National Academy Press.

McLaughlin, M. J. (1996). Consolidating categorical program resources to support local school improvement: Issues and perspectives. *Journal of Education Finance, 21*, 506-527.

McLaughlin, M. J. (1997). State policies in an era of standards-based reform: Where are the students with disabilities? [Special issue]. *NASDSE Liaison Bulletin, 27*(7).

McLaughlin, M. W., & Shepard, L. A. (1995). *Improving education through standards-based reform* (a report by the National Academy of Education Panel on Standards-Based Education Reform). Stanford, CA: National Academy of Education.

National Commission on Teaching and America's Future. (1996). *What matters most: Teaching for America's future*. New York: Carnegie Corporation of New York & Rockefeller Foundation.

Odden, A., Monk, D., Nakib, Y., & Picus, L. (1995). The story of the education dollar: No academy awards and no fiscal smoking guns. *Phi Delta Kappan, 77*, 161-168.

Rhim, L. M., & McLaughlin, M. J. (1997, March). *State level policies and practices: Where are the students with disabilities?* College Park: University of Maryland, Institute for the Study of Exceptional Children and Youth.

Slavin, R., & Fashola, O. (1998). *Show me the evidence! Proven and promising programs for American schools*. Thousand Oaks, CA: Corwin.

Smith, M. S., & O'Day, J. (1991). Systemic school reform. In S. H. Fuhrman & B. Malen (Eds.), *The politics of curriculum and testing* (pp. 233-268). New York: Falmer.

U.S. Department of Education. (1995). *To assure the free appropriate public education of all children with disabilities* (17th annual report to Congress on the implementation of the Individuals with Disabilities Education Act). Washington, DC: Office of Special Education Programs.

Vermont Department of Education. (1993). *The common core of learning*. Montpelier, VT: Author.

FOUR

Special Education Funding and Integration
CASES FROM EUROPE

COR J. W. MEIJER

SIP JAN PIJL

SIETSKE WASLANDER

Most countries hold the view that children with special needs should be educated in the mainstream. Though different terminology is used to describe this aim (inclusion, integration, nonsegregation), the general objective is the same: to maximize the quality and quantity of interaction between the disabled and nondisabled (Organisation for Economic Cooperation and Development [OECD], 1995a). Throughout this chapter, the term *integration* will be used. This term is in keeping with linguistic usage and educational practice in most European countries.

AUTHORS' NOTE: This chapter is partly based on Meijer, Pijl, & Hegarty, 1994; Pijl & Dyson, 1998; and on Pijl & Meijer, 1994.

Research shows that countries differ in their degrees of success of integrating students with special needs into regular education. Major differences have been described not only in quantitative terms but also in terms of educational organization and actual provisions (OECD, 1995a; Pijl & Meijer, 1991). A wide range of factors contributes to this variation between and within countries, a number of which have been described and analyzed (e.g., Meijer, Pijl, & Hegarty, 1994; OECD, 1995a; Pijl, Meijer, & Hegarty, 1997). Variation between countries stems from factors such as legislation, attitudes, history of special education, and population density. Recently, the focus has been on the impact of educational funding on integration.

Several researchers now subscribe to the view that the way in which special education is funded partly accounts for the nature of the education delivered (Danielson & Bellamy, 1989; Dempsey & Fuchs, 1993; Meijer, Peschar, & Scheerens, 1995; Parrish, 1994). Still, the scientific study of funding and integration has only just begun. The challenge of such work is threefold: to provide empirical evidence of the connections between funding and integration; to develop an analytical framework to explain how abstract funding models affect everyday education practices of integration; and, ultimately and ideally, to make adequate predictions about the effects of changes in funding on integration.

Our modest aims in this chapter are to take two initial steps toward linking funding and integration. The first step is to look for empirical clues in four European countries. The second step is to begin developing an analytical framework to provide an analytical guide for future studies. Before we begin, however, our choice of countries, data sources, and methodology require some explanation.

Our approach is inductive rather than theory driven for several reasons. The most obvious reason is that a theory to explain how funding and integration are related has yet to be developed. In our view, for a theory to be of more than just scientific value, it must be built on empirical data. However, in the case of international comparative research on funding and integration, data gathering is difficult. Not all countries keep statistics on special education and integration, let alone similar statistics. Therefore, gaps in data are inevitable. We adopt a case study approach, because this enables us to do justice to the information that is available and allows us to point out important country-specific idiosyncrasies. The cases also provide an empirical foundation for an analytical framework.

The four European countries we focused on here are Austria, England, Denmark, and the Netherlands. All these countries have an explicit integration policy, and recent research data on the funding of special needs education are available. Another motive behind our choice of these countries was the need to look at a variety of integration policies and practices. After all, connections between funding and educational consequences must hold up within a wide range of circumstances to enable inductive reasoning. The case descriptions are primarily based on data gathered for several research projects (Meijer et al., 1994; Pijl, 1996; Waslander & Meijer, 1996). Although the particular focus of these projects differed, integration policies and funding of special needs education were always included as topics. The data we drew on include interviews with key persons in the countries in question, policy documents, education statistics, and other relevant literature.

To provide the case studies with common elements, we applied a so-called *actor* approach. This approach has proven to be a powerful sociological tool to study the mutual influence of acting entities and their contexts (e.g., Boudon, 1979). Acting entities are called *actors* and can be individual people, groups of people, or organizations. The basic idea is that actors and the actions they take are affected by incentives and disincentives in the context, whereas actions on their part shape the context and may also provide incentives and disincentives for other actors. The dynamics of social processes can thus be studied by alternately treating context and actors as cause and effect in the analysis so that mutual dependencies between different actors are examined as well.

In our case, an actor is a person or organization involved in providing special needs education. The various actors have different tasks, responsibilities, and more or less autonomy to make their own judgments and decisions. Actors have their own interests and goals, which may or may not be in step with official organizational goals or national or local policy. For example the primary goal of schools, their governing bodies, and local education authorities will be to educate students.

However, they will also try to secure the continuity of their own organizations and the job security of the professionals working for them. Actors are thus likely to develop strategic behavior, that is, act in their own interest, which is not necessarily the common interest. The extent to which actors can pursue their own goals partly depends on how much autonomy they have in the decision-making process. An elaborate system of formal rules does not rule out strategic behavior, however, as one authorized option may be more favorable to actors than another, also authorized, option. The behavior of actors involved in special education is directly related to incentives and disincentives provided by the contexts in which they operate. Although incentives and disincentives take many forms, the operating funding system is a particularly influential component. The link between funding and integration can thus be seen as financial incentives and disincentives that have an impact on a chain of actors, who make their own decisions and act on their own behalf, which results in more or less integration of children with special needs.

Looking at integration in this way reveals the difficulty of realizing national or local policy goals. Chances of achieving policy aims largely depend on how all the different actors evaluate the potential negative and positive effects in the context of their own situation (Meijer et al., 1995). Any attempted change in policy evokes strategic behavior on the part of teachers, governing bodies, local education authorities, and other actors as they attempt to minimize anticipated negative effects on their organizations and work. The case studies that follow describe funding and integration policies and practices in four European countries and point out the ways in which strategic behavior links funding to integration.

Austria

Austria consists of nine states. The federal government has a great deal of influence in education, whereas the states are mainly responsible for implementing centrally developed regulations.

The percentage of pupils, 6 to 14 years old, in special schools is 2.4%. There are over 500 special schools with some 18,500 pupils. Most of these pupils (66%) attend schools for the learning disabled and mentally retarded, whereas the others attend one of 10 other special school types.

The integrated classroom is an important instrument in integrating special and mainstream education in Austria. Within a regular school, the integrated classroom generally comprises 20 pupils, 4 of whom have special needs, and is taught by both a regular teacher and a special education teacher. The curriculum is usually adapted for the special needs pupils. In rural areas in particular, pupils are integrated individually. In such situations, the regular teacher is supported by a special education teacher. In practice, this support teacher ("Stutzlehrer") spends a great deal of time working one to one with the pupil. Depending on the specific needs of the pupil, a certain number of hours per week are available for this. In 1995-1996, there were 617 integrated classrooms (2,400 pupils) and around 3,500 special needs pupils in regular education with external guidance by a support teacher. The total number of integrated pupils was thus some 6,000 (0.8%) in the 6 to 14 age group.

In general, registering a pupil in special education is determined by a commission consisting of a regular school head teacher, a special education representative (such as the support teacher), school psychologist, school doctor, and other specialists, if necessary. Parents have the right to be consulted and may propose bringing in other commission members. The commission gathers the available information on the pupil and ensures that supplementary research is carried out if necessary. An important criterion for the commission is whether or not there is an impairment. This criterion is not precisely elaborated, and the commission's decision is described by informants as not being very objective. If, according to the commission, there is an impairment, this automatically implies that a pupil has special needs. This label is not elaborated in terms of disabilities or limitations and only indicates that extra effort is needed in education.

In principle, parents have a free choice between regular and special education for their child. Statistics indicate that around one quarter of parents now opt for integration (approximately 6,000 pupils in regular education as against 18,672 in special schools). Regular schools are legally obliged to accept pupils who register, unless they can demonstrate that they are not capable of providing adequate education for the pupil in question. Parent associations feel that in some integrated classrooms, the integration is spurious. A group of special needs pupils is taught by the special education teacher in a corner of the classroom while the other pupils pay attention to their own teacher. Strategic behavior on the part of the school has been particularly noticeable with respect to integrated classrooms. If an integrated classroom loses one of the four special needs pupils, the pressure on finding a new pupil is intense. After all, the school is threatened with losing its integrated classroom and the attendant funding. Referring one of the school pupils for diagnostic assessment is one way of trying to retain the class. Schools also split large classes of 35 pupils by having an integrated classroom. In such cases, it is not primarily a matter of integration, more a matter of intraschool organization. Conferring a special needs label on a pupil often covers his or her entire school period. The school gains no advantage from undertaking steps that might lead to the withdrawal of this label and the corresponding financing.

Integrating special needs pupils into regular education has had consequences for the way special schools function. In addition to educating their own pupils, these schools are being increasingly called on to help special needs pupils in regular education. Against all expectations, the increase in the number of special needs pupils in regular education has hardly reduced the number of pupils placed in special schools. In the 1988-1989 school year, 2.68% of all 6 to 14-year-olds attended special schools, whereas that percentage was 2.41 in 1995. It is evident that the rising number of special needs pupils in regular education and the stable number of pupils in special schools means an increase in the overall total of special needs pupils. The relative proportion of this group, compared to the relevant age group, has risen from 2.68% in 1988-1989 to 3.2% in 1995-1996. It is uncertain whether this increase would also have occurred had only places in special schools been available. Bearing in mind that the number of pupils in special schools has been decreasing over the last 20 years, far in advance of the integration process, the Austrian government presumes that the large majority of currently integrated pupils—without the current regulations—would have been in regular schools without any additional resources.

To prevent a further increase in the number of special needs pupils, attempts have been made to influence admission committees. Regions are regularly informed of the figures on special needs in their area. Many allocation committees are being asked to justify decisions, and inspection authorities are asked to supervise procedures and decisions and so forth. If these restrictive measures do not help, there is the possibility that funding for special needs pupils will be paid to the regions as a lump sum based on a ratio of 2.7%.

Financial provision for educating special needs pupils in Austria is characterized by direct funding. There are various arrangements for pupils in special schools, in integrated classrooms, or in regular education with support teachers. Of these three alternatives, special education is the most cost efficient. In a special education class, the student-teacher ratio is 7 to 1. For the integrated classroom, the policy is one extra teacher for every four special needs pupils. For the external supervision of pupils with learning or behavioral problems or both, 3 extra teaching hours per week are available; for pupils with sensory handicaps, 4 hours; and for pupils with serious mental handicaps, there are between 6 and 8 hours a week (a full week comprises 23 teacher hours). In certain cases, it is possible to deviate from this regulation; for example, 12 extra teaching hours are allocated for educating blind pupils. The higher costs involved in providing integration possibilities are accepted as a means of getting the integration process off the ground. The increase in the number of integrated classrooms, without the corresponding decrease in the numbers of pupils attending special schools, leads to increases in expenditure. However, the government's ability to reduce costs is limited: Having fewer integrated classrooms is directly opposed to the pursuit of integration into society, and any reduction in the level of provision would encounter much resistance from schools and parents.

In Austria, the funding model aims at supporting integration but also contains incentives for labeling and diagnosing more children as having special needs. In this country, integration policy has not resulted in a decrease in the percentage of children in segregated settings but rather, in an increase of special needs children in regular schools. Therefore, the total percentage of children with registered special needs has increased. Policy makers in Austria are now considering introducing a maximum regional budget to bring this development to a halt.

England

An important feature of the educational system in England is its high degree of decentralization in managing schools. The central government devolves an overall budget to the counties who then forward an amount of money to schools. Schools have far-reaching responsibilities in spending this budget. The Local Education Authorities (LEAs), paid directly by the county, arrange all special needs education.

The 1988 Education Reform Act introduced the national curriculum in England and Wales. An important component of the new policy was increased integration in regular education. The recommendation of integration was adopted into the 1981 Education Act. The law prescribed that although taking the wishes of parents into account, special needs pupils should, in principle, follow regular education. There are various options for providing education to pupils with sensory, physical, mental impairments, or behavioral problems (or a combination of these), including special schools, special classes linked to regular schools, or integration in regular education.

Only special needs pupils with a "statement of special needs" can be considered for special education. The LEA is responsible for issuing the statement. The procedure for issuing a statement is prescribed in the Code of Practice (Department for Education, 1994, pp. 52-69), but there are no clear criteria for the decision. The statement consists of a description of the special needs of the pupil, the special help required by the pupil, and the choice of school where this help can best be provided. Regular schools are generally not permitted to refuse pupils with statements from the LEA that claim they should be in regular education. However, if the school can prove that it is not capable of providing for the special needs of the pupil, placement is generally not enforced. Parents are closely involved in the whole procedure and have access to all relevant documents. In cases where the parents are not in agreement with the contents of the statement, with the inherent extra support for their child, or the advice regarding choice of school, they can appeal to a tribunal, which is also prescribed in the Code of Practice. The decision of the tribunal is final.

Within a number of regular schools, much experience has been gained with special needs pupils. In these schools, there are experienced and specially trained teachers, along with suitable educational tools and occasional building adjustments. The pupils are not placed in separate classes. They receive lessons in regular year groups. Schools that acquire this expertise and available facilities subsequently attract new pupils with similar problems. Being placed at these schools, often referred to as designated special provisions (DSP), is appealing to parents because pupils are given education by experienced teaching personnel and because the children can identify with other pupils with similar needs. Moreover, compared to placement in another regular school, no further resources are necessary for the training of staff and the purchase of material, so the costs per pupil can be lower due to economy of scale. A number of LEAs have adjusted the financial structure to protect the established expertise in these DSP. Even if there are few pupils, these schools are funded for a minimum number of placements. This means that the schools can employ teaching staff specifically geared to the pupil group in question.

The movement toward integration has led to a reduction in the number of pupils attending separate special schools. In general, the LEAs are aiming at an even greater reduction in this number. In Leeds, for example, one third of all special schools have closed within a period of 12 years. Here, 4% of pupils in the 5 to 16 age group have a statement, and one quarter of these attend a special school. A rise in the number of statements has been observed in Leeds: These have doubled in 5 years. The decline in the number of pupils in separate schools for special education has not led to a loss of special education expertise. Many of the teaching personnel employed in special schools now work within regular education or with the LEA school support service.

The financing of special needs in England is based on the age-weighted pupil unit (AWPU). The value of the AWPU is determined by the regional authorities. In general, the AWPU varies from £950 to £1,250 per year, per pupil. Schools have to pay all their costs from resources allocated via the AWPUs. The extra resources normally linked to a statement are paid out either as a fixed sum of money or as extra AWPUs. For example, in Northamptonshire, a system of six graded scales has been developed. If a school has at least 10% of Scale 1 pupils, the first scale entitles the school to 1 hour of classroom assistance per week. For the second scale, this is 4 hours (a full week is 24 hours). A Scale 1 pupil is defined, for instance, as being behind in reading, whereas a Scale 2 pupil is 2 or more years behind in reading and spelling or may have behavioral problems. Within Scale 3, a pupil with a statement (minor disabilities in the mainstream) counts for 3 times the number of AWPUs that would normally be assigned, whereas within Scale 4 (significant difficulties), this would be 4 times the number of AWPUs normally allocated, and so forth.

Thus, resources follow statements into schools. The statement procedure was introduced after 1982. Newly issued statements were given to relatively young pupils at that time. Because pupils normally retain their statements, once received, for their entire school career, the group of pupils with statements has continued to grow. It is only in recent years that increasing numbers of pupils with statements have been leaving secondary education. The LEAs hope that this means the increase in the number of statements issued will end. The problem with the statement system is that schools are penalized for success (the funding diminishes) and rewarded for failure (more statement finance).

Denmark

In the past few decades, reform to the system of special needs education and its administrative organization has been guided by three concepts (Danish Ministry of Education, 1992):

- Normalization—the challenge to society to allow handicapped people to lead a life as normal as possible
- Integration—the effort to treat handicapped and nonhandicapped people equally and to remove the special position of the handicapped
- Decentralization-regionalization—the effort to bring public services and decision making nearer to the people (i.e., to the municipality or local county)

Since the 1960s, laws have been enacted and measures taken that promote the normalization and integration of handicapped people, such as the foundation of the public school, the "Folkeskole." Decentralization has resulted in an increase of competency among municipalities and counties with regard to education, though within Government guidelines. Responsibility for Danish education is spread among the central authorities, provinces, and municipalities. Parliament determines the goals for different types of education and decides how financial resources are to be allocated among them.

The effort to integrate handicapped students in education and the policy to leave handicapped people in their own environments have resulted in large numbers of special needs students attending regular schools. Only 1.5% of all children receive special education in a segregated setting (Waslander & Meijer, 1996). This percentage includes children placed in (almost) full-time special classes. Relative to other countries, this percentage is quite low (Pijl & Meijer, 1991).

Denmark practices four types of integration: (a) twin schools, in which a regular school and a special school cooperate on a limited scale; (b) the regular school (i.e., the Folkeskole), with one or more special classes (center classes); (c) the regular school with a special education clinic; and (d) fully integrated education (Pijl, 1994). Twin schools are characterized by only a limited degree of social integration (Magne, 1987). Similarly, in the Folkeskole with one or more special classes, special and regular education are provided under one roof, but possibilities for integration are limited to social interaction. How much integration is realized in practice strongly depends on the situation. If there is only one special class in a school, for example, for pupils with learning difficulties, social integration is feasible. When there are a number of special classes (center classes), for instance, for mentally handicapped pupils, even purely social integration may not be achieved. In that case, the special classes operate mainly as separate units to give the group of pupils concerned a chance for personal development. Accordingly, these groups organize activities and holidays separately from the regular group.

The regular school with a clinic has been the centerpiece of the integration process for a long time. In principle, each regular school has a clinic or has access to one in the neighborhood. The clinic contains all available knowledge and materials on special education and places them at the disposal of pupils within the regular school. Pupils can attend the clinic for one or more subjects while their own class is engaged in the same subject(s). Because special education in a subject takes more time than regular education in the same subject, however, many types of attractive learning activities are eliminated. Thus, language teaching in the clinic, for example, is reduced to reading and spelling instruction. In addition, it has been found that pupils stay dependent on clinic instruction for much too long. To avoid these disadvantages, short, intensive courses are now used more frequently, in particular, for children with learning disabilities. For a limited period, the pupil has 10 to 15 lessons a week in the subject causing difficulty. The first experiments with these courses have been positive (Meijer, 1994).

Fully integrated education is defined as individual and group tutoring within the regular classroom. Special needs pupils stay in their own classes and receive extra assistance for part of the time, in small groups or individually. For this extra support, an itinerant special education teacher—for example, a reading consultant—can visit the school. In addition to giving specific pupil support, this teacher's task is also to advise the child's teacher.

The funding of special education in Denmark was recently described by Meijer (1994) and Waslander and Meijer (1996). The central government divides tax revenues among the various municipalities, including a nonrestricted budget for education. Municipalities also have their own tax incomes. The total amount of revenue at the disposition of the municipality covers various types of expenditures, including education. The amount of funding it allocates for education is a local policy decision. The responsibility for special needs students is shared by the municipalities and provinces. Municipalities (numbering about 300) are responsible for educating students with relatively mild special needs, whereas the provinces (14) cater to the more severe handicaps, having their own budgets to educate these children in special or regular schools. Usually, provinces are responsible for a maximum of 1% of all children from the severely handicapped category (Waslander & Meijer, 1996). The municipality must provide services for the remaining children. Funding may vary among municipalities according to local political decisions, but generally speaking, special education budgets in Denmark are relatively high (OECD, 1995b).

In the municipalities, school psychological offices identify needs and allocate resources for special education (Waslander & Meijer, 1996).

Special needs funding is allocated to schools in two ways. Every school receives a part of special provision funding as a lump sum based on total enrollment, and the rest of the special needs budget is allocated on the basis of individual assessment. The ratio between the lump sum and the individually allocated funds varies between municipalities. Identification and allocation are thus linked to the same organization (Waslander & Meijer, 1996).

Recently, the Danish government tried to enhance the power of the municipalities by proposing to transfer severe special needs funding from the provinces to the municipalities (Waslander & Meijer, 1996). Integrating the different budgets was seen as a step toward the further integration of special needs pupils. At the moment, it is unclear whether this proposal will be implemented, though municipalities favor the plan. However, provinces and parent organizations (for children with more severe needs) fear a reduction in expertise and a decrease in the quality of special provision (Waslander & Meijer, 1996). As a result of decentralization, municipalities have a high degree of autonomy, and this results in enormous regional differences in budgets, provision, and proportion of children in different settings. Some municipalities have twice the amount of budget for special needs provision than others. And although these regional differences are a source of concern, the central government lacks the power to change the situation (Waslander & Meijer, 1996).

The Danish funding system clearly demonstrates the advantages of decentralization of power and policies. Responsibility for the education of special needs children lies with the municipalities (mild special needs) and provinces (severe special needs). Although decentralization is one of the main factors contributing to integration in Denmark, the distinction between mild and severe special needs also causes dissension between municipalities and provinces. A recent proposal to integrate these different responsibilities and budgets is now being debated.

The Netherlands

The Dutch education system is based on the freedom of educators to found schools, to organize them, and to determine on what religion or conviction they are based. This is the reason for the wide variety of schools in the Netherlands (Ministry of Education & Science, 1989). The variety of Dutch schools has resulted in an enormous number of competent authorities, about 6,000 in all. Each municipality is the competent authority for the publicly run schools (35% of all schools) within its boundaries. The competent authority of denominational schools (65% of all schools) in a municipality is the school board (Ministry of Education & Science, 1989, pp. 89). Under the terms of the Constitution, all schools are funded equally. This financial equality has resulted in intricate legislation and regulation.

Another distinctive feature of the Dutch education system is its centralized policy. According to the provisions of the Constitution, central government controls education by means of legislation and regulations. It may do so directly by imposing qualitative or quantitative standards on schools or outcomes in student progress (or both) or indirectly by regulating the financial and other resources that schools receive from the government and the conditions with which they must comply (Ministry of Education & Science, 1989).

At present, Dutch schools are highly segregated. In the Netherlands, special education refers both to the largely separate system of special education and to the peripatetic supervision by visiting special needs teachers of a relatively small number of pupils in regular education. Special education has 14 different categories, including schools for the learning disabled, the educable mentally retarded, the deaf, the visually impaired, the physically handicapped, and the severely mentally retarded pupils. These 14 types of provisions are located in a system of special schools, though there are also departments attached to another type of special education (e.g., a department for children with severe speech disorders in a school for hearing impaired children). Provision for younger children with developmental difficulties may be located in departments attached to other school types for special education. In October 1994, 4.2% of pupils between the ages of 4 and 11 (Dutch primary school age) were receiving segregated special education (Pijl & Pijl, 1995). In 1972, this was a mere 2.2% (Meijer, Pijl, & Kramer, 1989). For a long time, the growth of the segregated special education sector was seen as reflecting the concern for pupils with special learning needs. Nowadays, this viewpoint is the subject of much debate. An increasing number of policy makers, educators, and parents favor integration.

In 1990, a new government policy was launched that focused on the education of two thirds of special needs pupils: those attending schools for learning disabilities and schools for the educable mentally retarded (Ministerie van Onderwijs en Wetenschappen, 1990). On a national level, some 300 clusters of both ordinary and special schools were formed. Most clusters were comprised of between 20 and 40 schools and included two special schools. As a result, regular and special schools began working together. Special needs coordinators were appointed in every regular school, training programs were launched, and new regulations for funding were drawn up.

The current system for funding special education is fairly straightforward: The number of teachers and teaching staff is based on the number of pupils the school has on a particular date. Decisions about eligibility and placement are the sole responsibility of an admissions committee. This committee is connected to each special school, and the staff hours available for the committee are directly linked to the number of children placed in the special school. The consequences of this arrangement are obvious: Admitting more pupils leads to an increase in staff. By providing a bonus for admitting pupils to special education, the government in fact promotes the segregation of special needs pupils. In terms of costs per pupil, segregated special education costs on average 4 times more than the education of a normal child, though this varies from 2.5 times more for a learning disabled child to 7 times more for a multiply handicapped child.

There are some regulations that provide special services for pupils returning from special schools to regular ones. The funding of these services depends on eligibility for special education, type of disability, and age. Funds are allocated to the special school staff and form the basis for their support of the regular school. No funding is available for the regular school. Although this regulation offers some incentives in reintegrating children from special schools to regular ones, the bonus is relatively small and restricted by several conditions.

For children with sensory or physical disabilities or for children with Down's Syndrome, additional funding can be obtained in the case of regular school placement. However, this is not permanent. A school has to apply to the government annually for a budget, and the amount received depends on the number of applications and the available budget. Until recently, a 4-year-old or 5-year-old child with Down's syndrome resulted in an extra 0.1 teacher. Thus, whereas the incentive for special school placement was relatively high, the reward for referring pupils from special to regular schools was relatively low. This partially explains the increase in special school placement rates in recent decades.

Because funding is now seen as a key factor for a successful integration policy, two innovations will be implemented in the coming years. First, concerning the learning disabled and educable mentally retarded, about half of the additional costs for special education will be allocated to clusters of collaborating regular and special schools. School clusters may now decide to use these funds for special provision in regular schools. Each of the 300 school clusters will be funded equally, based on the total enrollment in primary education. This has huge consequences because the percentage of children in the aforementioned categories varies from below 1% in some clusters to more than 6% in others. This funding system is to be implemented from 1998 onward, and by 2003, regions will have had to adapt their special education provision to the new funding structure. Some regions may have to close special schools where there is a high degree of segregated placements compared to other regions, whereas other areas may receive additional funds as a reward for a regionally effective integration policy.

Second, a separate line of policy development has recently been started for the remaining special needs students—those with sensory, physical, and mental disabilities and behavioral problems (Ministerie van Onderwijs, Cultuur en Wetenschappen, 1996). It is assumed that the current funding system hinders integrating these pupils into regular education as well. For these children, special services in regular settings will be encouraged. Means would be made available only after a positive decision by a body of specialists. If a pupil meets the criteria for a pupil-bound budget, parents and pupil can choose a school and take part in deciding how to use the funding. Parents' freedom of choice will be enshrined in legislation. An important factor in reinforcing the parents' position is that regular schools would not be allowed, in principle, to refuse pupils.

In summary, special schools have been funded on the basis of the number of children attending. Placement decisions are made by admissions committees, which are linked to special schools and whose positions also depend on the number of admitted children. This procedure clearly provides an incentive for segregation. Regular schools are not funded in the same manner, and resources do not follow special needs children into regular schools. New policies, however, are being developed to change this funding paradox. Currently, two new funding models are being introduced: a decentralized regional budget for mild special needs and a pupil-bound budget for severe special needs.

Summary and Discussion

These four case studies with profiles of countries illustrate that funding does have an impact on processes of integration. It is also clear that funding models can have unintended and undesirable effects and that the incentive structure of funding models can help explain discrepancies between policies aimed at integration and practices favoring pull-out.

The approaches of the aforementioned countries toward integration offer examples of actors behaving strategically and the consequences of this behavior for special needs education. To illustrate, we mention two cases. In the Netherlands, special schools received funding for each enrolled student, whereas regular schools had a much harder time obtaining additional funding for a special needs student. Segregation of students has been therefore advantageous for both regular and special schools. Funding policies thus encouraged the development of a large special education sector. The Dutch example illustrates the occurrence of mutual reinforcement when different actors favor the same option. The integrated classroom in Austria had a predetermined maximum number of special needs students. In case the number of special needs students changed, schools could aim to continue the integrated classroom by making the numbers fit the formal requirements again. The overall number of identified special needs students may therefore increase as a result of strategic behavior by schools. Although this appears to be in contrast with policy aims, actual practice may nevertheless support integration.

An analytical framework must now be developed that can explain in more detail how funding and integration are related. The actor approach points to strategic behavior as the crucial link. A next step is to assess whether, and how, particular funding models result in particular kinds of strategic behavior of particular actors. Before we can develop some understanding on this, more analytical tools are needed. To begin our analysis, we make three distinctions: the type of funding model, the aggregation levels, and the criteria a funding system has to meet.

With regard to funding models, a distinction can be made between input, throughput, and output funding (Meijer et al., 1995). Input funding is based on need, as determined by the number of students eligible for special needs education according to certain criteria, such as referral rates, achievement scores, and the number of disadvantaged children. In the second model, throughput funding, the allocation of money is not linked to particular students but rather, to tasks to be carried out or services to be delivered. Availability and development of support services are the main determinants. A third funding model is based on some measure of output. The underlying principle here is that money rewards good practice. For example, the fewer children referred to special schools or the higher student achievement, the more funds become available.

The three models create different incentives and disincentives. Input funding based on low achievement may invite or reinforce low achievement itself, because the more low achievers, the more money. The actual criterion that is used for funding will also make a difference. Input models are particularly vulnerable to strategic behavior whenever a discretionary assessment has to be made and especially when the criterion can be manipulated by the actor receiving the funds (Elster, 1992). Throughput funding has other disadvantages in that it may generate inactivity and inertia: Regardless of anything or what is accomplished, funds will be available. Output models have drawbacks too; such a model based on value added, for example, may encourage schools to open their doors to students with high potential and refer students with less potential to other parts of the system.

Thus, each funding model has its own advantages and disadvantages; there is no blueprint for the best model.

Apart from funding models, we need to distinguish between different levels of decision making or aggregation levels. An aggregation level can be a school, municipality, region, or so forth. In theory, the three models described earlier can be applied to all of these aggregation levels. For example, an input model based on the number of disadvantaged children can be used by a central ministry to allocate money over regions and can also be used by a local organization to allocate funds over schools. Moreover, all kinds of combinations of funding models are possible. For instance, a central ministry might apply an input model to allocate money over local organizations, whereas local organizations could use an output model to allocate money over schools. When analyzing funding, information is needed about the number of layers in the funding model and the specific characteristics of the model at each of the aggregation levels.

Adding to the complexities of the issue, different criteria can be applied to funding models, such as equality, efficiency, predictability, legitimacy, and so on (Hartman, 1992; O'Reilly, 1993; Parrish, 1994). Often, there is a trade-off between the different criteria. The importance attached to certain criteria may differ between actors: Officials in charge of finance are likely to give efficiency priority, whereas parents may rank adequacy highest. Related to this is the fact that the importance of criteria may differ with aggregation level: Efficiency may be most important to a central government, whereas a local organization may give priority to effectiveness.

The Gordian knot of funding and integration embodies diverse actors, different aggregation levels, various funding models, and a whole range of criteria. There are no simple answers as to what funding model best supports integration. However, despite all the complexities and the many differences between countries, our analyses do point to certain general considerations. As every funding model has its own benefits and flaws, solutions may be found by combining different funding models. The disadvantages of each of the models when operating separately can thus be reduced. At each aggregation level, the strengths of different models can be used. A combination of different models also enables checks and balances to be built into the system as a whole.

One of the most important criteria to be applied to a funding model for special needs education is efficiency. This usually means that money must be given to those who need it most. It has proved very difficult to achieve this aim by a funding model at a central level. Large-scale diagnostic and standardization systems are needed to establish where need is greatest. Even then, such funding can easily be used in unintended ways in practice, which calls for a whole system of controls. We therefore suggest some form of decentralization and a funding model with at least two layers. The first step of money allocation is then done by a central agency financing regional or local organizations, such as districts or school clusters. In the second step, this local organization distributes money among schools.

More specifically, our analyses of several funding models used in different countries in Europe (Waslander & Meijer, 1996) suggest that the following general principles seem to work out well in practice. In the first step of the allocation process, regions can be treated equally, provided a correction is made for differences in socioeconomic composition between areas. There is no evidence that the prevalence of children with special educational needs differs between regions when socioeconomic differences are taken into account. Funds can therefore be allocated simply on the basis of total enrollment in primary education or on some other population indicator.

The local organization then decides how to spend the money and designates which particular students should benefit from the special services. Preferably, this local organization also is responsible for the (independent) special needs expertise and is able to implement and maintain special needs provisions for those who require it. Furthermore, if staff of this local organization also regularly visit schools, some control over funding use may easily be carried out. In general, it seems that a throughput model is the most attractive option at this local level. The allocation of money can be linked to actual tasks to be carried out, whereas drawbacks such as inactivity and inertia can be prevented by staff of the local organization adopting control mechanisms. A further way to prevent inactivity and inertia of schools is to incorporate elements of output funding. Low output may then be used as a possible correction of the budget for a future period of time. However, some degree of budget stability across years is important.

Integration can be achieved more easily in a decentralized model than in a central approach. In a centrally prescribed plan, too much emphasis may be put on the organizational characteristics of that specific model without integration being realized in practice. Local organizations with some degree of autonomy may be far better equipped to change the system, thus a decentralized model is likely to be more cost-effective and provide fewer opportunities for undesirable forms of strategic behavior. Nevertheless, the central government has to clearly specify what goals must be achieved, but the way in which these are then achieved is left to local organizations.

Accountability is an important concern in a decentralized system, as shown in the case of Denmark. Apart from the fact that clients of the education system and taxpayers have a right to know how funds are spent, accountability can help secure efficient use of funds. Accordingly, some kind of monitoring and evaluation will be inevitable elements of an adequate funding system. The need for this is even greater in a decentralized model compared to more centralized options (Waslander & Meijer, 1996). Independent evaluation of the quality of education for special needs students is therefore part of such a model.

Our main conclusion is that funding systems do influence integration practices. Our studies in several European countries indicate that funding is a relevant topic in the integration debate. Policy makers in all countries we visited reflected more and more on the impact of particular funding systems on integration and on the forms of strategic behavior they may evoke. We suggest making strategic behavior the central focus when analyzing funding and integration. We also provided additional analytical tools to guide such an analysis in future studies. The challenge for the future is not to avoid or control strategic behavior but rather, to construct funding models in such a way that the strategic behavior it evokes supports policy goals.

References

Boudon, R. (1979). *La logique du social, introduction à l'analyse sociologique*. Paris: Librairie Hachette.

Danielson, L. C., & Bellamy, G. T. (1989). State variation in placement of children with handicaps in segregated environments. *Exceptional Children, 55*, 448-455.

Danish Ministry of Education. (1992). *Education in Denmark: A brief outline.* Copenhagen: Author.

Dempsey S., & Fuchs, D. (1993). "Flat" versus "weighted" reimbursement formulas: A longitudinal analysis of state-wide special education funding practices. *Exceptional children, 59*(5), 433-443.

Department for Education. (1994). *Code of Practice.* London: HMSO.

Elster, J. (1992). *Local justice: How institutions allocate scarce goods and necessary burdens.* New York: Russell Sage Foundation.

Hartman, W. T. (1992). State funding models for special education. *Remedial and Special Education, 13*(6), 47-58.

Magne, O. (1987). Skandinavien. In K. J. Klauer & W. Mitter (Eds.), *Vergleichende Sonderpädagogik, Handbuch Sonderpädagogik, Band II* (pp. 316-336). Berlin: Carl Marhold Verlagsbuchhandlung.

Meijer, C. J. W. (1994). Denemarken [Denmark]. In S. J. Pijl & C. J. W. Meijer (Red.), *Integratie in internationaal perspectief* [Integration in international perspective] (p. 97-130). Groningen: RION.

Meijer, C. J. W., Peschar, J. L., & Scheerens, J. (1995). *Prikkels* (Incentives). De Lier: Academisch Boeken Centrum.

Meijer, C. J. W., Pijl, S. J., & Hegarty, S. (Eds.). (1994). *New perspectives in special education.* London: Routledge.

Meijer, C. J. W., Pijl, S. J., & Kramer, L. J. L. M. (1989). Rekenen met groei. Ontwikkelingen in de deelname aan het (voortgezet) speciaal onderwijs (1972-1987) [Account with growth: Developments in participation of (secondary) special education.] *Tijdschrift voor Orthopedagogiek, 28,* 71-82.

Ministerie van Onderwijs en Wetenschappen. (1990). *Weer samen naar school [Together to school again].* Den Haag: SDU.

Ministerie van Onderwijs, Cultuur, & Wetenschappen. (1996). *De rugzak: Beleidsplan voor het onderwijs aan kinderen met een handicap* [The backpack: Policy plan to educate children with a handicap]. Den Haag: SDU.

Ministry of Education and Science. (1989). *Richness of the uncompleted: Challenges facing Dutch education.* The Hague: SDU.

O'Reilly, F. E. (1993). *State special education finance systems, 1992-93.* Palo Alto, CA: American Institutes for Research, Center for Special Education Finance.

Organisation for Economic Cooperation and Development. (1995a). *Integrating students with special needs into mainstream schools.* Paris: Author.

Organisation for Economic Cooperation and Development. (1995b). *Education at a glance: OECD-indicators.* Paris: Author.

Parrish, T. B. (1994). *Fiscal issues in special education: Removing incentives for restrictive placements.* Palo Alto, CA: American Institutes for Research, Center for Special Education Finance.

Pijl, S. J. (1994). Denmark. In C. J. W. Meijer, S. J. Pijl, & S. Hegarty (Eds.), *New perspectives in special education: A six country study of integration* (p. 25-39). London: Routledge.

Pijl, S. J. (1996). *Het leerling gebonden budget in het buitenland* [The pupil-bound budget in other countries]. Groningen: Groningen Institute for Educational Research.

Pijl, S. J., & Dyson, D. A. (1998). Pupil-bound budgets in education: A three country study. Manuscript submitted for publication.

Pijl, S. J., & Meijer, C. J. W. (1991). Does integration count for much? An analysis of the practice of integration in eight countries. *European Journal of Special Needs Education, 6,* 100-111.

Pijl, S. J., & Meijer, C. J. W. (1994). *Integratie in internationaal perspectief: Een studie naar bronnen voor het regulier onderwijs* [Integration in an international perspective: A study of resources of mainstream schools]. Groningen: RION.

Pijl, S. J., Meijer, C. J. W., & Hegarty, S. (Eds.). (1997). *Inclusive education: A global agenda.* London: Routledge.

Pijl, Y.J., & Pijl, S. J. (1995). Ontwikkelingen in de deelname aan het (voortgezet) speciaal onderwijs [Developments in attendance of (secondary) special education]. *Pedagogische Studiën, 2,* 102-113.

Waslander, S., & Meijer, C. J. W. (1996). *Middelen: Wat WSNS uit het buitenland kan leren over beleid, geld en verevenen* [Means: What WSNS can learn from other countries about policy, money and equalization]. De Lier: Academisch Boeken Centrum.

PART II

Methodological and Policy Profiles From the States

FIVE

The Patterns of Expenditures on Students With Disabilities
A METHODOLOGICAL AND EMPIRICAL ANALYSIS

JAY G. CHAMBERS

More than half of the states in the United States have either made, or are seriously considering, changes to their funding mechanisms for special education services. With the emphasis on reducing incentives for identification and placement of students in special education programs and services, many states have either adopted, or at least considered, a census-based approach to funding. A census-based approach funds special education not on the basis of counts of special education students but rather, on the total count of students enrolled in the district. A census-based funding model assumes that all districts have approximately the same percentage of special education students and then provides a fixed amount of additional resources based on this assumption. Unfortunately, what this approach fails to recognize is that not all special education students cost the same to educate.

What is required is a better recognition of the factors that reflect educational needs among not only special education students but all students. These need characteristics should be based on criteria that are as objectively measured as possible, so that funding formulas based on these need factors do not significantly influence the identification or placement of students in service models.[1] It is ultimately the subjectivity of the criteria for classification of children that creates the incentives for misplacement of students in programs. This does not occur through the malice of school decision makers but rather, as a result of a normal response to the responsibility of classifying children who are at the margin of various criteria. The goal of decision makers is often simply to obtain the best funding possibilities for meeting the needs of the students in their districts—a goal that most anyone of good intent would undoubtably pursue.

Expenditure differences arise out of differences in student needs.[2] Moreover, students may be categorized according to their own characteristics (e.g., age, grade levels, disabilities, levels of need) or according to their placements or service assignments (which we shall refer to as their service prototypes).[3] Each way of categorizing students reveals significant information about the patterns of expenditure variation. Whereas the state may select one way of categorizing students for the purpose of funding or reimbursement, the various factors that contribute to the patterns of variation are important in understanding the equity implications of alternative funding mechanisms. Differences in the distribution of students with respect to various need categories may have dramatic effects on costs. School systems enrolling more high-need students than other school systems will tend to exhibit higher per-student expenditures.

State policy makers need to understand the factors that are associated with variations in the patterns of expenditure across school systems as well as the patterns of cost variations across categories of students. Only with this understanding can decision makers at the state and local levels evaluate the goals and objectives and the impact that alternative funding mechanisms might have in achieving these goals and objectives.

The purpose of this chapter is to examine the patterns of variation in expenditures for students with disabilities in relation to student need characteristics. The goal is to illustrate how student needs relate to patterns of expenditure. The patterns of variation observed in this study raise questions about the concept of an "average student" with disabilities that underlies the "additional resources" commonly used in the development of census-based funding of special education.

The second section examines the institutional context for the study and discusses the study methodology. This study uses the individual student as the unit of analysis. Thus, the focus is not so much on the expenditures on special education per se but rather, on the expenditures for providing all educational services to students with different disabilities and needs.

The third section explores the role played in the determination of expenditures by the types of service delivery mechanisms (the prototype) and the alternative ways of classifying student needs. This study introduces some crude measures of student need based on the perception of primary service providers of the specific curricular, behavioral, and physical needs of special education students. Outcomes or other indicators of the quality of services being provided are not explicitly considered in this analysis because of the difficulty of comparing such measures across students with differing needs. Rather, the focus is on patterns of variation in the expenditures for students with different types of characteristics, which are ultimately dependent on the decisions of school officials with regard to placement and the design of service delivery systems.

The last section presents a summary of the results and points to future directions of policy and research based on this analysis.

The Context and Study Methodology

This chapter is based on a larger study for the Commonwealth of Massachusetts conducted by the Center for Special Education Finance (CSEF; Chambers, Parrish, Hikido, & Dueñas, 1995).[4] The CSEF study was conducted in the wake of the Education Reform Act passed by the Massachusetts state legislature in June 1993. Central to the Reform Act was the establishment of a funding formula to provide all schools with adequate and equitable education resources.

Prior to the 1993 Education Reform Act, special education funding in Massachusetts relied on a system of weights based on student placement. Under the current state funding formula, additional funds for special education are allocated to school systems based on the percentage of the entire student population that is presumed to require special education services.

One rationale for this type of formula is that it does not provide a fiscal incentive to identify and label students as needing special education. The formula was also designed to support a philosophy of inclusion by eliminating incentives for separate placements for students with disabilities.

As a result of education reform, there has been an increase in the state share of education costs and a heightened interest in understanding the costs and uses of education funds. The report on which this chapter is based (Chambers et al., 1995) provides a detailed analysis of the revenues, expenditures, and uses of funds in special education.

The Data and Samples

The CSEF study includes data collected for a sample of approximately 1,300 special education students attending 81 elementary, middle or junior high, and high schools randomly selected from within 25 school districts selected from a stratified random sample of the three different types of schools systems (i.e., local kindergarten-12th grade, elementary, and regional school systems) in Massachusetts. The sample school systems were selected with probability proportional to district size (i.e., larger districts had a greater chance of being selected). Three of the school systems in the original sample did not wish to participate in the study and were replaced with a randomly chosen school system from the same stratum as the school system choosing not to participate.

The original study includes data collection from the sample districts, the sample schools, and a sample of special education service providers. In addition to completing a Special Education Teacher-Service Provider Questionnaire, each respondent also completed an Information About a Special Education Student form for three randomly selected students from his or her class or caseload.[5] District special education directors also provided information on a sample of special education students served in out-of-district placements. The student-level data collection provided information on the services a student received and the number and type of school staff providing these services. In total, CSEF staff collected information on 415 teachers-service providers (80.3% response rate) and 1,297 students (80.2% response rate). School-level and district-level data were obtained from 100% of the participating schools and districts.

Statewide data sets, the school summary, and end-of-the-year reports provided additional information regarding special education enrollments, out-of-district student placements, and tuition expenditures.

Study Methodology

This study used a resource cost model approach to data collection and analysis. The resource cost methodology is a bottom-up approach to gathering data on resources.[6] The importance of this methodology is both the way resources are measured (i.e., by the physical ingredients) and the way the information is organized. Resources are organized according to the way services are delivered to clients (or students, in the case of schools). For example, instead of gathering data on the total dollars expended for teachers' services, the resource cost methodology gathers information on the full-time equivalent (FTE) number of teachers and organizes the counts by assignment to self-contained classrooms, departmentalized classrooms, or the provision of resource services.

Collecting data on nonpersonnel resources is more difficult. School-level data are sometimes impossible to obtain because accounting records are not tracked to the school level. Moreover, records that can be tracked to the school level often vary by program (e.g., categorical versus general fund moneys). Thus, data on nonpersonnel resources are not as reliable as data about staff. However, personnel account for over 90% of education resources at the school level and thus are the most important education resource provided to students. Therefore, the lack of completely reliable nonpersonnel expenditure data does not represent a significant loss of information.[7] This study consequently focuses on personnel expenditures. Average expenditure figures presented in this chapter are intended to reflect statewide estimates.[8]

Another feature of the data presented in this chapter is that the effects of differences across school systems in the salaries and benefits paid to school personnel were removed from the analysis. All expenditure estimates used an estimated statewide average salary for each different employee job title represented in the data. For example, all teachers were assigned the same salary and benefit rate regardless of the school system in which they teach. Each of the other categories of service providers (e.g., speech therapists, instructional aides, counselors) was treated in a similar fashion. Thus, none of the differences observed may be attributed to any factors (e.g., labor market conditions or teacher quality) that might affect the levels of salaries and benefits across local school systems within the state. The remaining differences in expenditures are those associated only with differences in the quantities and combinations of different kinds of personnel used in the provision of services to children with various disability conditions or special needs.

Expenditure Differences Among Students With Disabilities

The figures presented in this section focus on the total personnel expenditures on all instructional and related services provided to students with and without disabilities. The analysis examines several ways of classifying special education students for the purpose of sorting out the factors underlying the variations in expenditures. The analysis goes beyond categorizing students simply by prototype and permits one to cross-categorize students by service prototype, levels of need, and type of disability.[9]

No account is taken in these figures of the expenditures for program coordination, supervision, or administration at the school site or the school system level. All of these data reflect exclusively the instructional and related service components of expenditure, including hours of time related to direct services, preparation, assessment, evaluation, and any other out-of-class time spent by the service providers related to direct service provision.

Conceptual Framework for
Classifying Students With Disabilities

Conceptually, each student exhibits a certain set of attributes that reflect educational, behavioral, and medical-physical needs. These student attributes are translated through the process of assessment and evaluation into a set of needs for instructional and related services. The degree of need will affect the intensity of services. Intensity of service may be defined by a multitude of factors, including the number and types of personnel involved in service provision, the number of hours per week of service received from each type of personnel, and the level of individual attention received in the process of service provision (e.g., as reflected in class sizes, group sizes, or caseloads).

Ideally, student needs would be based on an objective set of personal attributes or competencies. Unfortunately, the literature in this field provides little foundation for identifying such a set of objective indicators. Most of the literature relies on the use of student disabilities as a way of categorizing students for the purpose of cost or expenditure analysis.[10]

The analysis presented in this section categorizes students in a number of ways for the purpose of exploring variations in costs. Specifically, student data are organized by type of environment, grade level, service prototype, primary disability, and student need. Each of these is described briefly:

Type of environment: This refers to departmentalized versus nondepartmentalized settings. Middle-junior high and high schools are traditionally organized in departmentalized environments in which the school day is divided into separate class periods.[11] Elementary schools are more commonly organized as nondepartmentalized settings.[12] However, in some instances, certain higher grade levels in an elementary school are organized like departmentalized courses. Moreover, certain categories of students (e.g., severely disabled) may be served in self-contained environments regardless of grade level.

Grade levels: Within departmentalized and nondepartmentalized environments, students with disabilities are categorized according to the following grade levels: preschool, kindergarten, primary grades 1 through 3, intermediate grades 4 through 8, traditional high school grades 9 through 12, and ungraded. For some individual students, grade levels were not recorded; these are designated as missing.

Service prototype: The service prototype is the most common method for classifying students with disabilities in Massachusetts. The service prototype reflects a combination of a type of placement (e.g., regular classroom, outside the regular classroom, separate school) and the percentage of time spent in that placement. The service prototype represents one way of describing the intensity of service needs for a special education student by describing the setting in which the student is served and the relative amount of time the student spends in that setting. Massachusetts previously used this method as a basis for distributing special education funding to local school systems.

Primary disability: Special education students are also categorized according to primary disability using the federal categories specified under the Individuals with Disabilities Education Act (IDEA). CSEF requested the student disability label to permit the ultimate comparisons that might be made with other state or national data on costs.[13] It has been argued that labels can be stigmatizing to students and that they do not provide all of the necessary information about needs for services and their related costs. Nevertheless, disability labels do provide some, although limited, information about the types and intensities of instructional and related services, especially in combination with other methods of categorization. The empirical analysis to follow will provide some interesting insights into the value of disability in sorting out the variations in cost.

Student need: The last mode of categorization is based on the subjective response of the special educator who was asked to rate each student in the sample according to the student's level of need for curricular, behavioral, and medical-physical adaptations in the learning environment necessary to provide instructional services. For each of these three areas of need, the teacher was asked to designate one of the following four levels of adaptation: none, minor, moderate, or major. No further definitions or criteria were provided. Although these responses are clearly subjective, they provide yet another dimension that may be helpful in identifying sources of varying service needs and hence, costs. In addition to using the three separate categories of adaptation (i.e., curricular, behavioral, and medical-physical), a composite index was also devised using the average of the three index values.[14]

Patterns of Expenditure by Prototype and Need

What are the patterns of variation in relation to these different ways of categorizing students? How do expenditures relate to placement or prototype? What characteristics of students generate the need for certain configurations of services and therefore expenditures? How do teachers' perceptions of student needs for adaptations of curriculum materials, behavioral supports, and medical-physical supports relate to instructional and related service costs? This section examines each dimension (e.g., prototype, disability, or need) independently.

Figures 5.1, 5.2, and 5.3 present the average per-student expenditures for instructional and related services for students served in internal versus external assignments. The internal assignments are divided between nondepartmentalized (traditionally elementary) environments and departmentalized (traditionally secondary school) environments. Within each of these contexts, students are categorized by placement (i.e., service prototype) and by their own personal characteristics (i.e., grade level, disability, and level of need). The level of need is the composite index of the level of adaptation of curriculum materials, behavioral supports, or medical-physical supports required for each student.

As a benchmark for these special education expenditure data, regular education expenditure data are presented in the figures for the internal assignments (i.e., elementary instruction in Figure 5.1 for nondepartmentalized and middle-junior high and high school instruction in Figure 5.2 for departmentalized). The instructional expenditures for regular education programs are derived from the school-level analyses described in Chambers et al. (1995).[15]

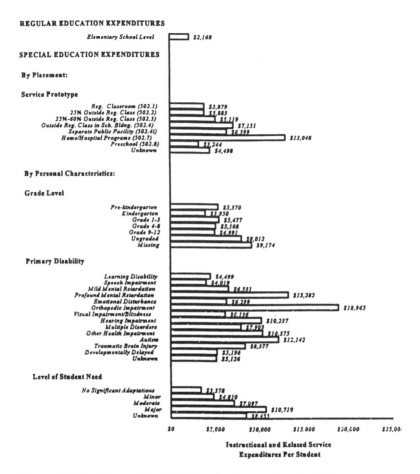

Figure 5.1. Regular and Special Education Instructional and Related Service Personnel Expenditures per Student in Nondepartmentalized Settings Across Placements (Service Prototypes), Grade Levels, Disabilities, and Levels of Student Need

SOURCE: Adapted from Chambers et al. (1995).
NOTE: Regular education expenditures are derived from the CSEF Resource Allocation forms; special education expenditures are based on CSEF Information About a Special Education Student surveys.

Expenditures by Prototype

Variations in the expenditures across prototypes reflect variations in the percentage of time spent in the regular classroom combined with the type of setting or facility (e.g., separate public or private

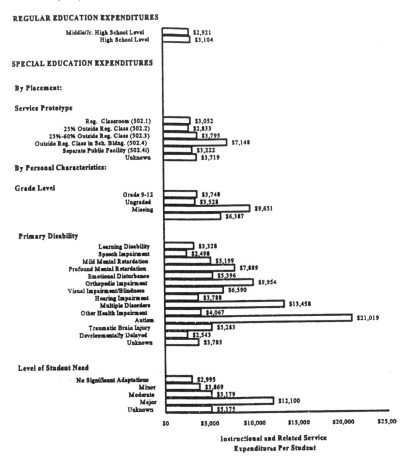

REGULAR EDUCATION EXPENDITURES

Middle/Jr. High School Level — $2,921
High School Level — $3,104

SPECIAL EDUCATION EXPENDITURES

By Placement:

Service Prototype

Reg. Classroom (502.1) — $3,052
25% Outside Reg. Class (502.2) — $2,833
25%-60% Outside Reg. Class (502.3) — $3,795
Outside Reg. Class in Sch. Bldg. (502.4) — $7,148
Separate Public Facility (502.4i) — $3,222
Unknown — $3,719

By Personal Characteristics:

Grade Level

Grade 9-12 — $3,748
Ungraded — $3,528
Missing — $9,651
$6,387

Primary Disability

Learning Disability — $3,328
Speech Impairment — $2,498
Mild Mental Retardation — $5,199
Profound Mental Retardation — $7,889
Emotional Disturbance — $5,396
Orthopedic Impairment — $9,954
Visual Impairment/Blindness — $6,590
Hearing Impairment — $3,788
Multiple Disorders — $13,458
Other Health Impairment — $4,067
Autism — $21,019
Traumatic Brain Injury — $5,283
Developmentally Delayed — $2,543
Unknown — $3,785

Level of Student Need

No Significant Adaptations — $2,995
Minor — $3,869
Moderate — $5,179
Major — $12,100
Unknown — $5,175

$0 $5,000 $10,000 $15,000 $20,000 $25,00

Instructional and Related Service
Expenditures Per Student

Figure 5.2. Regular and Special Education Instructional and Related Service Personnel Expenditures per Student in Departmentalized Settings Across Placements (Service Prototypes), Grade Levels, Disabilities, and Levels of Student Need

SOURCE: Adapted from Chambers et al. (1995).
NOTE: Regular education expenditures are derived from the CSEF Resource Allocation forms; special education expenditures are based on CSEF Information About a Special Education Student surveys.

facilities). The data from these samples of students show that, in general, more restrictive, segregated placements are more costly than less restrictive placements. The average annual expenditure per student for regular elementary school students was around $2,200. For regular middle-junior high and high school students, the expenditure

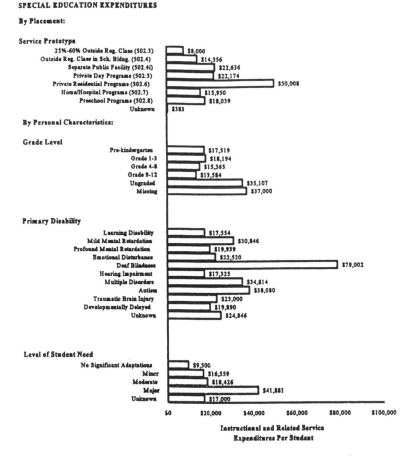

Figure 5.3. Regular and Special Education Instructional and Related Service Personnel Expenditures per Student in Out-of-District Environments Across Placements (Service Prototypes), Grade Levels, Disabilities, and Levels of Student Need

SOURCE: Adapted from Chambers et al. (1995).
NOTE: Regular education expenditures are derived from the CSEF Resource Allocation forms; special education expenditures are based on CSEF Information About a Special Education Student surveys.

was approximately $2,900 and $3,100, respectively. For students with disabilities served in nondepartmentalized environments who spend virtually all of their time in the regular classroom, the average per student expenditure was about $3,900 for all instructional and related services. This is about 1.8 times the expenditure for instructional services for regular education students. Excluding home-hospital programs, this expenditure per student ranged up to $7,151 for special education students served outside the regular class in the regular school building, which is about 3.3 times the expenditure for regular educational services.

Whereas the expenditures for regular education instruction at the secondary levels were higher than regular education expenditures at the primary level, the expenditures for serving students with disabilities were relatively lower at the secondary level. This is probably due to the fact that special education students with greater needs generally do not move to departmentalized environments that are typical in secondary schools. With the exception of the home-hospital programs, the expenditure on service prototypes for students served by the school systems within which they reside ranged from about $2,800 to $7,200 per student. That is, within the departmentalized environment, students with disabilities classified by their prototype exhibited expenditures that ranged from being virtually identical to regular education instructional expenditures to approximately 2.4 times regular education expenditures per student. This extreme ratio was for students with disabilities served outside the regular class within the regular school building (see Prototype 502.4 in Figure 5.2).

As one would expect, the expenditures by prototype for those students served outside the local school system (the out-of-district environments presented in Figure 5.3) in which they resided were significantly higher than those for students served within the school system. For example, the per-student expenditures for students served outside the local school system in separate public facilities or private day programs ranged between $22,000 and $23,000. The average expenditures of private residential programs were just in excess of $50,000 per student. These external placements ranged in cost from about 2.7 to almost 24 times the cost of regular education.

Average Expenditures by Student Characteristics

The data presented in Figures 5.1, 5.2, and 5.3 reveal considerable variation in per-student expenditures across different categories of students with disabilities. The smallest range of variation is observed across grade-level classifications. Kindergarten programs for special education children tended to be the least costly, in part, because the children did not attend school full time. Kindergarten programs even for regular students tended to be half-day programs. Programs for nondepartmentalized students tended to be more costly in general than those for departmentalized students in upper grade levels, primarily because the most severely disabled students were generally not served in traditional upper-grade environments. Ungraded students were generally the most severely disabled and hence the most costly, and they were served, more often than not, in self-contained classroom environments.

The patterns of expenditure with respect to differences in the index of student needs are as one would expect. In each of the figures, the expenditures are shown to increase with the levels of adaptations required. Students requiring major adaptations of their environment were the most costly to serve, followed by those with moderate, minor, and no significant adaptations required. For students served in nondepartmentalized environments, expenditures ranged from a low of $3,378 for students requiring no significant adaptations to a high of $10,710 for students requiring major adaptations. For departmentalized environments, expenditures ranged from a low of $2,995 to a high of $12,100, whereas for external assignments, expenditures ranged from a low of $9,500 to a high of $41,881.[16]

Most states in the United States have used student disability as a way of categorizing special education students. As shown in the following discussion, disability categories told only a portion of the story about what led to expenditure differences between students. Nevertheless, at least some significant percentage of the variance in expenditures may be explained by disability, and categorizing students in this fashion can provide a basis for comparison across states.

As shown in most studies of special education expenditures, the least expensive students were those categorized as learning disabled or speech impaired, which combined, accounted for about 50% to 60% of the students with disabilities.

According to the analysis of Massachusetts's expenditures, learning disabled students in nondepartmentalized settings were more than twice (2.08 = $4,499/$2,168) as expensive to serve as regular education students, whereas for learning disabled students in departmentalized settings, the expenditures were only about 7% to 14% higher than those for regular students.[17] Among the nondepartmentalized settings, average per-student expenditures for instructional and related services ranged from $4,019 for a child with a speech impairment to as much as $18,965 for a child with an orthopedic impairment. The expenditures on students with disabilities in departmentalized settings ranged from a low of $2,498 for speech-impaired students to a high of $21,019 for students classified with autism. For students served in external assignments, these expenditures ranged from a low of $17,325 for hearing-impaired students to a high of $79,002 for deaf-blind students.

Among students served in the nondepartmentalized settings, the instructional and related services expenditures per student were all over $10,000 for students classified as profoundly mentally retarded, visually impaired or blind, orthopedically impaired, hearing impaired, other health impaired, and autistic. Among students served in the departmentalized settings, the instructional and related services expenditures per student were over $10,000 only for students classified as having multiple disorders or autism. Both of these categories include relatively small percentages of the students with disabilities served in departmentalized settings: about 3% with multiple disorders and less than 1/5 of 1% for autism.

Patterns of Expenditure Differences:
A Multidimensional Analysis

Although a substantial portion of the variance in the expenditures for instructional and related services may be explained by certain conventional ways of categorizing students, an even more substantial portion of the variance is left unexplained by systematic differences in the characteristics of students. Table 5.1 displays the percentage of the variance in instructional and related service expenditures explained by alternative ways of categorizing students with disabilities. Multivariate regressions were run using the data on the instructional and related service expenditures for individual students with disabilities. No data on individual regular education students were available

TABLE 5.1 Percentage of the Variance in Instructional and Related
Service Expenditures Explained by Alternative Ways of
Categorizing Special Education Students: School Year
1994-1995

Method of Categorizing Students	Students Served in Internal Assignments		External Assignments (outside the local school system)
	Nondepartmentalized Environments	Departmentalized Environments	
Placement			
1. Service prototype	22%	31%	52%
Student characteristics			
1. Grade level	1	17	14
2. Primary disability	23	38	25
3. Need for adaptation of curriculum, behavioral supports, and medical-physical supports	30	25	45
4. All student characteristics combined (i.e., 1, 2, & 3)	37	43	61
Sample size	674	563	60

SOURCE: Adapted from Chambers et al. (1995), CSEF Information About a Special Education Student surveys.

NOTE: Percentages reflect the adjusted R-square calculated for the weighted least squares regression with the dependent variable being the natural log of the cost of instructional and related service expenditures per pupil. The weights used in the regression analysis represent the number of students in the population represented by each student in the sample. The adjustment is for the degrees of freedom used in calculation of the regression equation.

for this analysis. Five separate equations were run for each of the three groups of students categorized by type of assignment: students in external (out-of-district) assignments and students in nondepartmentalized versus departmentalized internal (within district) assignments.

The results displayed in Table 5.1 reveal that the differences in the expenditures for instructional and related services for students with disabilities served in nondepartmentalized settings could be explained about as well with knowledge of a student's service prototype (22% of variance explained) or primary disability (23% of variance explained). The level of need explained about 30% of the variance for students served in nondepartmentalized settings.

Among students in departmentalized settings, primary disability explained about 38% of the variance, followed by service prototype, with 31% of variance explained, and the level of need, with about 25% of the variance explained. However, knowledge of a student's grade level, by itself, did not convey much information about the patterns of variation in the expenditures on special education services.

For students in external assignments, the statistical analysis revealed that knowledge of the limited set of service prototypes applicable to these students explained a greater percentage of the variance (52%) than did knowledge of student disability, which explained only 25%. Knowledge of a student's level of need explained approximately 45% of the variance.

Table 5.2 provides additional detail on the patterns of variation in the per-pupil expenditures for instructional and related service personnel for students with disabilities. The explanatory variables in the regression equations on which these parameter estimates were based include all student characteristics. These characteristics included the student's age as reflected in grade level; the student's level of need for curricular adaptation, behavioral supports, and physical-medical supports; the student's primary disability; and whether the student had more than one disability designated or not. The reader is reminded that only students with disabilities were included in this regression analysis. The service prototype to which the student was assigned was intentionally excluded from this regression because presumably, this assignment would be based on these other student characteristics and were within the control of local school decision makers. The adjusted R-square indicates that more than 40% of the variance in instructional and related service expenditures is explained by these equations for students in the internal assignments, and more than 60% of the variance is explained for students in external assignments.[18]

Grade Level

Among those students with disabilities served in internal assignments, the only statistically significant grade-level effect corresponded to the preschool and kindergarten programs, which were about 27% to 33% less expensive than primary grades 1 through 3, probably for the most part because they were generally part-time programs.

TABLE 5.2 The Relationship Between Instructional and Related
Services Expenditures and the Characteristics of Students
With Disabilities (based on multivariate ordinary least
squares regression estimates)

Description of Independent Variables	Students Served in Internal Assignments				External Assignments	
	Nondepartmentalized		Departmentalized			
	Parameter Estimate	t-stat	Parameter Estimate	t-stat	Parameter Estimate	t-stat
Base cost	$2,694	97.23	$2,838	52.20	$25,267	24.33
Student Classification	Effect (in percentage)		Effect (in percentage)		Effect (in percentage)	
Grade level						
Preschool	–32.5	–2.40	n. a.	n. a.	n. a.	n. a.
Kindergarten	–27.4	–3.24	n. a.	n. a.	n. a.	n. a.
Primary grades 1 through 3	—		—		—	
Grades 4 through 8	2.6	0.74	7.1	0.57	– 47.0	–2.63
Grades 9 through 12	16.0	1.30	–7.6	– 0.65	–22.2	–1.27
Need for curriculum adaptation						
None	—		—		—	
Minor	16.5	1.83	– 8.4	– 0.80	– 40.4	–1.19
Moderate	31.3	3.32	12.0	1.06	–26.2	– 0.76
Major	33.4	3.34	16.8	1.25	–35.1	–1.22
Unknown	82.2	4.18	13.8	0.46	n. a.	n. a.
Need for behavioral support						
None	—		—		—	
Minor	19.8	3.97	0.6	0.12	29.7	1.83
Moderate	17.3	3.42	9.7	1.39	71.5	2.22
Major	33.3	4.80	52.7	3.59	82.5	2.56
Unknown	–18.7	–1.77	–2.9	–0.20	n. a.	n. a.
Need for physical-medical support						
None	—		—		—	
Minor	1.5	0.27	–3.8	– 0.40	27.6	0.83
Moderate	17.2	2.19	–20.5	–1.99	42.3	1.82
Major	43.7	3.70	4.3	0.20	52.6	1.65
Unknown	13.3	1.39	6.8	0.77	–1.7	– 0.07
Primary student disability						
Learning disabled	—		—		—	
Speech impairment	1.0	0.12	–18.6	– 0.31	n. a.	n. a.
Mild mental retardation	24.9	3.83	30.8	3.60	6.5	0.22
Profound mental retardation	90.0	4.68	107.4	3.56	–38.5	–1.47
Emotional disturbance	15.3	2.18	27.3	2.17	–11.3	– 0.48
Orthopedic impairment	167.9	6.36	268.0	2.66	n. a.	n. a.
Visual impairment-blindness	2.5	0.15	109.0	2.43	n. a.	n. a.

TABLE 5.2 *Continued*

Description of Independent Variables	Students Served in Internal Assignments				External Assignments	
	Nondepartmentalized		Departmentalized			
	Parameter Estimate	t-stat	Parameter Estimate	t-stat	Parameter Estimate	t-stat
Base cost	$2,694	97.23	$2,838	52.20	$25,267	24.33
Student Classification	Effect (in percentage)		Effect (in percentage)		Effect (in percentage)	
Deaf-blind	n. a.	n. a.	n. a.	n. a.		-2.09
Hearing impairment	102.2	3.14	25.1	0.89	40.2	0.76
Multiple disorders	10.1	1.06	279.3	6.11	36.5	0.92
Other health impairment	97.1	2.40	24.6	0.96	n. a.	n. a.
Autism	24.8	0.61	360.3	3.12	-6.5	-0.21
Traumatic brain injury	47.0	1.63	19.3	0.58	-42.8	-0.85
Developmentally delayed	4.0	0.80	-41.0	-7.20	-38.8	-1.21
Unknown	12.1	1.15	15.1	2.09	-5.7	-0.13
Number of disabilities						
Primary disability only	—		—		—	
One additional disability	18.3	4.14	10.2	1.55	-11.9	-0.88
Two additional disabilities	17.8	2.67	12.9	1.30	223.8	1.86
Three or more additional disabilities	26.2	3.01	15.5	1.12	12.3	0.52
		F-Stat		F-Stat		F-Stat
R-square	0.43	14.98	0.47	15.44	0.79	4.85
Adjusted R-square	0.40		0.44		0.63	
Mean: Dependent variable (expenditure per pupil)	$4,695		$3,424		$21,837	
Sample size	673		562		59	

SOURCE: Adapted from Chambers et al. (1995), the Information About a Special Education Student Who is Served survey and the CSEF Resource Allocation forms.

NOTE: This analysis includes only those sample students located in Kindergarten through 12th grade school systems.

Weighting: These parameter estimates were weighted so that they reflect estimates for the population within Massachusetts.

Base cost: Base cost is based on the parameter estimate corresponding to the intercept term in the regression. It reflects the per-pupil expenditures on instructional and related services for a student with disabilities who is in the primary grades (1-3); has no special needs for curriculum, behavioral supports, or physical-medical supports; is learning disabled; and has no other disability conditions.

Percent effect: The figures in the columns below the label "Effect (in percentage)" are estimated from the actual regression parameters as follows. If β = regression parameter, then the effect in percentage = $100 * [exp(\beta) - 1]$ where exp = the exponential function.

Pupil Needs

The need for curricular adaptations appeared to have significant impact only on the expenditures on serving students with disabilities in nondepartmentalized settings, for the most part, in elementary school settings. Both moderate or major curriculum adaptations seemed to be associated with approximately the same expenditure differential of just over 30% (t-ratios 3.3). It is interesting that those whose differential needs were missing were associated with an 80% higher expenditure (t-ratio of 4.18). No statistically significant differential was associated with minor curricular adaptations. Among students in departmentalized settings, the magnitudes of the differentials associated with curricular adaptations were all below 17%, and none of these were statistically significant. Among students in nondepartmentalized settings, the need for behavioral supports appeared to be associated with an expenditure differential of between almost 20% (t-ratio = 3.97) for minor needs up to a more than 33% cost differential (t-ratio = 4.80) for major needs. There was virtually no significant difference in expenditure between minor and moderate needs. Among students in departmentalized settings, only those perceived as having major needs for behavioral supports exhibited any differential expenditures, but these differences were quite substantial, at more than 50% (t-ratio = 3.59).

For students in nondepartmentalized settings, moderate needs for physical or medical supports were associated with an expenditure differential of about 17% (t-ratio = 2.19), whereas major needs exhibited a 43% differential (t-ratio = 3.70). No statistically significant differential was associated with minor needs. Though the magnitudes were relatively large (ranging from 27% to more than 50%), the needs for physical or medical supports among students with disabilities in external assignments were not statistically significant.

Student Disability

Among students in nondepartmentalized settings, 6 of the 12 disability categories exhibited positive and statistically significant expenditure differences when compared with learning disabled. Significant differences ranged from a low of 15.3% (t-ratio = 2.18) for emotional disturbance to a high of 167.9% (t-ratio = 6.36) for orthopedic impairment. In the middle of this distribution is profound mental retardation, exhibiting a 90% differential (t-ratio = 4.68), other health impairment with a 97.1% differential (t-ratio = 2.40), and hearing impaired at 102.2% (t-ratio = 3.14).

Among students served in departmentalized settings, 8 out of the 12 disability categories appeared to be associated with statistically significant expenditure differences related to students with learning disabilities. These expenditure differentials ranged from a low of about 27% (t-ratio = 2.17) for emotional disturbance to a high of 360% (t-ratio = 3.12) for students with autism. That is, autistic children, on average, exhibited expenditures about 4.6 times those for students with learning disabilities in nondepartmentalized settings. Children with multiple disorders or orthopedic impairments exhibited expenditures that are about 279% (t-ratio = 6.11) and 268% (t-ratio = 2.66) higher, respectively, than those for students with learning disabilities in departmentalized settings. Children with profound mental retardation exhibited expenditures more than 100% higher than those with learning disabilities in these settings.

Last, among students in nondepartmentalized settings, those with more than one disability exhibited higher expenditures for instructional and related services ranging from about 18% for one or two additional disabilities (t-ratios of 4.14 for one additional and 2.67 for two additional disabilities) to more than 26% (t-ratio = 3.01) for students with three or more disabilities.

Comparison to Regular Education Cost

Table 5.3 was developed for the purpose of comparing the expenditures for serving students with disabilities with the expenditures for regular education students. The data in Table 5.3 combine the information on the expenditures for serving regular education students shown in Figures 5.1 and 5.2 with the analysis of variations in the average expenditures for instructional and related services for students with disabilities shown in Table 5.2. The regular education cost factors in the first row of Table 5.3 are calculated as the ratio of the base expenditure for a student with disabilities (from Table 5.2) for the corresponding instructional setting (i.e., nondepartmentalized, departmentalized, and external) to the expenditure for regular education students at the grade ranges commonly served in that setting. For each setting, the base expenditure for a student with disabilities corresponds to a student in the primary grades (1-3) who exhibits no special needs for curricular adaptations, behavioral supports, or physical-medical supports and who is classified as learning disabled with no other disabilities.[19] Each regular education cost factor (top row) relates specifically to students in the setting in which the student was served (i.e., nondepartmentalized, departmentalized, or external assignments).

For nondepartmentalized students, this ratio was 1.24, which is determined by the ratio of the average per-pupil expenditure on students with disabilities in nondepartmentalized settings (i.e., $2,694 from Table 5.2) to the average per-pupil expenditure on regular education students at the elementary level (i.e., $2,168 from Figure 5.1). For departmentalized students, this regular education cost ratio was 0.93, which is the ratio of the average per-pupil expenditure on students with disabilities in departmentalized settings (i.e. $2,838 from Table 5.2) to the average per-pupil expenditure on regular education students at the middle and high school levels (i.e., $3,044 = .33 × $2,921 + .67 × $3,104, from Figure 5.2).[20] For external assignments, the regular education cost ratio was 9.70, which was the ratio of $25,267 to the overall average expenditure per pupil for regular education students of $2,606 [= ($2,168 + $3,044)/2].

The remaining rows in Table 5.3 present the special education cost factors corresponding to each specific characteristic of a student with disabilities. This special education cost factor reflects the ratio of the expenditure for serving a student with disabilities with the corresponding characteristic, relative to the base expenditure for a student with disabilities, all else equal. That is, the expenditure or cost impact of each characteristic was isolated, hypothetically, from every other characteristic.

The ratio of the expenditure for serving a student with disabilities with any given combination of student characteristics relative to regular education was calculated by selecting the regular education cost factor and multiplying it times each of the combination of special education cost factors corresponding to each student characteristic. That is, to use these figures to calculate the expenditure for a given type of student, one would have to select the appropriate combination of student characteristics and multiply the various ratios together to estimate the implicit cost ratio to regular education.[21] Clearly, one must take care in using this table not to create combinations of student characteristics that do not exist, but the data at least provide some idea of the sources of the expenditure variations that exist for students with disabilities.

For example, consider a student with disabilities who is served in a 5th grade nondepartmentalized setting (special education cost factor = 1.03), exhibits minor needs for curriculum adaptation (special education cost factor = 1.17), is learning disabled (special education cost factor = 1.00) and has no additional disabilities. This student has a regular education cost factor of 1.49 (= 1.24 × 1.03 × 1.17).[22] If this same student were to require moderate behavioral supports (special education cost factor = 1.17), the regular education cost ratio would be 1.75 (= 1.24 × 1.03 × 1.17 × 1.17).

Now, consider a more severely involved student. A student in primary grades (1-3) who has minor needs for curriculum adaptation, major needs for physical-medical supports, is orthopedically impaired, and has 2 additional disabilities has a regular education cost factor of 6.61 (= 1.24 × 1.17 × 1.44 × 2.68 × 1.18). A student in primary grades (1-3) who has minor needs for curriculum adaptation, major needs for behavioral supports, is emotionally disturbed, and has no additional disabilities has a regular education cost factor of 4.39 (= 1.24 × 1.17 × 1.33 × 1.15). This same student in a secondary, departmentalized setting would have a cost factor of 1.66 (= 0.93 × 0.92 × 1.53 × 1.27).

Among the students with external assignments, the base regular education cost factor is 9.70. Add the disability of deaf-blindness to this base cost factor, and the regular education cost factor becomes 24.4 (= 9.7 × 2.52).

What do these numbers imply about the hypothetical average student with disabilities? The second to the last row in Table 5.3 presents the special education cost factor corresponding to the hypothetical average student with disabilities (i.e., the average combination of the characteristics presented in Table 5.3) in each type of setting. The last row in Table 5.3 presents the overall average regular education cost factor for the average student with disabilities. For example, the average student with disabilities served in nondepartmentalized

TABLE 5.3 The Ratios of Expenditures for Instructional and Related Service Personnel for Various Categories of Students With Disabilities Relative to Regular Education Students (based on multivariate ordinary least squares regression estimates)

	Students Served in Internal Assignments				External Assignments	
	Nondepartmentalized		Departmentalized			
	Regular Education		Regular Education		Regular Education	
Cost Factor	Cost		Cost		Cost	
Descriptions	Factors	Significance	Factors	Significance	Factors	Significance
Ratio of base expenditure for a student with disabilities to regular education student	1.24	***	0.93	***	9.70	***

Characteristics of Students With Disabilities	Special Education Cost		Special Education Cost		Special Education Cost	
	Factors	Significance	Factors	Significance	Factors	Significance
Grade level						
Preschool	0.68	**	n. a.		n. a.	
Kindergarten	0.73	***	n. a.		n. a.	
Primary grades 1 through 3	1.00		1.00		1.00	
Grades 4 through 8	1.03		1.07		0.53	***
Grades 9 through 12	1.16		0.92		0.78	
Need for curriculum adaptation						
None	1.00		1.00		1.00	
Minor	1.17	*	0.92		0.60	
Moderate	1.31	***	1.12		0.74	
Major	1.33	***	1.17		0.65	
Unknown	1.82	***	1.14			
Need for behavioral support						
None	1.00		1.00		1.00	
Minor	1.20	***	1.01		1.30	*
Moderate	1.17	***	1.10		1.71	**
Major	1.33	***	1.53	***	1.82	**
Unknown	0.81	*	0.97			
Need for physical-medical support						
None	1.00		1.00		1.00	
Minor	1.01		0.96		1.28	
Moderate	1.17	***	0.79	**	1.42	*
Major	1.44	***	1.04		1.53	*
Unknown	1.13		1.07		0.98	

TABLE 5.3 *Continued*

	Students Served in Internal Assignments				External Assignments	
	Nondepartmentalized Regular Education Cost		Departmentalized Regular Education Cost		Regular Education Cost	
Cost Factor Descriptions	Factors	Significance	Factors	Significance	Factors	Significance
Ratio of base expenditure for a student with disabilities to regular education student	1.24	***	0.93	***	9.70	***
Characteristics of Students With Disabilities	Special Education Cost		Special Education Cost		Special Education Cost	
	Factors	Significance	Factors	Significance	Factors	Significance
Primary student disability						
Learning disabled	1.00		1.00		1.00	
Speech impairment	1.01		0.81			
Mild mental retardation	1.25	***	1.31	***	1.06	
Profound mental retardation	1.90	***	2.07	***	0.61	
Emotional disturbance	1.15	**	1.27	**	0.89	
Orthopedic impairment	2.68	***	3.68	***		
Visual impairment-blindness	1.02		2.09	**		
Deaf-blind					2.52	**
Hearing impairment	2.02	***	1.25		1.40	
Multiple disorders	1.10		3.79	***	1.36	
Other health impairment	1.97	**	1.25			
Autism	1.25		4.60	***	0.94	
Traumatic brain injury	1.47		1.19		0.57	
Developmentally delayed	1.04		0.59	***	0.61	
Unknown	1.12		1.15	**	0.94	
Number of disabilities						
Primary disability only	1.00		1.00		1.00	
One additional disability	1.18	***	1.10		0.88	
Two additional disabilities	1.18	***	1.13		3.24	*
Three or more additional disabilities	1.26	***	1.16		1.12	
Average student with disabilities	1.74	***	1.29	***	0.86	***
Average ratio to regular education	2.17	***	1.21	***	8.38	***

SOURCE: Adapted from Chambers et al. (1995), the Information About a Special Education Student Who is Served survey and the CSEF Resource Allocation forms.
NOTE: This analysis includes only those sample students located in Kindergarten through 12th grade school systems.

(continued)

TABLE 5.3 *Continued*

Ratio of base cost for a student with disabilities to regular education cost: This ratio is equal to the base cost of serving a student with disabilities divided by the base cost of serving a regular education student. The base cost for a student with disabilities assumes the student is in the primary grades (1-3), exhibits no special needs, and is learning disabled with no additional disabilities. This base cost is derived from the intercept term for each of the three regression equations and is presented in the top row of Table 5.2. The values are $2,694 for nondepartmentalized, $2,838 for departmentalized, and $25,267 for external assignments. The estimates of per-pupil expenditures for regular education are based on the school-level analysis of regular education services for elementary ($2,168) and secondary ($3,044) students (see Figures 5.1 and 5.2). The average of the elementary and secondary figures ($2,606) is used as the regular education benchmark for those students with disabilities served in external assignments. Cost factors: The cost factors presented are calculated from the regression coefficients corresponding to the dichotomous variables representing the student characteristics. The cost factors reflect the ratio of the cost of serving a student with disabilities with a certain characteristic relative to the base cost of serving a student with a disability. If β = regression coefficient, then the cost factor is calculated by the expression $\exp(\beta)$ where $\exp$ = the exponential function.
Statistical significance: * = 0.10; ** = 0.05; *** = 0.01.

settings exhibits a special education cost factor of 1.74. Multiplying this special education cost factor by the regular education cost factor of 1.24 (Row 1 of Table 5.3), one can estimate the average ratio of the costs of serving a student with disabilities in a nondepartmentalized setting at 2.17 (= 1.74 × 1.24). Similarly, for students with disabilities served in departmentalized settings, the average ratio to regular education is 1.21 (= 0.93 × 1.29). For students served in external assignments, this regular education cost factor is 8.38 (= 9.70 × 0.86). Viewed in this fashion, one can see that there is a considerable difference in this ratio across these three settings.

The goal of these analyses is to be able to estimate the expenditures required to serve students with different sets of need characteristics. To be completely successful in this venture means that adding information about the specific service prototype to the regression equations on which Tables 5.2 and 5.3 are based would add relatively little to the explanatory power of the equation. But what happens when we add service prototype to each equation? Unfortunately, whereas the student characteristics do explain a substantial portion of the variance in expenditures, the addition of service prototype still adds significantly to the explanatory power of the equation. The adjusted r-square of the equation for students in nondepartmentalized settings increases from .43 to .51 with the addition of service prototype variables to the equation. The adjusted r-square of the equation for students in departmentalized settings increases from .47 to .54 with the addition of service prototype variables to the equation. In both cases, the prototype adds 0.07 to the r-square, and some of the service prototype indicators are statistically significant.[23] Clearly, more elaborate and precise indicators of pupil needs will be required to explain fully the variations in expenditures. For example, one might include more specific indicators of the nature of the curricular adaptations (e.g., the use of braille texts), the types of physical-medical supports (e.g., need and frequency of catheterization), or the nature of behavioral problems experienced (e.g., depression or hyperactivity).

Inclusion and Student Need

The previous analyses have demonstrated some systematic patterns of variation in costs of services to students with disabilities in relation to their placements, perceived needs, age levels, and specific disabilities. What seems clear from this analysis is that no one specific factor captures student needs and hence cost variations. Knowledge of student disability does contribute some information about student needs and hence costs; however, there are significant variations in costs within prototype groupings related to the levels of needs and student disabilities.

Assigning students to a disability category, as well as assessing their levels of curricular, behavioral support, and physical-medical support needs is, to some degree, a subjective process. What are the factors that affect this process of assigning students to a need category?

One hypothesis is that teachers working in more inclusive environments will tend to perceive students as having lower levels of need than they would if they were in less inclusive environments.[24] To test this hypothesis, the following analysis was carried out. First, an average level of student need was calculated for each school. This estimate was based on the index values reflecting the levels of adaptations of curricular materials, behavioral support, and physical-medical support needs assigned to the sample of students with disabilities in each of the sample schools for this study. Thus, each school had a single index value that is intended to reflect the average level of need of its students with disabilities.

Second, each school was assigned an index value reflecting the level of inclusion being implemented in the school. One aspect of defining inclusive practice was that more services were provided to students with disabilities within the regular classroom than outside the regular classroom. That is, rather than being served in separate environments (special classes or pull-out resource programs), students with disabilities spent more time within the regular classroom and were served by resource teachers or instructional aides. Rather than having the student go to the teacher, the teacher went to the student. The measure of inclusion used for this analysis is the percentage of the instructional and related service budget for special education spent on resource teachers or instructional aides who went into the regular classroom to provide services.[25]

Third, schools were identified by grade levels served in order to control for differences in the general school environment and delivery systems common to these grade levels that might affect the results of this analysis.

Table 5.4 presents the correlation of average student needs with the measure of inclusion. All three correlations are negative, although only the correlation for elementary schools is statistically significant. These results are consistent with the hypothesis that special education teachers employed in elementary schools with more inclusive practices rate their students as having lower levels of need. This is evidence that the environment within which students are served and the philosophy underlying the approach to serving special education children may affect the ways in which these children are perceived. These results are consistent with either one hyposthesis or a combination of two hypotheses:

Students in more inclusive schools actually have lower needs.

or

Students in more inclusive schools
are perceived as having lower needs.

Without more objective data on the measurement of student needs, it was not possible to distinguish between these two hypotheses. To distinguish between them would require the consistent measurement

TABLE 5.4 Relationship Between Inclusion and Student Needs: School Year 1994-1995

Type of School	Correlation Between Student Need and Inclusionary Practice	Level of Statistical Significance	Number of Sample Schools
Elementary School	− 0.37	.016	41
Middle-Junior High School	− 0.15	.584	15
High School	− 0.20	.364	22

SOURCE: Adapted from Chambers et al. (1995), the Information About a Special Education Student Who is Served survey and the CSEF Resource Allocation forms.
NOTE: How to interpret this table—an example: The –0.37 suggests that schools classified as being more inclusive exhibit lower levels of student needs according to the teachers. The level of significance of .016 indicates that there is a probability of 1.6% that a correlation this far from zero could have occurred by chance. In other words, a negative correlation like the one in the table is likely to hold true for the population of elementary schools in Massachusetts. The sample size on which this statistic is based includes 41 schools.

of student needs across all schools by a party who could observe the students independently of the school environment within which they are served. The perceptions of student needs by the teachers within each school could then be compared to those of the more objective external reviewers.

Summary and Conclusions

An understanding of the factors affecting expenditure differences is critical for state policy makers considering issues related to funding alternatives. The analysis contained in this chapter indicated that although a substantial portion of the variance in expenditures for serving students with disabilities may be explained by certain conventional ways of categorizing students, an even more substantial portion of the variance was left unexplained by systematic differences in the observable characteristics of students.

The analysis revealed systematic differences in expenditure related to primary disability as well as the levels of need for adaptation of curricular materials, behavioral supports, and physical-medical supports as reported by teachers. All else equal, students for whom additional disabilities were reported beyond their primary disability exhibited higher expenditures, ranging from 10% to 26% depending on the number of disabilities and the severity of involvement. Among the students served in nondepartmentalized settings, the need for physical-medical supports exhibited a wider range of expenditure variation (i.e., from 1% to 44% difference) than did the differences in expenditure associated with the adaptation of curriculum or behavioral supports (i.e., which range from about 17% to 33%). Among the students served in departmentalized settings, these expenditure differences were generally smaller, suggesting lower levels of involvement.

Controlling for differences in curricular, behavioral, and physical-medical support needs, expenditure differences associated with disability varied considerably between students served in nondepartmentalized versus departmentalized settings. Whereas expenditure differences for students with mild mental retardation and emotional disturbance were of similar orders of magnitude between students served in nondepartmentalized versus departmentalized settings, expenditures for students with other disabilities differed significantly in expenditures between these two types of settings. This evidence was consistent with the notion that students in departmentalized settings were less severely disabled than those in nondepartmentalized settings.

Last, results were consistent with the notion that the environment within which students are served and the philosophy underlying the approach to serving special education children may affect the ways in which these children are perceived, especially at the elementary level. Specifically, the evidence was at least consistent with the hypothesis that teachers working in more inclusive schools may perceive children to exhibit lower levels of need than those located in less inclusive schools. More research would be required to determine the impact of these changes in teacher perceptions of need on the educational process and ultimately on student outcomes.

What do the results of this analysis mean for census-based funding? Census-based funding assumes that the variations in the percentage of students identified with disabilities and the average resources required to serve those students do not vary all that much across local school districts. The data presented in this chapter show the potential for variations in the average resources currently expended to serve students with disabilities. Whereas approximately half of the students with disabilities are classified as learning disabled and the variations in expenditures within this category are relatively small, the remainder are distributed among the other disability categories. This chapter suggests that there is considerable potential for variations across districts and schools in the patterns of expenditure for students with disabilities associated with variations in the composition of students according to disability categories and needs for curricular, behavioral, and physical-medical supports. Census-based funding can potentially result in substantial overfunding and underfunding of special education services across districts serving different compositions of students. To determine the potential impact of census-based funding, further research is needed to understand how services, expenditures, and the composition of student needs vary across schools and districts and what implications these variations have for the relationship between expenditures and revenues.

Five assumptions underlie the analysis presented in this chapter: (a) Student needs can be defined in terms of specific student characteristics; (b) they can be objectively measured or assessed (i.e., operationalized); (c) there is a specific relationship between the desired outcomes for students, the service requirements needed to achieve those outcomes, and characteristics that define student needs; (d) one can accurately measure the cost of a particular type of service; and (e) school decision makers understand these relationships and attempt to assign students and school inputs to services in an optimal fashion, given available resources and prices of school inputs.

The next steps in this research involve more extensive investigation into these assumptions. A more extensive and detailed set of student characteristics needs to be identified and measured. More work needs to be done to explore the relationship between the desired outcomes for certain types of students, the observed student need characteristics, and the service requirements. That is, which types of services in what levels of intensity are required to produce certain outcomes for students who exhibit certain need characteristics? How do these service requirements change in the face of changing fiscal constraints and differences in the relative prices of the school inputs that make up the service? The goal is to associate service expenditures with need characteristics that are determined in the most objective possible way. School funding systems may then be based on the counts of children with these various combinations of need characteristics. The more objective the process of determining the presence of need characteristics in a child, the less ability local decision makers will have to influence the processes of identification and placement of these children. By making this process of assessment more objective and basing the school funding system on the assessment of needs, one can also ensure that local districts have sufficient funding to meet the needs of special populations of children.

Notes

1. The Florida Department of Education (FDE) undertook a study (1996) focused on the development of objective criteria for classifying special education students for the purposes of determining needs for services, their costs, and the level of state funding to be provided.

2. Underlying this simple statement is the notion that student needs are intrinsic: Student needs can be defined in terms of specific student characteristics; They can be objectively measured or assessed (i.e., operationalized). There is a specific relationship between the desired outcomes for students, the service requirements needed to achieve those outcomes, and characteristics that define student needs. One can accurately measure the cost of a particular type of service. Moreover, the analysis implicitly assumes that school decision makers ultimately understand these relationships and make optimal decisions about the assignment of students to services, given the total resources and prices of the school inputs that are available to them.

3. This terminology, the *service prototype*, is adopted to conform to that of the Commonwealth of Massachusetts, whose data provide the basis for the analyses contained in this chapter.

4. Copies of the full report on which this chapter is based (Chambers et al., 1995) may be obtained from the author at the Center for Special Education Finance located at the American Institutes for Research, John C. Flanagan Research Center, PO Box 1113, Palo Alto, California, 94302.

5. Instructions were provided to each respondent on how to select the students at random from their classes or caseloads.

6. Initially, this was referred to as the ingredients approach by Levin (1983) because of its focus on the physical ingredients allocated for programs and services. As this methodology has been used and enhanced by Chambers and Parrish (1982, 1984, 1994) over the years, it has come to be known as the resource cost model approach.

7. Based on the overall estimates of nonpersonnel expenditures presented in the final report to Massachusetts (Chambers et al., 1995), every $100 of expenditure on personnel generates, on average, an additional $9.36 expended on nonpersonnel resources. See Figure II-6a (Chapter II) and Table C-4a (Appendix C), and Footnote 11 in Chapter III of the final report (Chambers et al., 1995) for a further discussion.

8. All data from the sample of students have been weighted so that the descriptive statistics represent estimates of the values for the statewide population from which the samples are selected.

9. With minor exceptions, which are noted, the data presented in this chapter are derived from the CSEF surveys titled Information About a Special Education Student.

10. A team at the FDE has developed a promising new approach that links student needs to types and intensities of services and, ultimately, costs (see Florida Department of Education, 1996).

11. In the most common models of the departmentalized environment, both regular and special education students are enrolled in anywhere from five to seven class periods, each of which focuses on a different subject or specialized set of skills. This environment is referred to as departmentalized because the courses are most commonly organized into separate departments by subject area.

12. Nondepartmentalized environments are characterized by self-contained classrooms, organized by grade level(s), in which students are assigned to classrooms staffed, most often, by one full-time teacher who provides instruction in most of the primary academic and, in some cases, nonacademic subjects. In some instances, classes or subsets of subjects are team taught or are instructed by subject matter specialists.

13. Despite the fact that disability labels have not commonly been used in the Massachusetts funding model, the vast majority of teachers responding on behalf of the students were able to identify the primary disability according to one of these labels.

14. A factor analysis was done on these three dimensions, and it was found that the three dimensions tend to move together. Only a single factor was identified, thus permitting consolidation into a single index as an average of the three dimensions. This index is used in parts of the analysis presented in the text.

15. That is, regular education costs are based on the school site data from the sample of schools included in this study and reflect the average costs of instructional services for regular elementary, middle-junior high, and high school students. The cost data for students with disabilities are based on the information taken from the individual student information forms.

16. More detailed breakdowns of the levels of need and their relationships to costs can be found in Appendix F of the report to the Massachusetts Department of Education (Chambers et al., 1995). Multiple regression analyses were performed to examine the relationships between costs and all student characteristics and to identify statistically significant relationships between various categories of students.

17. These figures are based on the ratio of instructional and related service expenditures for learning disabled students relative to the regular education expenditures for middle-junior high and high school expenditures. For the middle-junior high schools, the ratio is 1.14 = $3,328/$2,921, whereas for the high school, the ratio is 1.07 = $3,328/$3,104.

18. The difference in the R-square in Table 5.2 and the overall R-square in the last column of Table 5.1 is due to the addition of the variables indicating the number of disabilities assigned to each student.

19. This is the antilog of the intercept in the regression equation.

20. The value $3,044 is the weighted average of the middle-school-level and high-school-level figures from Figure 5.2. The high-school-level average per-pupil expenditure is $3,104 for grades 9 through 12, and the middle school average per-pupil expenditure is $2,921 for grades 7 and 8. The weighted average of these two figures is determined as follows: $3,044 = .33 × $2,921 + .67 × $3,104, where the weights reflect the number of grade levels represented by each number.

21. The reason why the implicit cost ratio to regular education is the product of the other ratios is as follows: In the regression equation, $\ln y = \alpha + \beta_1 x_1 + \ldots + \beta_p x_p$, where $x_1, \ldots x_p$ are dichotomous covariants, α represents the base cost of a special education student, and β_i represents the special education cost factor for x_i. A student with $x_1 = 1$ and $x_2 = 1$ and all the other $x_i = 0$ would have a total cost of $y = \exp(\alpha + \beta_1 + \beta_2)$. Let c = the cost of regular education. Then the student's regular education cost ratio is given by the following expression:

Regular education cost ratio = y/c

$$= \frac{\exp(\alpha + \beta_1 + \beta_2)}{c}$$

$$= \frac{\exp(\alpha) \times \exp(\beta_1) \times \exp(\beta_2)}{c}$$

Rearranging terms, one arrives at the following expression:

$$= \frac{\exp(\alpha)}{c} \times \exp(\beta_1) \times \exp(\beta_2) \text{, where } \frac{\exp(\alpha)}{c}$$

= the ratio of the base expenditure for a student with a disability to the average expenditure for a regular education student.

22. The reader will recall that calculating the regular education cost factor for a given type of student with disabilities requires the use of the ratio of the base regular education cost factor of 1.24.

23. It is important to recognize that this analysis implicitly makes two assumptions: that (a) there is a unique relationship between student characteristics, service requirements, and the desired outcomes for students with disabilities and (b) school decision makers behave in an optimal fashion in the way they assign students to services. An alternative explanation for the additional explanatory power of service prototype in the analysis is that there are differences across districts in the perceptions of the way student needs relate to service requirements, the fiscal constraints, or the relative prices of the inputs used to provide the optimal services. The author is grateful to Cassandra Guarino for pointing this out and for suggesting that this assumption be made explicit in the discussion.

24. The author wishes to thank Margaret McLaughlin for suggesting this hypothesis.

25. These estimates of this percentage are based on school-level data on special education expenditures rather than student-level data on costs.

References

Chambers, J. G., & Parrish, T. B. (1982). *The development of a resource cost model funding base for education finance in Illinois, Volume I: Executive summary and Volume II: Technical report* (Prepared for the Illinois State Board of Education). Stanford, CA: Associates for Education Finance and Planning.

Chambers, J. G., & Parrish, T. B. (1984). *The development of a program cost model and a cost-of-education index for the State of Alaska: Final Report, Volumes I-IV.* Stanford, CA: Associates for Education Finance and Planning.

Chambers, J. G., & Parrish, T. B. (1994). Modeling resource costs. In S. Barnett & H. Walberg (Eds.), *Cost analysis for Educational Decision Making.* Greenwich, CT: JAI.

Chambers, J. G., Parrish, T. B., Hikido, C., & Dueñas, I. (1995). *A comprehensive study of education for the Commonwealth of Massachusetts: Final report.* Palo Alto, CA: American Institutes for Research, Center for Special Education Finance.

Florida Department of Education. (1996). *Proposed funding model, final report, 1994-1995.* Tallahassee, FL: Author.

Levin, H. M. (1983). *Cost effectiveness: A primer.* Beverly Hills, CA: Sage.

S I X

Special Education Finance in Pennsylvania

ROBERT E. FEIR

Pennsylvania—long a leader in special education—enacted major revisions of both its special education program rules and financing system in 1990 and 1991. The purpose of this chapter is to analyze the impact of these changes—particularly the fiscal changes—during the first 4 years of implementation. Results during the first 2 years of the reforms suggested that the aims of policy makers in 1990 and 1991 generally were being realized, although not uniformly throughout the state (Feir, 1995; Hartman, 1994; Montgomery & DeSera, 1996), but by 1994-1995 (the latest year of complete data), the picture was somewhat less clear.

Background

Three years before Congress passed the initial Education for All Handicapped Children Act in 1975,[1] Pennsylvania entered into a federal court consent agreement to locate and educate all children with mental retardation in the state.[2] Less than a year before the state entered into this so-called PARC consent agreement, the General Assembly replaced the 67 county school superintendents with 29 intermediate units (IUs; regional education service agencies), and the IUs soon took on the major responsibility for planning and operating special education programs.

State Board of Education regulations governing special education programs included provisions for mainstreaming but emphasized separate program operation; in fact, to be eligible for special education funding, programs were required to be offered outside of regular classes.[3] Throughout the development and expansion of special education in this country, Pennsylvania had the distinction of being the only state with a statutory requirement to pay 100% of the excess costs of educating special education students and the further distinction of defining both gifted children and those with disabilities as eligible for special education (National Association of State Directors of Special Education, 1982).

This fiscal policy provided incentives to open increasing numbers of special education programs, and some more arcane aspects of the statute made it more advantageous for those programs to operate under the aegis of the intermediate units.[4] These incentives resulted in many needed programs, but also in overidentifying, labeling, and maintaining students in special education longer than necessary, placement in more restrictive settings than necessary, and a drift of expenditures from other categories into special education (Moore, Walker, & Holland, 1982).

During the 1980s, special education programs in Pennsylvania grew rapidly, and the statutory requirement to fund 100% of them outstripped the General Assembly's budgetary inclination in a time of increasing demands for prison construction, medical assistance and other welfare programs, and senior citizen programs.

Elementary and secondary school enrollments declined every year during the 1980s, but special education enrollments increased in 6 of those 10 years, resulting in a major increase in the percentage of all public school students receiving special education services.

Although it was invisible to most people for several years, a crisis in special education finance began to brew in the early 1980s. At the end of the 1981-1982 fiscal year, the state was $2 million short in its obligations to school district special education funding. The deficit was rolled over and paid out of 1982-1983 appropriations. By the end of the 1987-88 fiscal year, the debt had grown to $50 million. These shortfalls were temporary, and school districts and intermediate units essentially loaned the money to the state until payments could be made early in the succeeding fiscal year. Classes did not close, and teachers did not work without being paid, so the issue did not lend itself to general public attention. By 1988-1989, the debt was $104 million, and serious attention began to be paid by the Department of Education and legislators, who appropriated $99 million, the amount they thought would be needed to pay the debt. The 1989-1990 budget was another $89 million short, and the failure of the General Assembly to accept the governor's proposals for change in 1990-1991 resulted in an additional shortfall of $147 million.

Policy Changes: 1990-1991

Two sets of policy changes were enacted in 1990 and 1991. On July 1, 1989, the State Board of Education was directed by the legislature to revise the special education program regulations no later than March 1, 1990. The General Assembly wanted the regulations to provide for "fiscal accountability, prudent management, appropriate education support services and special classes to meet the needs of pupils, and assurance of continued service" to children enrolled in special education programs.[5]

The new regulations, representing the first major change in 14 years, were adopted February 27, 1990, and became effective 4 months later.[6] The most significant change was to focus on instructional needs of students rather than on their deficits. Referral for special education evaluation would need to be preceded by either instructional interventions of an instructional support team (IST) or a parental demand for immediate evaluation. This change was designed to lead to regular class success for more students and a reduction in unnecessary or inappropriate referrals for special education evaluation and placement. The State Board's revised regulations also included several innovations for students eventually placed in special programs. The special education curriculum was required to mirror the regular education program to the maximum extent feasible. Special services could be provided in regular classrooms and still be eligible for special education funding (the funding aspect of this change was made moot by subsequent changes in the funding system). Parental authority was increased, and the regulations provided for early intervention and postsecondary transition services, more refined individualized education plans (IEPs), and behavior management for students needing it. Aversive discipline was prohibited, and students completing their IEPs would receive a regular high school diploma.

The State Board attempted to make available a wider array of services to meet student learning needs so that the most expensive option—testing for and placement in special education—would not be the only one available to school districts. However, only legislative action could eliminate or revise the incentives implicit in the full excess costs system of special education funding.

In his 1990-1991 budget message, the governor proposed a new method of funding special education programs. He offered to appropriate sufficient funds to cover excess costs for 1 year but with the funds distributed according to a formula based on local wealth and total enrollment—not special education students or actual expenditures for special education—and with no assurance that future increases would be related to cost increases (Casey, 1990). The General Assembly did not accept the proposed change but did enact a modified version as part of the state budget the following year.

The new formula, which took effect in 1991-1992, is not related to actual expenditures for special education or to numbers of students receiving special education services.[7] Most of the funding is distributed on the basis of a two-part formula. In 1991-1992, each district received $525 for 17% of its average daily membership (ADM; presumed to be children with mild disabilities and gifted students) and $7,000 for 1% of its ADM (presumed to be children with severe disabilities). These amounts were in addition to general aid, and the special education formula did not include a wealth-based equalization factor, as the governor had proposed. In subsequent years, the percentages of ADM and the dollar amounts per student have been revised by the General Assembly as the basis for appropriation increases (in 1994-1995, the final year of this study, the reimbursements were $1,035 for 15% of ADM and $12,500 for 1%). Districts may use these funds to provide programs directly or in consortia with other districts or to contract with IUs for the operation of programs.

The new funding law provides that 5% of the annual appropriation be paid to IUs to maintain core services and that a contingency fund be controlled by the Secretary of Education to assist districts with severe, unanticipated local problems. The contingency fund has ranged from 1% to 2% of the annual appropriation since its inception in 1991-1992. During 1991-1992, additional payments were targeted to three IUs that had operated 100% of the special education programs in their regions. These were Philadelphia, Pittsburgh, and Schuylkill County. The payments continued for Philadelphia and Pittsburgh through 1994-1995 but now are being phased out.

For 1991-1992 only, the General Assembly included two additional elements: (a) to provide a cost-based inflation factor of 5% and (b) to ensure that the new formula initially would distribute at least 3.5% more state funds to each IU region than in the 1990-1991 fiscal year. The cost of these factors was $28 million.

Last, in passing the 1991-1992 budget, the General Assembly appropriated $147 million to pay off its prior year's obligation and increased state funding of special education by 32% over 1990-1991. In addition, the legislation phased out district obligations to pay part of the prior year's regular education costs of students in special education programs operated by IUs. In 1991-1992, 75% of this so-called tuition recovery (valued at $150 million) was forgiven, and it was eliminated completely in 1992-1993.

Since the adoption of the formula in 1991-1992, the General Assembly has not altered its general approach to funding special education except to adjust the formula factors and the size of the contingency fund.[8] In addition, it adopted a recommendation by the governor for 1994-1995 to appropriate $10.5 million to assist several hard-pressed districts that had net special education expenditures as a percentage of their total expenditures exceeding 150% of the state average.[9] This supplement also is being phased out.

Four Years of Implementation

The remainder of this chapter is concerned with the implementation of the new special education policies from 1991-1992 through 1994-1995, using data obtained from the Pennsylvania Department of Education for all 500 operating school districts. Data elements include enrollment; numbers of students receiving special education, including the location of the service delivery and provider of the service; total school district expenditures; special education expenditures; and state support of special education expenditures through the new formula.[10]

Although it would be interesting to study the effects of the transition between 1990-1991 (the last year under the old system) and 1991-1992 (the first year under the new formula), to do so runs considerable risks. Under the old system, most state funds were distributed to IUs; under the new system, almost all funds are distributed to districts. Under the old system, districts paid IUs for the regular education costs of special education students through tuition recovery, and those payments were made for the prior year programs based on 2-year-old tuition rates; under the new system, tuition recovery has been eliminated. Under the old system, although full excess costs were paid by the state, payments often were made in years subsequent to those in which obligations were incurred, and the basis of payments to IUs and districts differed somewhat; under the new system, state payments are for current costs and are unrelated to actual expenditures incurred by districts and IUs. For all of these reasons, a more limited analysis of the early implementation of the new system is undertaken here.

It should be noted, however, that the 1991-1992 state budget and changes in special education funding were not adopted by the General Assembly until August 5, 1991, only a couple of weeks before the opening of school for most districts. As a result, there was almost no time for districts to revise special education pupil placements or alter program types or operating agencies during 1991-1992. Therefore, although it is recognized that few direct comparisons to the previous system can be derived from this study, it is very likely that 1991-1992 implementation was very similar in most districts to pre-reform operations.

Policy Objectives

Three separate, albeit not unrelated, policy objectives were identified by policy makers in the early 1990s (Casey, 1991; Pennsylvania
State Board of Education, 1990; Task Force, 1988). The first objective—
and the one foremost in the minds of state legislators and the governor—was to control the escalating state expenditures for special
education. The second objective was to give school districts greater
control over special education expenditures and remove the excess
costs disincentive for economizing so that the escalation of local costs
for special education might be slowed as well. The third objective was
to reduce the number of students identified for special education
programs through the introduction of instructional support and to
increase the percentage of students who received their special education services in regular classes, both of which were anticipated to
reduce reliance on more expensive services.

The analysis presented here is aimed at determining the degree to
which policy makers' goals have been achieved.

Controlling State Costs

There is no question about the effectiveness of the special education
formula in capping the growth in state expenditures for special education. What the state spends each year is no longer a function of
spending decisions by 500 operating school districts and 29 IUs. It is,
rather, a function of the budgetary decisions of the governor and the
General Assembly.

When the governor first proposed a formula to fund special education, the Department of Education predicted that without such a
change, the accumulated deficit owed to districts could actually exceed what was then a half billion dollar annual special education
appropriation in less than 5 years. Although some found this prediction alarming, the fact is that net school district expenditures for
special education (i.e., local spending not reimbursed through the
state special education formula)—spending that would have been a
state responsibility under the old excess costs system—actually to-
taled $489.4 million in 1994-1995.

TABLE 6.1 Average Annual Percentage Increases in Pennsylvania
State General Fund Expenditures for Special Education
Prior to and Following Implementation of Formula
Funding

State General Fund Appropriation	Average Percentage Increase 1981-1982 through 1991-1992	Average Percentage Increase 1991-1992 through 1994-1995
Special education (including instructional support teams)	16.51	4.98
Approved private schools (including charter schools for deaf and blind)	8.96	1.75

The state no longer incurs annual $100 million deficits. It no longer needs to appropriate double-digit percentage increases for special education. In fact, since appropriating the 32% increase needed to make the transition to the new formula, the legislature has increased the special education line item of the budget only modestly each year. Table 6.1 demonstrates these facts by showing average annual state general fund appropriations increases before and after implementation of the special education formula.

Impacts on Local Finance

What impact has the change in special education policy had on local school districts, in terms of school finance and service delivery? The most obvious impact is that special education now costs school districts more than it did in the past. Under the excess costs system, school districts bore practically no costs in excess of the regular education costs of students receiving special education. By design, the new formula reduces the state's relative share of the obligation for special education finance and shifts that burden to the school districts. In 1991-1992, school districts spent $413.7 million and in 1994-1995, they spent $489.4 million of local funds on special education.

In terms of whether the new funding system with its revised incentive structure has enabled districts to control their own local costs of

TABLE 6.2 Summary of Special Education Expenditure Data,
1991-1992 through 1994-1995

Category	1991-1992	1994-1995
Per-pupil special education expenditures:		
Median	$ 443	$ 493
Minimum	214	218
Maximum	1,484	1,655
Special education expenditures		
as a percentage of total:		
Median	7.84	8.00
Minimum	3.20	3.35
Maximum	18.66	20.35

providing special education, the results are a good deal more mixed. Between 1991-1992 and 1994-1995, the 19.82% increase in special education expenditures by districts was considerably greater than the 14.30% increase for total school district expenditures. On a per-pupil (not per-special education pupil) basis, the median special education expenditure increased from $443 in 1991-1992 to $493 in 1994-1995. For the median school district, special education expenditures as a percentage of total spending increased from 7.84% to 8.00%. These increases are elaborated somewhat in Table 6.2.

Of the 500 districts, 120 realized absolute reductions in per-pupil special education expenditures, ranging from $0.30 to $380 (or from 0.06% to 36.70%). Nearly one half of the districts (239) realized absolute reductions in per-pupil net special education expenditures (special education expenditures less the state reimbursement). By comparison, only 42 districts experienced reductions in overall spending per pupil during the period under study. Although more districts reduced spending on special education than the number that reduced their total spending, most districts did experience increases in special education spending, special education spending per pupil, and special education spending as a percentage of the total budget.

When this study was initially undertaken, it was hypothesized that the following factors would likely relate to a district's ability or inability to control its special education costs:

District wealth: A district with a high aid ratio (i.e., a district with low property and personal income wealth per student) is likely to have the fewest resources to spend on education in general or on special education.

Total expenditures per pupil: A district that spends a great deal on education in general is likely to spend a great deal on special education.

Special education pupils: A district with a high percentage of students receiving special education is likely to spend a relatively large amount of its budget to educate these students. The policy changes were designed in part to reduce the percentage of students placed in special education programs, the result of which should be reduced budget shares devoted to those programs.

Level of intervention: A district organizing most of its special education in part-time and full-time special classes is likely to incur higher costs than a district relying primarily on regular class instruction and itinerant services, which are less expensive to deliver. The policy changes were designed in part to shift special education services from part-time and full-time special classes to regular class and itinerant instruction, the result of which should be reduced spending on special education.

Program control: A district that relies largely on IUs and approved private schools (APSs) is less likely to be able to control program costs than a district that operates the special education programs for most of its students. The policy changes were designed in part to shift program control from IUs and APSs to school districts, the result of which should be reduced spending on special education.

As indicated earlier, expenditure, enrollment, district wealth, level of intervention, and program control data for all 500 operating districts for 1991-1992 and 1994-1995 were analyzed.

The variables of primary focus (referred to later as *expenditure variables*) for purposes of this study were (a) 1991-1992 and 1994-1995 special education expenditures per pupil, (b) 1991-1992 and 1994-1995 special education expenditures as a percentage of total district expenditures, (c) the percentage change in special education expenditures per pupil from 1991-1992 through 1994-1995, and (d) the change in special education expenditures as a percentage of total district expenditures from 1991-1992 through 1994-1995.

The variables hypothesized to be strongly associated with these (referred to later as *contextual variables*) for purposes of this study were (a) the 1991-1992 and 1994-1995 aid ratio (a measure of district wealth per pupil), (b) total expenditures per pupil, (c) special education students (including the gifted) and students with disabilities as percentages of total enrollment and (d) the changes in such percentages, (e) the percentage of students receiving special education in regular classes and itinerant programs and in part-time and full-time special classes and (f) the changes in those percentages, (g) the percentages of students receiving special education in district-operated, IU-operated, and APS-operated programs, and (h) the changes in those percentages.

Pearson correlation coefficients were calculated to determine relationships among the expenditure and contextual variables and the patterns of such relationships. The results of these analyses are described in the discussion to follow and summarized in Table 6.3.

All the contextual variables correlated significantly with per-pupil special education expenditures in both years. The largest correlations for both years were with total district expenditures, percentage of special education students served by APSs, percentage of students in special education (including gifted programs), percentage of students with disabilities, and percentage of special education students served in part-time and full-time special classes. These correlations were all positive.

Three of the contextual variables correlated significantly and positively with the percentage change in special education expenditures per pupil. These were the change in the percentage of pupils with disabilities, the change in the percentage of special education students served by IUs and APSs, and the change in the percentage of special education students served by IUs.

All but two of the contextual variables correlated significantly with special education spending as a percentage of total district expenditures in 1994-1995, and all but three did in 1991-1992. The highest correlations for 1994-1995, all of which were positive, were with percentage of students with disabilities, percentage of special education students served in part-time and full-time special classes, per-

TABLE 6.3 Correlations Between Expenditure and Contextual Variables

Contextual Variable	SE$/ Pup 1991-1992	SE$/ Pup 1994-1995	Change SE$ /Pup	SE% Tot$ 1991-1992	SE% Tot$ 1994-1995	Change SETot
AR	−.26*	−.22*		.14*	.11*	
Tot$	.58*	.57*		.08	.10*	
SE%Pup	.49*	.49*	.09	.35*	.37*	.10*
Dis%Pup	.43*	.46*	.18*	.51*	.56*	.20*
PT/FT%	.33*	.38*	.03	.45*	.46*	.04*
R/I%	−.26*	−.18*	−.03	−.39*	−.27*	−.01
%IU	−.14*	−.12*	.10*	−.02	−.02	.15*
%APS	.57*	.54*	.08	.38*	.36*	.10*
%IU-APS	−.11*	−.10*	.10*	.001	−.004	.15*

* = Correlation is significant at the .05 level.
Variable names: SE$/Pup = Special education expenditures per pupil. SE%Tot$ = Special education spending as a percentage of total district expenditures. AR = Aid ratio (measure of local property and income wealth per pupil; higher aid ratios indicate lower wealth per pupil). Tot$ = Total district expenditures per pupil. SE%Pup = Percentage of district pupils in special education (including gifted programs); change = change in percentage of district pupils in special education (including gifted programs), 1991-1992 to 1994-1995. Dis%Pup = Percentage of district pupils with disabilities; change = change in percentage of district pupils with disabilities, 1991-1992 to 1994-1995. PT/FT% = Percentage of special education pupils served in part-time and full-time special classes; change = change in percentage of special education pupils served in part-time and full-time special classes, 1991-1992 to 1994-1995. R/I% = Percentage of special education pupils served in regular classes and itinerant programs; change = change in percentage of special education pupils served in regular classes and itinerant programs, 1991-1992 to 1994-1995. %IU = Percentage of special education pupils served by IUs; change = change in percentage of special education pupils served by IUs, 1991-1992 to 1994-1995. %APS = Percentage of special education pupils served by approved private schools; change = change in percentage of special education pupils served by approved private schools, 1991-1992 to 1994-1995. %IU-APS = Percentage of special education pupils served by IUs and approved private schools; change = change in percentage of special education pupils served by IUs and approved private schools, 1991-1992 to 1994-1995.

centage of students in special education (including gifted programs), and percentage of special education students served by APSs. For 1991-1992, the highest correlations were with percentage of students with disabilities, percentage of special education students served in part-time and full-time special classes, percentage of special education students served in regular classes or itinerant programs (negative correlation), percentage of special education students served by APSs, and percentage of students in special education (including gifted programs).

Five contextual variables showed significant positive correlations with the change in special education spending as a percentage of total expenditures. These were the change in the percentage of pupils with disabilities, the change in the percentage of special education students served by IUs and APSs, the change in the percentage of special education students served by IUs, the change in the percentage of special education students served by APSs, and the change in the percentage of students in special education (including gifted programs). What do the data indicate with regard to the hypotheses stated previously?

District wealth: In both 1991-1992 and 1994-1995, high aid ratios (low-wealth districts) showed significant negative correlations with total spending and special education spending per pupil and positive correlations with special education as a percentage of total expenditures.

Total expenditures per pupil: This variable showed the strongest correlation of any of the contextual variables with 1991-1992 and 1994-1995 special education expenditures per pupil and correlated significantly, but to a lesser degree, with special education expenditures as a percentage of total expenditures for 1994-1995.

Special education pupils: The percentage of pupils with disabilities showed the strongest correlation with special education spending as a percentage of total spending in 1991-1992 and 1994-1995 and correlated significantly with special education expenditures per pupil in 1991-1992 and 1994-1995. Special education enrollment (including gifted pupils) as a percentage of total enrollment correlated significantly with special education expenditures per pupil and with special education as a percentage of total spending in both years. Increases in the percentage of pupils with disabilities showed the highest correlations, with both increases in special education expenditures per pupil and special education spending as a percentage of total expenditures.

Level of intervention: As predicted, part-time/full-time and regular/itinerant service variables both correlated significantly with special education expenditures—on a per-pupil basis and as a share of total budgets in both years. Districts relying more heavily on part-time and full-time classes experienced higher costs; those relying on regular class and itinerant instruction experienced lower costs. Changes in the degree of reliance on these placement types were not correlated significantly with changes in per-pupil special education expenditures or special education spending as a share of total expenditures.

Program control: The percentage of pupils served by APS programs correlated significantly with special education spending per pupil and as a share of a district's total budget in 1991-1992 and 1994-1995. However, the percentage served in IU programs correlated negatively and significantly with special education expenditures per pupil in both years. On the other hand, increased percentages of students served in IU programs correlated positively and significantly with increases in special education expenditures per pupil and increases in special education spending as a percentage of total spending.

Having examined all 500 operating districts, it seemed especially useful to concentrate more attention on those districts that were not able to achieve the policy objective of controlling special education costs by 1994-1995. Therefore, I looked most closely at districts at least 1.645 standard deviations above the mean—presumed to be the top 5% of districts (25 districts) in a normal distribution—on the following measures: (a) 1994-1995 per-pupil special education expenditures, (b) 1994-1995 special education spending as a percentage of total district expenditures, (c) the change in per-pupil special education expenditures from 1991-1992 through 1994-1995, and (d) the change in special education spending as a percentage of total district expenditures from 1991-1992 through 1994-1995. The means, standard deviations, and numbers of districts meeting these criteria are displayed in Table 6.4.

Districts meeting these criteria were examined with respect to wealth (aid ratio), size (enrollment), growth (percentage increase in enrollment from 1991-1992 through 1994-1995), population density (1990 Census data), and the contextual variables showing strong correlations in the correlation analysis that has been described. The distribution of districts meeting these criteria among the quintiles of 500 districts will be shown in Tables 6.5 through 6.8.

Nearly three dozen districts were more than 1.645 standard deviations above the mean for 1994-1995 per-pupil special education expenditures. Table 6.5 shows that these districts were predominantly wealthy, large, and urban (high population density). They were high

TABLE 6.4 Districts More than 1.645 Standard Deviations Above the
Mean on Four Dependent Variables

Variable	$\overline{X}$	SD	1.645 SD	Cases More than 1.645 SD > $\overline{X}$
1994-1995 special education expenditures per pupil	$536.81	$182.55	$837.10	35
1994-1995 special education spending as percentage of total expenditures	8.18	2.17	11.75	29
Percentage change in special education expenditures per pupil	18.70	19.92	51.47	34
Change in special education spending as percentage of total expenditures	0.06	1.33	2.25	25

per-pupil spenders in general, had high percentages of students with disabilities, and were more inclined to serve them in part-time and full-time special classes rather than in regular classes or itinerant programs. They also placed high percentages of students in APSs. This latter factor, which showed the second highest correlation with per-pupil special education expenditures (see the earlier correlation analysis), is in part a function of geography. Almost all the APSs are located in Allegheny County in southwestern Pennsylvania and the five counties in southeastern Pennsylvania, including Philadelphia and its suburbs. Of the 35 districts spending the most per pupil on special education, 29 were located in those six counties.

There were 29 districts showing more than 1.645 standard deviations above the mean for 1994-1995 special education spending as a percentage of total district expenditures. They included 19 of the 35 with the highest per-pupil special education expenditures. Table 6.6 shows that the 29 were predominantly large and urban. They were high spending districts in general with large percentages of students with disabilities. As in the previous analysis, they relied on part-time and full-time placements and APSs more than on regular classes and itinerant programs to serve students in special education. Of these 29 districts, 16 were located in the six counties with the greatest concentration of APSs.

TABLE 6.5 Selected Characteristics of Districts More Than 1.645
Standard Deviations Above the Mean for 1994-1995
Special Education Expenditures Per Pupil

Characteristics	*Number of Districts Ranked by Quintile*[a]					
	I	*II*	*III*	*IV*	*V*	*N*
Aid ratio	3	5	6	5	16	35
1994-1995						
total enrollment	17	7	2	4	5	35
Enrollment growth,						
1991-1992 through						
1994-1995	8	9	7	4	8	35
Population density						
(1990 Census)	30	4	1	0	0	35
Total district expenditures						
per pupil	29	4	2	0	0	35
Percentage of district						
pupils with disabilities	18	6	8	2	1	35
Percentage of special						
education pupils served						
in regular classes,						
itinerant programs	6	7	4	4	14	35
Percentage of special						
education pupils served						
in part-time and						
full-time classes	18	8	2	3	4	35
Percentage of special						
education pupils						
served in approved						
private schools	24	8	1	2	0	35
Expected N if randomly						
distributed	7	7	7	7	7	35

a. There are 100 of Pennsylvania's 500 operating school districts in each quintile. Quintile I is the highest (e.g., the highest aid ratios, which are the poorest districts; the highest enrollments, which are the largest; etc.).

Nearly three dozen districts were more than 1.645 standard deviations above the mean for percentage change in special education expenditures per pupil from 1991-1992 through 1994-1995. Table 6.7 shows that these were predominantly wealthy, rapidly growing districts with increasing percentages of pupils with disabilities.

Last, about two dozen districts were more than 1.645 standard deviations above the mean for the change in special education spending as a percentage of total expenditures from 1991-1992 through

TABLE 6.6 Selected Characteristics of Districts More Than 1.645 Standard Deviations Above the Mean for 1994-1995 Special Education Spending as Percentage of Total Expenditures

Characteristics	Number of Districts Ranked by Quintile[a]					
	I	II	III	IV	V	N
Aid ratio	5	7	8	5	4	29
1994-1995						
total enrollment	12	7	2	5	3	29
Enrollment growth, 1991-1992 through 1994-1995	3	8	6	7	5	29
Population density (1990 Census)	20	3	2	4	0	29
Total district expenditures per pupil	13	5	3	5	3	29
Percentage of district pupils with disabilities	22	5	1	1	0	29
Percentage of special education pupils served in regular classes, itinerant programs	3	3	4	5	14	29
Percentage of special education pupils served in part-time and full-time classes	18	6	2	2	1	29
Percentage of special education pupils served in approved private schools	16	3	5	4	1	29
Expected N if randomly distributed	5.8	5.8	5.8	5.8	5.8	29

a. There are 100 of Pennsylvania's 500 operating school districts in each quintile. Quintile I is the highest (e.g., the highest aid ratios, which are the poorest districts; the highest enrollments, which are the largest; etc.).

1994-1995. Table 6.8 shows very little in terms of discernible patterns among these school districts.

Changing Service Delivery Patterns

The special education regulations adopted by the State Board of Education in 1990 encouraged more regular class service and required

TABLE 6.7 Selected Characteristics of Districts More Than 1.645
Standard Deviations Above the Mean for Percentage
Change in Special Education Expenditures Per Pupil,
1991-1992 through 1994-1995

| Characteristics | Number of Districts Ranked by Quintile[a] | | | | | |
	I	*II*	*III*	*IV*	*V*	*N*
Aid ratio	4	8	5	6	11	34
1994-1995 total enrollment	8	8	5	4	9	34
Enrollment growth, 1991-1992 through 1994-1995	17	6	3	6	2	34
Population density (1990 Census)	3	10	6	9	6	34
Change in pupils with disabilities as percentage of total enrollment	10	6	6	8	4	34
Change in percentage of special education pupils served by intermediate units	4	9	8	6	7	34
Expected N if randomly distributed	6.8	6.8	6.8	6.8	6.8	34

a. There are 100 of Pennsylvania's 500 operating school districts in each quintile. Quintile I is the highest (e.g., the highest aid ratios, which are the poorest districts; the highest enrollments, which are the largest; etc.).

prereferral instructional support to ensure more appropriate and less costly service delivery. These regulatory changes have entered into the broader context of national discussions of inclusion. How much did inclusionary special education service increase from 1991-1992 through 1994-1995? The data in Table 6.9 suggest there was relatively little change in service delivery patterns during these 4 years.

In the aggregate, the percentage of special education students served in regular classes increased by 1.25 percentage points, whereas service in regular or itinerant and part-time or full-time classes each decreased by less than one quarter of a percentage point. Nearly twice as many districts increased the use of regular class service as the number that decreased this type of service, and 70 districts increased their use for at least 5% of their special education students. This indicates some shift toward the provision of special education in regular classes. With less than 4% of all special education students

TABLE 6.8 Selected Characteristics of Districts More Than 1.645 Standard Deviations Above the Mean for Change in Special Education Spending as Percentage of Total Expenditures, 1991-1992 through 1994-1995

Characteristics	Number of Districts Ranked by Quintile[a]					
	I	II	III	IV	V	N
Aid ratio	2	6	10	3	4	25
1994-1995 total enrollment	3	7	5	3	7	25
Enrollment growth, 1991-1992 through 1994-1995	7	8	3	6	1	25
Population density (1990 Census)	5	4	5	7	4	25
Change in pupils with disabilities as percentage of total enrollment	7	4	4	7	3	25
Change in percentage of special education pupils served by intermediate units	2	6	6	6	5	25
Expected N if randomly distributed	5	5	5	5	5	25

a. There are 100 of Pennsylvania's 500 operating school districts in each quintile. Quintile I is the highest (e.g., the highest aid ratios, which are the poorest districts; the highest enrollments, which are the largest; etc.).

being served in regular classes, however, and 3.5 times as many being served in full-time special education classes by 1994-1995, it is fair to say that the service delivery pattern that year was not very different than 4 years earlier.

There were, however, significant shifts in patterns of program control, as can be seen clearly in Table 6.10. School districts assumed control from IUs of a large number of special education programs during the period of this study.

There were also slight decreases in the total special education population, from 269,969 in 1991-1992 to 269,670 in 1994-1995, and in the number of students with disabilities, from 191,690 in 1991-1992 to 188,082 in 1994-1995. Although these decreases were very small, total district enrollments increased by almost 100,000 students during the period, so they represented reductions of nearly one percentage point

TABLE 6.9 Summary of Special Education Service Delivery Patterns, 1991-1992 and 1994-1995

Service Delivery Type	1991-1992	1994-1995
Percentage of special education		
pupils served in regular classes:	1.91	3.16
Minimum (253 districts in 1991-1992;		
169 in 1994-1995)	0.00	0.00
Maximum	70.38	59.74
Percentage of special education pupils		
served in regular classes and		
itinerant programs:	53.11	53.03
Minimum	12.12	4.46
Maximum	90.26	94.38
Percentage of special education pupils		
served in full-time and part-time		
special classes:	31.85	31.64
Minimum	3.15	1.57
Maximum	80.29	81.88

in the percentage of total enrollment in special education and the percentage of all students with disabilities.

Conclusions

Several conclusions can be drawn from the research presented here. First, changes in state special education policy in Pennsylvania succeeded in capping the state's growing obligation to support special education.

TABLE 6.10 Summary of Special Education Program Control, 1991-1992 and 1994-1995

Agency Operating Program	1991-1992	1994-1995
Percentage of special education		
pupils served by school districts	66.31	79.77
Percentage of special education pupils		
served by intermediate units	32.14	18.89
Percentage of special education pupils		
served by approved private schools	1.55	1.34

Second, school districts were less successful in limiting their growing obligations to these programs. In the aggregate, both district special education and net special education expenditures increased more from 1991-1992 through 1994-1995 than did total school district spending, and special education as a share of total budgets increased slightly. On the other hand, more districts were able to reduce per-pupil special education spending (120 districts) and net special education spending (239 districts) than total district spending (42 districts) during the period, suggesting that the results of these reforms have been inconsistent at the local level.

Third, districts least able to control costs were those with high-cost educational programs in general, high percentages of students with disabilities, and high percentages of students receiving special education services in part-time or full-time classes and in APSs.

Fourth, fiscal policy changes adopted by the General Assembly were designed to reduce school district reliance on IUs, and this clearly has occurred. The effect on special education costs, however, has been much less clear. Increased reliance on IUs correlated significantly with increased per-pupil special education spending and with increased special education spending as a percentage of total expenditures, but the percentage of students served by IUs in 1994-1995 correlated negatively with per-pupil special education expenditures. It may be that the insignificant changes in program delivery patterns—regardless of which agency operated the classes—overwhelmed any savings that might have been realized by districts assuming responsibility for their own special education programs.

Fifth, program policy changes adopted by the State Board were designed to reduce special education placements and to increase the percentage of students receiving their special education in regular classes. Between 1991-1992 and 1994-1995, there was a small reduction in the number of special education students and a small increase in the percentage served in regular classes. Other research now suggests that a decade of implementation of the IST approach may result in the reductions in special education placements and the increased service in regular classrooms that policy makers had anticipated in 1990 (Hartman & Fay, 1996).

All of the research reported in this chapter is purely quantitative. It cannot address issues of program quality, student achievement, or parent and educator satisfaction. All of these are legitimate and important areas of research if a complete picture of the efficacy of the special education program and fiscal policy changes adopted by Pennsylvania in 1990 and 1991 is to emerge.

Notes

1. 20 U.S.C. 1400 et seq.
2. *PARC v. Commonwealth,* 334 F. Supp. 1257 (E.D. Pa. 1971) and 343 F. Supp. 279 (E.D. Pa. 1972).
3. 22 Pa. Code, Chapter 13.
4. Section 2509 of the Public School Code of 1949 (24 P.S. 25-2509).
5. Act of July 1, 1989 (Pub. L. 253, No. 43).
6. 22 Pa. Code, Chapter 14.
7. Act of August 5, 1991 (Pub. L. 219, No. 25).
8. Acts of July 9, 1992 (Pub. L. 392, No. 55), June 7, 1993 (Pub. L. 49, No. 16), and Act 1994-6A.
9. Act 1994-6A.
10. Data regarding school district expenditures were extracted from district annual financial reports. Data regarding special education placements and services were taken from PennData, the Department's special education management information system. Data regarding total district enrollments were from the districts' annual enrollment reports to the Department. Data regarding aid ratios were provided by the Department's Bureau of Basic Education Fiscal Administration.

References

Casey, R. P. (1990). *1990-91 general fund budget.* Harrisburg, PA: Office of Budget.
Casey, R. P. (1991). *1991-92 general fund budget.* Harrisburg, PA: Office of Budget.
Feir, R. E. (1995, March). *Pennsylvania's special education formula: Early results.* Paper presented at the Annual Meeting of the American Education Finance Association, Savannah, GA.
Hartman, W. T. (1994). *A continued analysis of Pennsylvania's new special education funding formula.* Harrisburg, PA: Pennsylvania Department of Education.
Hartman, W. T., & Fay, T. A. (1996). *Cost-effectiveness of instructional support teams in Pennsylvania* (Policy Paper No. 9). Palo Alto, CA: American Institutes for Research, Center for Special Education Finance.

Montgomery, D. L., & DeSera, M. (1996). *A profile of special education finance reform in Pennsylvania*. Palo Alto, CA: American Institutes for Research, Center for Special Education Finance.

Moore, M. T., Walker, L. J., & Holland, R. P. (1982). *Finetuning special education finance: A guide for state policy makers*. Washington, DC: Educational Testing Service.

National Association of State Directors of Special Education. (1982). *A description of state funding procedures for special education in the public schools*. Washington, DC: Author.

Pennsylvania State Board of Education. (1990). *Report on special education*. Harrisburg, PA: Author.

Task Force on the Education of Students with Disabilities. (1988). *Quality education: Preparation for life*. Harrisburg, PA: Pennsylvania Department of Education.

SEVEN

The Allocation of Resources to Special Education and Regular Instruction in New York State

HAMILTON LANKFORD

JAMES WYCKOFF

Many researchers, policy makers, and practitioners believe that despite the expenditure of substantial additional resources, today's public elementary and secondary students are performing only modestly better than students did 10 or 20 years ago.[1] They often argue that too few resources are reaching the classroom and that when money is spent on classroom uses, it is not spent productively to

AUTHORS' NOTE: This chapter is a revised version of a more detailed analysis that appeared under the title, "The Allocation of Resources to Special Education and Regular Instruction," in *Holding Schools Accountable,* edited by Helen Ladd and published by the Brookings Institution (1996). We have benefited from the comments of Jane Hannaway, Helen Ladd, participants at the Brookings Institution conference, and seminar participants at the University of Kentucky, the University of Maryland, and Williams College. The chapter was written while Lankford was in residence at the Mellon Project on Higher Education Finance at Williams College and Wyckoff was an NSF/ASA fellow at the U.S. Bureau of the Census.

increase achievement. To evaluate this argument, it is necessary to examine how school districts spend their money. But despite hundreds of production function studies exploring the relationships between overall inputs and outcomes, there is little understanding of the forces behind the allocation of school district expenditures. Few of the production function studies employ detailed data on inputs, and virtually none take account of the entire range of expenditures made by school districts.

However, researchers have recently begun using state databases to examine how districts allocate expenditures.[2] This chapter will focus most heavily on expenditure data from New York State, which provide some support for the notion that an increasing portion of the budget went to administrative and special education uses at the expense of classroom instruction. For example, the share of resources spent on regular teaching in New York State fell from 53.1% in the 1979-1980 school year to 48.8% in the 1992-1993 year; over the same time period, the share of resources spent on special education expanded from 5.0% to 11.3%. What has driven the large increases in special education expenditures? Have these increases reduced resources going to regular classrooms, or have other factors, such as enrollments and revenues, also changed to mitigate the effect of increased special education allocations?

This chapter addresses these questions and more generally examines the relationships among regular instructional expenditures, special education spending, spending in other budget areas, school district revenues, and enrollments for regular and disabled students.

Special Education in Public Schools

The education of disabled children became a major concern of school districts in 1975 with the enactment of Pub. L. 94-142, the Education for All Handicapped Children Act (currently, the Individuals with Disabilities Education Act). Although prior legislation had drawn attention to concerns about educating disabled students, Pub. L. 94-142 initiated a period in which the federal government became much more active in the regulation and financing of special education.[3] For example, the law called for federal reimbursement to the states for each special education student, without regard to the handicapping condition.[4] Although the federal government provides about 8% of the average per pupil expenditure for disabled students, the federal presence and regulation have led to substantially increased involvement by state and local governments (Parrish & Verstegen, 1994, p. 3). On average, states pay for 56% and local governments pay 36% of special education expenditures. However, there has been wide variation in the state portion of special education expenditures, varying from 85% in Alabama to 17% in Oregon (O'Reilly, 1993, p. 13). To some extent, this variation reflects different approaches to financing special education.

State funding formulas for special education basically take one of four formulas: flat grant, pupil weighted, resource based, or cost based. Flat-grant formulas provide a fixed payment per special education student that may vary by type of disability. Pupil-weighted formulas assign specific weighting factors to various classifications of special education students based on estimates of the cost of providing services to these students. Resource-based formulas reimburse districts for specific resources, such as teachers. Cost-based formulas reimburse districts for some portion of their actual special education costs. These formulas affect the net cost to school districts of classifying students in various special education categories. Recently, some states, including Pennsylvania, have moved to reimbursement systems that provide lump sum payments to districts based on total district enrollment, independent of both the number of students identified as disabled and the actual expenditures for these students. In such a case, a district bears the entire cost of increments in special education expenditures.

The number of students identified as disabled grew at a steady pace between 1980 and 1992, increasing by 24% over the period.[5] In contrast, total enrollments increased by less than 1% during this period. As a result, the number of special education students rose from 9.6% of all students in 1979-1980 to 11.8% in 1991-1992. The composition of special education students across categories changed as well. In 1979-1980, 22% of special education students were mentally retarded and 32% had some specific learning disability. By 1991-1992, mental retardation accounted for just 11% of the disabled, whereas 45% had some specific learning disability.

The shifting composition of types of special education students reflects the fact that the classification of learning disabilities has undergone profound changes over the last 20 years as researchers have learned more about causes and treatment. Advances in diagnostics for learning disabilities have resulted in the classification of children as learning disabled who previously would have gone unidentified.[6] Disagreement remains on the definition of what constitutes a learning disability, and there is latitude as to which students are identified as special education students. As a result, changes in special education enrollments may reflect changes in the choices made by teachers, administrators, parents, and students.

Expenditure data at the national level for special education students are very limited and out of date. As part of its report to Congress on the implementation of Pub. L. 94-142, the U.S. Department of Education did report special education expenditure data from 1981-1982 through 1987-1988.[7] However, no national special education expenditure data have been collected since 1988, and the existing data have insufficient detail about how the remainder of school district budgets are allocated across functional categories and over time. Therefore, we have turned to state data for our analysis. The remaining analysis considers special education enrollment and financial data and detailed budgeting data for school districts of the state of New York.

Enrollment of special education students in New York State mirrored the national trend by growing substantially over the period from 1979-1980 to 1992-1993. Special education student enrollments increased by 65% over this period, whereas enrollments of regular students decreased by 13%. Special education students are classified into a number of categories, including emotionally disturbed, speech impaired, mentally retarded, and learning disabled. The first three categories have remained fairly constant as a share of total enrollments, but the share of New York students identified as learning disabled rose from less than 1% of total enrollment in 1979-1980 to more than 7% of total enrollment by 1992-1993.

Even within many disability categories, there is fairly wide variation in the placement setting (and hence, cost) to which the student is assigned. For example, New York categorizes its public school placements according to whether students are pulled out of regular classes at least two periods a week but not more than 20% of the time,

TABLE 7.1 The Relationship Between Type of Disability and Placement, All Public Nonresidential Special Education Students, New York State, 1992-1993[a]

| Type of Disability | Percentage of All Nonresidential Special Education Students | Placement Setting | | |
		Less Than 20%[b]	20% to 60%[c]	More Than 60% and Special Public Day[d]
Learning disabled	59.9	25.2	36.0	38.8
Speech impaired	13.7	49.1	11.4	39.5
Emotionally disturbed	12.2	10.8	15.4	73.8
Mentally retarded	6.0	7.2	8.0	84.8
Multiply disabled	3.8	8.1	8.3	83.6
Total all disabilities	100.0	25.5	26.6	47.9

a. Authors' calculations were from the state summary of the PD-4 survey made available to us by the New York State Education Department in January, 1994.
b. Pulled out of regular classes at least two periods a week but not more than 20% of the time.
c. Pulled out of regular classes 20% to 60% of the time.
d. Pulled out of regular classes at least 60% of the time or attending special day schools.

out of regular classes between 20% and 60% of the time, out of regular classes at least 60% of the time, or attending special public day schools.[8] The relationship between type of disability and treatment setting is shown in Table 7.1.[9] Students with learning disabilities accounted for 59.9% of all public nonresidential special education placements during the 1992-1993 school year and were fairly evenly divided between the various placement settings. However, most (nonresidential) students with emotional disturbance, mental retardation, or multiple disabilities are placed in higher cost settings, which means either outside regular classes at least 60% of the time or in a special public day school.

There appears to be wide variation across districts in the rate of identification of special education students as well as in placement settings. Table 7.2 shows that during the 1992-1993 school year, the special education identification rate was about twice as high in districts at the 90th percentile as in districts at the 10th percentile (13.7% v. 7.3%). Large differences in identification rates, in total and for each placement setting, have existed through time, as is shown by comparing the 1979-1980 distribution with that for 1992-1993. The data behind this table suggest some other connections as well. School districts with a higher incidence of students pulled out at least 60% of the time

TABLE 7.2 Rate of Identification of Nonresidential Special Education Students, by Placement Settings as a Percentage of All Students, New York State School Districts, 1979-1980 and 1992-1993

	1979-1980		1992-1993	
Placement Setting	10th Percentile	90th Percentile	10th Percentile	90th Percentile
Outside classroom 20% or less	0	3.6	0	3.1
Outside classroom 20% to 60%	0	3.4	2.4	7.7
Outside classroom 60% or more	0.7	3.9	1.9	6.8
All placements	2.0	8.5	7.3	13.7

are likely to have fewer students pulled out 20% to 60%. A similar relationship exists between the students pulled out 20% to 60% and the students pulled out less than 20%.[10] This suggests the possibility that districts may have discretion to alter the classification of students at the margin. The wide variation in identification rates also suggests this possibility.

The policy environment for special education in New York State, like that in most states, is complex and idiosyncratic. New York has four different formulas that specifically provide aid for special education students and several other formulas—such as for transportation aid—that reimburse school districts for a portion of certain costs that are often larger on a per-pupil basis for special education students than for regular students. As a result of the different formulas, floors and ceilings, adjustments for wealth, save-harmless provisions, and so on, there is wide variation in the additional state aid that a district can receive when it identifies an additional student to receive special education. For most of the aid, districts receive nonmatching reimbursements, although in some limited cases, the state matches a school district's allowable expenditures. Given that much of the aid results from something called the "public excess-cost formula," which gives districts additional reimbursements based on the number of students in each special education classification, there may be a financial incentive to categorize students as needing special education.[11] Districts would have such an incentive to the extent that the reimbursement exceeds the cost of providing the services required for that placement. That incentive will tend to be greater for districts with higher aid ratios (lower wealth) and higher approved operating expenditures per pupil, as long as certain ceilings and cutoffs are not reached. A district in the top 10% of state aid reimbursement per special education student had twice the financial incentive to classify a student for special education as did a district in the bottom 10%. Of course, financial incentive is just one of the reasons that some school districts might have larger special education enrollments than others.

The growth in special education student enrollment and expenditures has led many to assert that special education expenditures have increased at the expense of resources for regular students. During the early 1990s, many school districts were experiencing the fiscal pressures of reduced growth in state aid and mounting resistance to property tax increases. In this climate, large increases in school budgets became less tolerable, and it has become conventional wisdom that increased spending on special education has crowded out spending on regular students.[12] To explore this issue, we next examine special education spending per pupil over time and its relationship to per-pupil spending on regular students.

Per-Pupil Expenditures
for Regular and
Disabled Students

The debate in the education production function literature over whether money matters for educational performance considers the relationship between expenditures and achievement. Invariably, empirical studies make no distinction between resources allocated to regular students and those going to disabled students who may not be tested for achievement. Nor do such studies distinguish whether resources allocated to regular students are ending up in the classroom or in administration, transportation, and other uses. If a disproportionate share of increased spending is not arriving in the classrooms of regular students, then researchers who use total per-pupil expenditures on education may systematically understate the effect of such expenditures. To understand how resource allocations to regular class-rooms have changed over time, it is necessary to isolate expenditures made on behalf of regular students.

There are very few estimates along these lines. Several studies have produced detailed estimates of the cost of special education for particular districts at a point in time, but none appear to have examined these costs or expenditures in a systematic or consistent way over time (e.g., Chaikind, Danielson, & Brauen, 1993; Chambers & Dueñas, 1994; Kakalik, Furry, Thomas, & Carney, 1981; Moore, Strang, Schwartz, & Braddock, 1988; Rossmiller, Hale, & Frohreich, 1970.)

Allocation of Resources

As a starting point, consider Table 7.3, which divides expenditures in New York State and New York City into 13 categories. From the 1979-1980 school year until 1992-1993, total real educational expenditures in New York State (excluding New York City) rose by $3.2 billion. Over that same time, the share of total spending going to regular teaching fell from 53.1% to 48.8%, whereas the share going to disabilities teaching rose from 5.0 to 11.3%. If regular instruction had maintained its share of total spending, it would have received an additional $700 million in 1992-1993. Where did this money go? Some of it may have gone to central administration, pupil personnel services, other educational support, transportation, and curriculum development, all of which slightly increased their share of total educational expenditures over this time frame. However, special education is by far the largest source of new spending. In fact, slightly more of the increase in total spending was allocated to instruction for special education students than to instructional spending for regular students. The importance of special education spending is magnified in New York City, where the increase in regular teaching expenditures was about half of that for special education teaching.[13]

However, Table 7.3 does not account for enrollment changes that occurred over the period; it simply indicates the changing share of total dollars. Regular enrollments in districts outside New York City

TABLE 7.3 Allocation of the Real Increase in Education Expenditures in New York State and City Between 1979-1980 and 1992-1993[a]

Expenditure Category	1980 Share of Total Expenditure (by percentage)	1993 Share of Total Expenditure (by percentage)	Real Change in Expenditure (in thousands of dollars)	Share of Real Change (by percentage)
New York State				
(excluding New York City)				
Teaching, regular	53.1	48.8	1,073,591	33.3
Teaching, disabilities	5.0	11.3	1,099,305	34.1
Tuition	0.7	1.2	100,513	3.1
Central administration	3.1	3.5	156,423	4.9
Building supervision	4.9	4.5	93,156	2.9
Curriculum development	0.5	0.6	28,338	0.9
Pupil personnel services	3.9	4.1	157,072	4.9
Other educational support	2.0	2.3	102,777	3.2
Operations and maintenance	10.6	8.6	47,043	1.5
Miscellaneous	3.6	4.1	191,114	5.9
Transportation	5.5	5.6	189,990	5.9
Insurance	0.6	0.9	60,117	1.9
Debt	6.4	4.5	–75,619	–2.3
Total	100.0	100.0	3,233,819	100.0
New York City				
Teaching, regular	54.3	47.7	562,806	28.5
Teaching, disabilities	6.9	18.6	1,045,638	53.0
Tuition	0.6	3.8	263,193	13.3
Central administration	2.2	3.3	132,449	6.7
Building supervision	7.2	3.0	–184,435	–9.3
Curriculum development	0.2	0.2	7,863	0.4
Pupil personnel services	2.7	2.5	35,034	1.8
Other educational support	1.0	0.3	–33,193	–1.7
Operations and maintenance	9.6	8.8	126,957	6.4
Miscellaneous	2.5	1.8	–7,527	–0.4
Transportation	6.0	6.4	148,383	7.5
Insurance	0.0	0.0	–302	0.0
Debt	6.9	3.5	–123,312	–6.2
Total	100.0	100.0	1,973,555	100.0

SOURCE: Authors' calculations were based on data from annual financial reports (ST-3) of the New York State Department of Education.
a. All dollar amounts have been adjusted to 1993 dollars using the state and local government purchases component of the implicit price deflator for gross domestic product (U.S. Council of Economic Advisors, 1995).

decreased by 20% over the 1980-1993 period, whereas special education enrollments increased by 70%. As a result, it is necessary to recompute these differences on a per-pupil basis.

Estimates of expenditures per pupil for regular and disabled students are presented in Table 7.4 for New York City and the remaining school districts in New York State. For the first row, overall expenditure per pupil is simply total expenditures divided by average daily enrollment over the school year (as defined by the State Education Department), regardless of the status of students. However, dividing up expenditures between regular and special education students is not straightforward. Because most special education students spend some portion of their day in regular classrooms, spending on teaching for special education students must include both instruction expenditures for those students in placements outside regular classrooms and a prorated share of the instructional expenditures for regular classrooms and of other educational expenditures.

One assumption is that regular and special education students in a regular classroom each receive the same level of service. In this case, a special education student in a regular classroom would receive $1/n$th of the resources, where n is the total class size. A similar assumption could be made with respect to nonteaching resources: Regular and special education students share equally in pupil personnel services, administration, operations, and maintenance. This assumption is reflected in the estimates of per-pupil spending on teaching and overall per-pupil spending for both New York State and City, reported in the section of Table 7.4 identified as "Resource use assumption 1."

An alternative assumption would be that special education students receive more resources per pupil than regular students, with the difference depending on the severity of the disability. A natural step here is to assign varying weights to students in the three categories of placement settings: that is, those who spend less than 20% of their time outside regular class, those who spend 20% to 60% outside regular class, and those who spend more than 60% outside regular class. Based on studies that examine the costs of providing special education, we believe that the estimates of spending per pupil in these three categories with weights of 1.1, 1.5, and 2.5 are the most plausible.[14] For example, a special education student who spends 20% to 60% of time

TABLE 7.4 Estimated Per Pupil Expenditures for Regular and Special Education Students, by Assumptions About Resource Use, New York City and State, 1980 and 1993 (amounts in 1993 dollars)

Resource Use Assumption	New York State (excluding New York City)			New York City		
	1980	1993	*Percentage Change*	1980	1993	*Percentage Change*
Overall Expenditure	6,228	9,295	49.2	6,317	7,799	23.5
Resource use assumption 1[a]						
Spending on teaching						
Per regular student	3,427	4,902	43.1	3,631	4,125	13.6
Per special education student	6,909	11,027	59.6	7,376	16,396	122.3
Total spending						
Per regular student	6,015	8,544	42.0	6,060	6,545	8.0
Per special education student	9,497	14,668	54.4	9,805	18,817	91.9
Resource use assumption 2[b]						
Spending on teaching						
Per regular student	3,375	4,734	40.3	3,554	4,002	12.6
Per special education student	7,708	12,235	58.7	8,414	17,474	107.7
Total spending						
Per regular student	5,757	7,602	32.0	5,781	6,188	7.0
Per special education student	12,490	17,806	42.6	13,588	21,958	61.6
Resource use assumption 3[c]						
Spending on teaching						
Per regular student	3,349	4,653	38.9	3,517	3,943	12.1
Per special education student	8,099	12,809	58.2	8,917	17,989	101.7
Total spending						
Per regular student	5,662	7,388	30.5	5,655	6,028	6.6
Per special education student	13,905	19,408	39.6	15,299	23,361	52.7

a. Assumes that each full-time-equivalent (FTE) pupil uses same quantity of resources outside special education classrooms.
b. Assumes that the FTEs of special education students spending less than 20% of their time outside regular classes have a weight of 1.1 (10% more resources than regular students), those pulled out 20% to 60% of the time have a weight of 1.5, and those pulled out 60% or more have a weight of 2.5.
c. Assumes that the FTEs of special education students spending less than 20% of their time outside regular classes have a weight of 1.15, those pulled out 20 to 60% have a weight of 1.75, and those pulled out 60% or more have a weight of 3.25.

outside a regular classroom will use 1.5 times as many regular class-room resources while in a regular class as other students, a multiple that does not count the resources spent directly on special education. In Table 7.4, the rows labeled "Resource use assumption 2" use these weights and show that spending on teaching for regular New York State students increased by about 40% over the 1980-1993 period, whereas teaching expenditures for special education students in-creased by 59%. Thus, spending on teaching for special education students is increasing nearly 50% more rapidly than spending for regular students. Total spending per regular student increased from about $5,800 in 1980 to $7,600 in 1993, a 32% increase, whereas total spending per special education student increased from $12,500 to $17,800, a 43% increase.

The final portion of Table 7.4, "Resource use assumption 3," offers a scenario where the costs of special education students are assumed to be higher. Here, the spending weights for the three categories are 1.15, 1.75, and 3.25.

Expenditures in New York districts outside New York City show substantial increases across all the per-pupil measures, regardless of the weightings employed. However, expenditures reported for New York City suggest that special education per-pupil spending has shown dramatic increases, both for teaching and in total, whereas per-pupil expenditures for regular students have barely increased. According to the second resource use assumption (our intermediate case), total spending on regular students increased from $5,800 per pupil in 1980 to $6,200 in 1993, an increase of 7%. Special education expenditures grew from $13,600 per pupil in 1980 to $22,000 in 1993, an overall growth of 62%. Although regular students in New York City and the rest of the state received about the same resources in 1980, by 1993, regular students in New York City were receiving nearly 20% fewer dollars than those residing in districts outside the city. It appears that per-pupil expenditures in regular classrooms in New York City have suffered in comparison to those outside New York City, whereas per-pupil special education spending has ballooned.

The rapid increase in special education expenditures in New York City is often attributed to a consent decree filed on behalf of Jose P., a disabled student, which has been in force since 1980.[15] As a result of this decision, virtually every aspect of policy and administration of special education in New York City is protected by the consent decree and subject to negotiation with the plaintiff's legal representation. As a result, the Board of Education for New York City has very little discretion over special education expenditures.[16] Therefore, the remainder of the school district budget—the nonspecial education portion—is subject to the fiscal pressures that face the city. This is likely to account for much of the disparity in the growth of per-pupil spending between special education and regular students reported in Table 7.4.[17]

These estimates illustrate vividly why measuring educational resources by average expenditure per student, as is often done in policy discussions and production function studies, can be so misleading. Compare overall expenditures per pupil at the top of Table 7.4 with total spending for regular students. For districts outside New York City, overall expenditures per pupil in 1993 ($9,295) overstate our best estimate of expenditures per regular student ($7,602) by 22%. For New York City, overall expenditures per pupil are too high by 26%. Perhaps more important are the overestimates of the growth in expenditures for each type of student. Overall expenditures per pupil grew by 49% from 1980 to 1993 in districts outside New York City. However, our intermediate estimate of the growth of total spending per pupil is 32% for regular students and 43% for special education students.[18] Thus, the simple measure of overall expenditure per pupil overstates growth by about 50% for regular students and 30% for special education students. In New York City, the overall expenditure growth of 23.5% overstates actual growth for regular students by 16 percentage points, or 200%. During the period from 1980-1981 to 1992-1993, 11 states had overall enrollments that declined by at least 5% (New York declined 6%; National Center for Education Statistics, 1994, pp. 52-53). These averages undoubtedly mask much larger enrollment reductions in some districts in these and other states. Special education enrollments have generally been increasing in most districts. As a result, it is likely that many places are experiencing the phenomenon of increasing special education and declining regular enrollments, causing overall per-pupil expenditure growth rates to exceed either regular or special education per-pupil growth rates. Furthermore, the effect is likely to be larger in many places than indicated here, as our results are for an average of 655 districts.

TABLE 7.5 Special Education Expenditures and Enrollments in Selected Periods, 1980 to 1993

Item	1980	1985	1989	1993
New York State				
(excluding New York City)				
Special education spending				
(1000s of dollars)	1,413,974	2,084,514	2,811,727	3,434,640
Special education enrollments	113,207	151,940	161,520	192,895
Outside the classroom				
60% or more of the time	50,031	65,806	76,300	85,258
Outside the classroom				
20% to 60% of the time	32,058	52,857	56,142	81,027
Outside the classroom				
20% or less of the time	31,118	33,277	29,078	26,610
New York City				
Special education spending				
(1000s of dollars)	853,004	1,563,265	1,914,402	2,154,699
Special education enrollments	62,775	97,907	96,447	98,130
Outside the classroom				
60% or more of the time	51,913	60,624	57,757	57,705
Outside the classroom				
20% to 60% of the time	10,238	18,761	17,999	31,382
Outside the classroom				
20% or less of the time	624	18,522	20,691	9,043
Total				
Special education spending				
(1000s of dollars)	2,266,978	3,647,780	4,726,130	5,589,339
Special education enrollments	175,982	249,847	257,967	291,025
Outside the classroom				
60% or more of the time	101,944	126,430	134,057	142,963
Outside the classroom				
20% to 60% of the time	42,296	71,618	74,141	112,409
Outside the classroom				
20% or less of the time	31,742	51,799	49,769	35,653

Decomposing the Growth in
Special Education Expenditures

Expenditures for special education students in New York State increased by 150% from 1979-1980 to 1992-1993, which is an average annual rate of 7.8% (see Table 7.5). What accounted for this extraordi-

TABLE 7.6 Growth in Total Expenditures for Special Education
Students, Decomposed Between Changes in Enrollment
and Changes in Expenditures per Pupil, Selected Periods,
1980 to 1993

Item	1980 to 1985	1985 to 1989	1989 to 1993
New York State (excluding New York City)			
Annual growth in expenditures			
for disabled students	8.1	7.8	5.1
Decomposition of change			
in expenditure			
Enrollment	79.2	22.9	89.7
Expenditures per pupil	20.8	77.1	10.3
Decomposition of change in enrollment			
Outside classroom 60%			
or more of the time	40.7	109.5	28.6
Outside classroom			
20% to 60% of the time	53.7	34.3	79.3
Outside classroom 20% or less			
of the time	5.6	−43.8	−7.9
New York City			
Annual growth in expenditures			
for disabled students	12.9	5.2	3.0
Decomposition of change			
in expenditure			
Enrollment	79.0	−8.3	15.4
Expenditures per pupil	21.0	108.3	84.6
Decomposition of change			
in enrollment			
Outside classroom 60% or more			
of the time	24.8	196.4	−3.1
Outside classroom 20% to 60%			
of the time	24.3	52.2	795.2
Outside classroom 20% or less			
of the time	50.9	−148.6	692.1

nary growth? Some insights are gained by decomposing the total
growth into two portions: one attributable to enrollment increases and
one resulting from increases in expenditures per disabled student.[19]
The results of this decomposition for New York districts over three
subperiods are shown in Table 7.6. In general, the three periods are
characterized by very different decompositions.

Consider first the top half of Table 7.6, describing the New York State districts outside New York City. The 1980-1985 period is characterized by relatively large growth in total expenditures for special education students.[20] About 80% of the expenditure increase during this period is attributable to increases in overall special education enrollments, and 20% results from increases in spending per pupil. This is the period with the highest growth in enrollment of students pulled out of classrooms at least 60% of the time (annual growth rate of 5.6%). These students, who are typically the most expensive to treat, accounted for 41% of the total increase in disabled enrollment during this period. In contrast, during 1989-1993 enrollment changes also accounted for the bulk of the increase in total expenditures, but the annual growth rate in the students pulled out at least 60% was half of that in the first period (2.8%), accounting for only 29% of the total growth in disabled enrollment. The reduction in the overall expenditure growth rate from 8.1% in 1980-1985 to 5.1% in 1989-1993 largely reflects the changing mix of special education students. Expenditure growth in the 1985-1989 period is driven by increases in expenditure per pupil, which results largely from a growth in the number of students pulled out at least 60% (109% of total).

In New York City, shown in the bottom half of Table 7.6, the pattern is quite different. During 1980 to 1985, the number of special education students exploded at an annual rate of 9.3%, with sizable increases occurring in all three disability groups. This enrollment growth accounted for most of the very large annual increases in spending on special education (nearly 13%). In the two later periods, total enrollment did not increase much at all, with annual growth averaging 0.2%. This implies that increases in expenditures per pupil drove most of the disabled spending increases over the two more recent periods. Because the number of high-cost students did not increase during these two periods, per-pupil spending increases were held down as well.

This descriptive work summarizes the financial setting that New York school districts faced with respect to the funding of special education and regular students, but it does not reveal how districts altered their budget allocations in response to changes in aid or in regular and special education enrollments. To examine these relationships and to explore allocations across budget categories, we now turn to a statistical model of school district finance.

A Statistical Model of
School District Finance

Several policy issues have been raised in this chapter: Are dollars reaching regular classrooms, or are they being diverted to other uses? Has special education crowded out spending on regular students? Are recent trends in special education enrollments and per-pupil expenditures likely to put substantial pressure on school district budgets? We address these questions by estimating the reduced-form linkages between enrollments and expenditures.[21]

To understand this model, share with us the assumption that budgetary decisions are made in two steps. In the first stage, total expenditures are determined on the basis of enrollments, the characteristics of the student population, state and federal aid, households' incomes and tastes, the property tax base, and other factors. In the second stage, the predetermined total expenditure is allocated across the various program and expenditure categories. As an approximation, this two-stage process is consistent with the budgetary process currently used by public school districts in New York. In the spring before the start of the school year, district officials formulate a tentative budget. The proposed budget is voted on by citizens in a referendum. Defeated budgets are revised and considered in repeat referendums. Because school officials are able to revise the initial budgetary plan over the summer and during the school year, the actual allocation of total expenditures may differ from the budget initially proposed.

To account for all these linkages, we have separately estimated models of state and federal aid, total expenditure determination, and the allocation of that total, using both present and lagged values of the explanatory variables.[22] In each equation, we employ a "fixed-effect" linear regression specification:

$$E_{it} = \alpha_t + \beta_0 X_{it} + \beta_1 X_{it-1} + \ldots + \beta_m X_{it-m} + d_i + \varepsilon_{it}.$$

In this formulation, E_{it} is the dependent variable, for example, total expenditure; in the case of the total expenditure regression, it would be for the ith district during period t. α_t is a constant term that can differ across years. X_{it-n} reflects the values of the time-varying explanatory variables for the ith district in period $t-n$. The total number of lags (m) may be large or small, depending on the nature of the dynamic process. β_0, β_1, . . . , β_m are vectors of parameters. d_i is a district-specific constant that captures the net effects of all measured and unmeasured attributes of the district that do not vary over the period.[23] The effects of the exogenous variables that determine expenditures and local taxes and the dynamic linkages in the process will determine the coefficients of the reduced-form model, which reflect the net effect of changes in the exogenous variables on expenditures.

With this framework in mind, the order of analysis works this way: the state and federal aid equations are functions of enrollments, income, property tax base, and student characteristics. Then, total educational expenditures are estimated based on the time-varying variables reflecting enrollments, student characteristics, state and federal aid, income, and the district's property tax base. We then divide up total expenditures into three categories: regular teaching, special education, and "other." For each of these categories, we then use a regression in which the time-varying explanatory variables are total expenditures, enrollments, and measures of student characteristics.[24] The specific variables employed and the parameter estimates are presented in Table 7.7. Here, the discussion will focus on the determinants of instructional expenditures for regular and special education classes.

As shown in the earlier decomposition of the growth in total special education expenditures, the periods before and after 1989 differ greatly. In addition, an expanding New York State economy during the mid-1980s afforded large increases in educational expenditures when enrollments were declining. By 1988, the economy had begun to slow, thereby limiting state and local tax increases. For example, state aid to local school districts grew at an annual rate of 4% between 1980 and 1989 but fell by 1.3% annually over 1989 to 1992. In 1989-1990, statewide enrollments began to increase for the first time in 18 years. These conditions produced a slowdown in the growth of real expenditures per pupil, which actually started to fall in 1991-1992. Thus, the fiscal and enrollment environments before and after 1988 were quite different. Several studies have provided evidence that school districts respond differently to enrollment increases and declines.[25] These results, along with the possibility that district responses may also be asymmetric with respect to improving and declining fiscal environments, motivated us to analyze the pre-1988 and post-1988 periods separately. Because the latter period mirrors current expenditure and fiscal trends, the following analysis focuses on the period since 1988.

An Estimation of the Use of
Additional Dollars and Crowding Out

An important debate in educational policy centers around whether schools make "good use" of additional dollars. Our analysis indicates the extent to which additional dollars would be allocated to regular and special education instruction—an important and not well understood piece of the puzzle. The estimated model indicates that, conditional on unchanged enrollments and other student characteristics, school districts are estimated to allocate 28 cents of an additional dollar of expenditure to regular teaching and 6 cents to special education (see Table 7.7). The remainder goes to other categories of expenditures or reduced taxes. Without more information, it is difficult to determine whether school districts are making good use of additional revenue, but these estimates certainly indicate that a smaller-than-expected share of new money is allocated to classroom uses. However, it does not seem that special education has a disproportionate claim on new revenue, either.

We estimate that a dollar of either federal or state aid increases total expenditures by about $0.80. It is surprising that this much of both kinds of aid "stick" in the school budget.[26] After all, the vast majority of state and federal aid is provided in a lump sum as opposed to a matching form, and school districts could readily offset such government aid by reducing local taxes, because local revenues make up over 50% of the total.

When school districts have revenue constraints, increases in spending in one area must come at the expense of spending in some other areas—the so-called crowding-out effect. One way of understanding how districts make these trade-offs is to examine the effects of additional enrollments on spending across categories. Table 7.7 indicates how instructional and noninstructional spending would change if enrollments for each type of student were to increase by one student with other enrollments remaining unchanged—first, if revenues

TABLE 7.7 Fixed-Effects Weighted Regression Results for Aid, Total Expenditures, Regular Teaching, and Special Education

Independent Variable	Federal Aid	State Aid	Total Expenditure	Regular Teaching	Special Education
Regular students t	257.2**	376.7	2,704.6**	632.9**	570.9**
	(4.32)	(0.89)	(6.70)	(2.97)	(4.35)
Regular students $t-1$	279.6**	880.3	−300.1	497.6*	−371.2*
	(3.81)	(1.93)	(−0.61)	(1.98)	(−2.40)
Regular students $t-2$	−238.5**	3,137.1**	−78.1	361.2	−591.0**
	(−4.22)	(8.92)	(−0.20)	(1.94)	(−5.14)
Special education 60% t	1,139.7**	−642.1	8,354.9**	−795.6	5,192.2**
	(5.68)	(−0.46)	(6.15)	(−1.12)	(11.92)
Special education 60% $t-1$	417.6	4,138.7**	−1,772.9	424.8	2,565.4**
	(1.92)	(3.07)	(−1.21)	(0.57)	(5.59)
Special education 60% $t-2$	−185.8	4,084.2**	336.3	307.7	1,199.0**
	(−0.95)	(3.36)	(0.25)	(0.46)	(2.90)
Special education 20% to 60% t	624.4**	−318.5	5,419.9**	390.4	1,945.5**
	(4.45)	(−0.26)	(5.71)	(0.79)	(6.37)
Special education 20% to 60% $t-1$	307.8	1,372.2	294.6	1,098.3*	343.2
	(1.90)	(1.37)	(0.27)	(1.98)	(1.01)
Special education 20% to 60% $t-2$	−153.0	4,517.5**	21.22	169.5	−373.4
	(−1.02)	(4.83)	(0.02)	(0.33)	(−1.17)
Special education < 20% t	400.5**	1,882.7	5,158.0**	557.9	1,085.5**
	(2.77)	(1.90)	(5.30)	(1.10)	(3.49)
Special education < 20% $t-1$	188.5	1,008.9	−478.4	648.8	−237.0
	(1.29)	(1.12)	(−0.49)	(1.31)	(−0.78)
Special education < 20% $t-2$	−393.2**	4,096.1**	305.9	154.4	−95.6*
	(−3.07)	(5.12)	(0.35)	(0.36)	(−2.23)
Full value ($000) t	0.0726	−1.6839**	2.565**		
	(1.66)	(−5.58)	(19.78)		
Full value ($000) $t-1$	0.000058	0.00062*			
	(−1.41)	(−2.38)			
Total personal income t	0.00249	−0.7328*	0.4259**		
	(0.24)	(−2.38)	(6.22)		
Total personal income $t-1$	0.01666*	0.1837**			
	(−2.13)	(3.76)			
Limited English proficient	435.5**	3,583**	1,077.1	−1,181.0*	−677.8*
	(2.94)	(3.85)	(1.01)	(−2.18)	(−2.03)
Regular student squared		0.1382**			
		(6.29)			
Special education 60% squared		3.526**			
		(2.69)			

TABLE 7.7 *Continued*

Independent Variable	Federal Aid	State Aid	Total Expenditure	Regular Teaching	Special Education
Special education		12.36**			
20% to 60% squared		(4.14)			
Special education < 20% squared		– 3.169**			
		(4.10)			
Black			1,348.4*	112.2	277.1
			(2.02)	(0.33)	(1.33)
Hispanic			–1,108.5	456.6	–1,242.3**
			(–1.75)	(1.47)	(– 6.37)
State aid			0.8029**		
			(32.97)		
Federal aid			0.7628**		
			(4.89)		
Total expenditure				0.2822*	0.0570**
				(19.66)	(6.44)
N	2,540	2,540	2,540	2,540	2,540
Adjusted R squared	0.96	0.99	0.99	0.99	0.99

* = Significant at the 5% level
** = Significant at the 1% level

remained unchanged and then, if local, state, and federal revenues did change in response to the additional student. For example, a permanent increase of one student in the number of regular students, with no change in revenue, is estimated to increase regular teaching by $1,492 (= 632.9 + 497.6 + 361.2), reduce special education by $391, and reduce noninstructional spending by $1,100.[27]

A similar analysis for the addition of a special education student provides no conclusive evidence that spending on regular students is reduced to accommodate the increased costs of that student. However, our expenditure data do not allow for a clear assessment. Although there is a modest ($63) decrease in regular classroom expenditures when the most expensive type of special education student is added (with no revenue increase), this indicates the effect on only this spending category, not the effect on regular students. At least some of these special education students spend a portion of their day in regular classes, requiring additional resources in that setting. To the extent that the additional special education student received some regular education services and regular education spending experienced a modest decrease, regular students would be at least somewhat worse off. The extent of crowding out with respect to the other two types of special education students is less clear. Because these students are spending increasing proportions of their day in regular classroom settings, it is difficult to determine whether the increased expense associated with regular teaching when enrollments increase is sufficient to compensate for resources going to the additional students. In the absence of significant negative effects on regular teaching, we are unable to draw firm conclusions.

Conclusion

Understanding how school districts allocate expenditures across types of students and budget categories is important in evaluating policies to improve educational productivity. This chapter focuses on two questions: What factors account for the large increase in special education expenditures that occurred in school districts in New York between 1980 and 1993? Have these increases reduced resources going to regular students? We believe we now have a better understanding of school district finances, although several issues remain unresolved.

The large growth in special education expenditures over the 1980 to 1993 period in New York resulted from a combination of increasing expenditures per disabled student and an increasing number of students with disabilities. The growth in expenditures per student reflected both a changing composition of special education students and increases in resources devoted to each type of student. In addition, it appears that institutional factors, such as regulations and court cases, have played a role in increasing special education expenditures. Our analysis clearly indicates that changing student composition and overall growth have played an important role in squeezing school district budgets and will continue to do so.

We have attempted to measure expenditures on regular and disabled students, both descriptively and econometrically. In neither case did we find clear support for the claim that special education expenditures crowd out spending on regular students. However, it is clear that descriptions of per-pupil expenditures that do not distinguish between regular and special education students substantially overstate the resources reaching regular students at a given time as well as changes over time. Thus, productivity analyses that do not account for this difference are likely to understate the effect of spending on outcomes of regular students.

We believe that the basic approach employed here is potentially applicable in considering a variety of related policy questions in educational finance. In descriptive work, we found that school districts appear to respond asymmetrically to enrollment changes for certain types of expenditures. For example, districts reduce spending on administration less when enrollments fall than they increase it when enrollments rise. If this result is robust to multivariate analysis, it would provide support for the notion that slack resources are consumed by an increasingly bloated administrative structure.

Last, and perhaps most important to the interpretation of the econometric results, would be the development of a complete structural model of school district economic behavior. Our model is clearly a reduced-form characterization of a more complicated budget determination process. With a structural understanding of this process, we can more comfortably attach behavioral interpretations to the empirical regularities documented here.

APPENDIX

Description of the Data

The 693 major school districts in New York in 1992-1993 compose our sample. District-level expenditure data are drawn from the annual financial reports (ST-3) for school years 1979-1980 through 1992-1993. Information regarding total student membership comes from the Basic Education Data System database. Disabled student counts are drawn from the Department of Education suspense file used in the calculation of state aid. See Lankford and Wyckoff (1996) for a detailed description of the data set.

The following are descriptions, means, and standard deviations of variables used in the regression analysis.

Variable	Definition	Mean
Total enrollment	Total number of students in district	2,327.1
Special education aid	Dummy if not on save-harmless X limited approved operating expenditures X aid ratio	2,183.0
School lunch	Number of eligible applicants to free and reduced-price school lunch program in district	640.8
Average class size	Mean class size for all common branch (K-6) classes in the district	21.7
Regular teaching	Expenditures on regular teaching in district	10,675,000
Special education	Expenditures on special education in district	2,200,300
Total expenditure	Total expenditures in district	21,554,000
State aid	Total state aid for education in district	8,985,100
Federal aid	Total federal aid for education in district	475,590
Regular students	Number of regular students in district	2,065
Special education 60%	Number of special education students out of regular class at least 60% of day in district	121

Variable	Definition	Mean
Special education	Number of special education students out of regular class between 20% and 60% of day in district	98
Special education < 20%	Number of special education students out of regular class less than 20% of day in district	43
Full value	Total full value of taxable property in district	725,200,000
Total personal income	Total personal income in county in which district is located	11,133,000
Limited English proficiency	Number of students who are categorized as limited English proficient in district	38
Black	Number of black students in district	208
Hispanic	Number of Hispanic students in district	82

Notes

1. See Hanushek and Rivkin (1994).

2. National data are notably weak in identifying many expenditure categories and do not provide consistent categorization over time. State data are more detailed. Lankford and Wyckoff (1995) employ school district data over a 13-year period in New York. Monk and Roellke (1994) examine very detailed school-level data for New York and Nakib (1994) examines school-level data from Florida. Also see Picus and Nakib (1993).

3. See Verstegen (1994) for a summary of the history surrounding the development and intent of Pub. L. 94-142.

4. Hartman (1980) has observed that this creates incentives for schools to identify and treat disabled students with the least severe disabilities to maximize net revenue. Some have suggested that these incentives lead to overidentification of special education students as a revenue source for school districts. See, for example, Parrish (1993) and Parrish and Verstegen (1994) for a discussion and summary of this research.

5. The following data on special education enrollments are found in U.S. Department of Education, Annual Report to Congress on the Implementation of Education of the Handicapped Act (1981, 1993).

6. Berninger and Abbott (1994) and Moats and Lyon (1993) describe the lack of common definition of learning disabilities and the resulting differences in identification rates.

7. In addition, Moore and others (1988) collected data from 80 school districts in 18 states for the 1985-1986 school year. Although well-designed and carried out, this analysis is now somewhat dated.

8. These are the four placement settings defined under the New York regular public excess-cost aid formula. This aid accounted for more than 80% of all state aid for special education in 1992-1993. In addition, there are private day schools, public and private

residential schools, and home and hospital living situations. These placements are generally the most expensive but represented less than 5% of the total special education enrollment in New York during the 1992-1993 school year.

9. The six disability types not shown in Table 7.1 each constitute less than 1% of public nonresidential special education students and 4% in total.

10. The rate of the first correlation is –0.28; the rate of the second is –0.14. However, there appears to be no relationship between the students pulled out at least 60% of the day and the students pulled out less than 20%.

11. Because the definitions employed to determine if a student should be classified as needing special education are open to wide variation in interpretation, the issue of whether school districts are influenced by the potential financial benefits has often been raised. For example, Leo Klagholz, education commissioner for New Jersey, recently was quoted as saying that "he believed the rise in the number of children in some categories (of special education) could be at least partially attributable to efforts on the part of local school districts to increase revenues from the state" (Braun, 1995, p. 1).

12. For example, Herman Badillo, New York City Mayor Rudolph Giuliani's special advisor on education finance, "says the Board of Education has allowed special education and bilingual programs to develop bloated payrolls, draining money from students in regular classrooms." The Board's budget director, Leonard Hellenbrand, "agreed that regular students had suffered as a result of court-ordered increases in special-education spending" (Dillon, 1994, p. 1).

13. A description of the data and definitions behind these statements is provided in this chapter's Appendix.

14. In 1980, the New York State Education Department conducted a detailed estimate of special education costs to determine the appropriate weights for each of the three special education classifications (less than 20%, between 20 and 60%, and greater than 60%) used in our analysis. Based on this analysis, the state developed weights of 1.13, 1.80, and 2.70, respectively. In addition, the ratio of special education expenditures to regular expenditures was about 2.2 in 1980 and 2.3 in 1993. This is consistent with previous cost studies (National Center for Education Statistics, 1994). In the case of regular teaching resources going to special education students, these weights are used together with the fraction indicating the portion of the day that these students are in regular classes.

15. *Jose P. v. Ambach*, 669 F.2d 865 (2d Cir. 1982), on remand, 587 F. Supp. 1572 (E.D.N.Y. 1984).

16. Information about the circumstances of special education in New York City is based on a conversation in November 1994 with Rebecca Cort, New York City coordinator for special education services, New York State Education Department.

17. For a detailed analysis of special education in New York City, see Fruchter, Berne, Marcus, Alter, and Gottlieb (1995).

18. That growth for both types of students can be below that for the overall expenditures per pupil may at first seem curious, but it is largely due to declining enrollments of regular students and increasing enrollments of special education students. Only when the mix of regular and special education students is unchanged will the percentage changes in total expenditures for regular and special education students necessarily bound the percentage change in the overall expenditure per pupil.

19. The basic decomposition formula is $1 = [S_2(E_2 - E_1) + E_1(S_2 - S_1)]/(T_2 - T_1)$, where S denotes expenditures per pupil, E denotes enrollment, T denotes total expenditures, and the subscripts reflect time periods. E can be replaced by its components, the three

disability groups, to further decompose the effects due to changes in enrollment. Ideally, we would like to have expenditures per pupil by special education classification to identify which group is responsible for increasing per-pupil costs. Such data are unavailable in New York.

20. As described in Note 19, the expenditure numbers reflect a prorating of regular classroom expenditures to the three types of special education students based on the portion of the time they are in regular classrooms. We use the weights in Table 7.4 under "Resource assumption 2."

21. A more detailed discussion of the model and statistical analysis is found in Lankford and Wyckoff (1996).

22. It is also possible that enrollments of both regular and special education students are affected by state and federal aid, total expenditures, and expenditures by category. We have not accounted for these potential relationships in the estimates presented, largely because the data necessary to incorporate such estimation were not completely available. In Hausman tests for endogeneity of special education enrollments in a more limited version of the model, we found evidence that the number of special education students in the equations for two expenditure categories (special education and building) probably suffer from endogeneity. We believe that not accounting for endogeneity is a potential problem of these analyses and see such modeling as an important item for future research.

23. More properly, $d_i = \delta W_i + \varepsilon_i$ is the "fixed effect," where the vector W_i represents those exogenous variables that are unchanged over the period analyzed. We use the fixed-effect specification for two reasons. First, our statistical analysis is motivated by an interest in how expenditures vary as a result of changes in enrollments. Fixed-effect estimation avoids statistical problems that arise when the individual effects are correlated with the error term. Second, a major advantage of the fixed-effect estimator is that the effects of the time-varying variables, such as enrollments, can be estimated without specifying or measuring any of the explanatory variables that are time invariant. In the current case, this is appealing because the selection of a complete set of variables would be somewhat arbitrary in the absence of an explicit theoretical model of expenditure determination, and data would be very difficult to obtain.

24. An instrumental-variables estimator is used in the model of expenditures by category because total expenditures is one of the explanatory variables.

25. Freeman and Hannan (1975) examine the differential effect of growth and decline in organizations. In particular, they believe that school districts will behave symmetrically with respect to hiring and firing of teachers (the direct component) but will behave asymmetrically with respect to the hiring and firing of administrators (the supportive component). McKee and Wintrobe (1993) argue that not only do administrators not face symmetrical hiring and firing decisions during time of organizational growth and decline, but consistent with Parkinson's law, the number of administrators actually expands during periods of organizational decline.

26. See Hines and Thaler (1995) for an excellent discussion of "flypaper effects."

27. If an enrollment increase were in place for at least 3 years, enrollments would be larger in periods t, t − 1, and t − 2. Thus, a permanent one-student increase in regular enrollments is estimated ultimately to increase regular teaching expenditures by $1,492 (= $632.9 + $497.6 + $361.2). The estimated $391 reduction in special education expenditures is calculated in a similar way. If total revenues and expenditures were unchanged, it would follow that other expenditures would have to fall by $1,101 (= $1,492 − $391). Accounting for changes in revenues, the enrollment change is estimated to

increase total expenditures by \$2,326 (= \$2,704.6 − \$300.1 − \$78.1). After accounting for the increase in total expenditures, the estimated total effect of the one-student increase in regular enrollment on regular teaching and special education expenditures are \$2,148 (= \$1,492 + 0.2822 × \$2,326) and \$258.4 (= −\$391 + 0.0570 × \$2,326), respectively. This implies that other expenditures are estimated to increase by \$436 (= −\$1,101 + (1 − 0.2822 − 0.0570) × \$2,326). Estimates of the effects of increasing special education enrollments can be calculated in similar ways.

References

Berninger, V. W., & Abbott, R. D. (1994). Redefining learning disabilities: Moving beyond aptitude-achievement discrepancies to failure to respond to validated treatment protocols. In G. R. Lyon (Ed.), *Frames of reference for the assessment of learning disabilities: New views on measurement issues* (pp. 163-183). Baltimore: Brooks.

Braun, R. J. (1995, March 19). Klagholz fears schools inflate special ed need. *Newark Star-Ledger*, p. 1.

Chaikind, S., Danielson, L. C., & Brauen, M. L. (1993, Winter). What do we know about the costs of special education? A selected review. *Journal of Special Education, 26,* 344-370.

Chambers, J. G., & Dueñas, I. E. (1994). *Impact of the Kentucky Education Reform Act on the special education costs and funding.* Palo Alto, CA: American Institutes for Research, Center for Special Education Finance.

Dillon, S. (1994, August 14). Badillo contends that the cost of special education is inflated. *The New York Times,* p. 1.

Freeman, J., & Hannan, M. T. (1975, April). Growth and decline processes in organizations. *American Sociological Review, 40,* 215-28.

Fruchter, N., Berne, R., Marcus, A., Alter, M., & Gottlieb, J. (1995). *Focus on learning: A report on reorganizing general and special education in New York city.* New York: New York University, Institute for Education and Social Policy.

Hanushek, E. A., & Rivkin, S. (1994). *Understanding the 20th century explosion in U.S. school costs* (Working Paper 388). Rochester, NY: University of Rochester, Rochester Center for Economic Research.

Hartman, W. T. (1980, Fall). Policy effects of special education funding formulas. *Journal of Education Finance, 6,* 135-159.

Hines, J. R., & Thaler, R. H. (1995, Fall). Anomalies: The flypaper effect. *Journal of Economic Perspectives, 9,* 217-226.

Kakalik, J. S., Furry, W. S., Thomas, M. A., & Carney, M. F. (1981). *The cost of special education* (A RAND Note). Santa Monica, CA: RAND.

Ladd, H. (Ed.). (1996). *Holding schools accountable.* Washington, DC: Brookings Institution.

Lankford, H., & Wyckoff, J. (1995, Summer). Where has the money gone? An analysis of school district spending in New York. *Educational Evaluation and Policy Analysis, 17,* 195-218.

Lankford, H., & Wyckoff, J. (1996). The allocation of resources to special education and regular instruction. In H. Ladd (Ed.), *Making schools accountable: Performance-based approaches to school reform* (pp. 221-257). Washington, DC: Brookings Institution.

McKee, M., & Wintrobe, R. (1993, July). The decline of organizations and the rise of administrators. *Journal of Public Economics, 51,* 309-327.

Moats, L. C., & Lyon, G. R. (1993, May). Learning disabilities in the United States: Advocacy, science, and the future of the field. *Journal of Learning Disabilities, 26,* 282-294.

Monk, D. H., & Roellke, C. (1994). The origin, disposition and utilization of resources within New York State public school systems: An update. *Proceedings from NCES Conference on Putting It All Together.* Washington, DC: National Center for Education Statistics.

Moore, M.T., Strang, E. W., Schwartz, M., & Braddock, M. (1988). *Patterns in special education service delivery and cost.* Washington, DC: Decision Resources Corporation.

Nakib, Y. (1994). Allocation and use of public K-12 education in Florida. In L. Picus & J. Wattenburger (Eds.), *Where does the money go? Resource allocation in elementary and secondary schools.* Thousand Oaks, CA: Corwin.

National Center for Education Statistics. (1994). *Digest of Education Statistics, (1994).* Washington, DC: Government Printing Office.

New York State Education Department. (1994). *Projections of public and non-public school enrollment and high school graduates to 2003-04 New York State.* Albany: State University of New York Press.

O'Reilly, F. (1993). *State special education finance systems, 1992-93.* Palo Alto, CA: American Institutes for Research, Center for Special Education Finance.

Parrish, T. B. (1993). *Federal policy options for funding special education* (Policy Brief). Palo Alto, CA: American Institutes for Research, Center for Special Education Finance.

Parrish, T. B., & D. A. Verstegen. (1994). *Fiscal provisions of the Individuals with Disabilities Education Act: Policy issues and alternatives* (Policy Paper). Palo Alto, CA: American Institute for Research, Center for Special Education Finance.

Picus, L., & Nakib, Y. (1993). *The allocation and use of educational resources at the district level in Florida* (Working Paper 38). Los Angeles: University of Southern California, Center for Research in Education Finance.

Rossmiller, R. A., Hale, J. A., & Frohreich, L. E. (1970). *Educational programs for exceptional children: Resource configurations and costs.* Madison: University of Wisconsin, Department of Educational Administration.

U.S. Council of Economic Advisors. (1995). *Economic Report to the President.* Washington, DC: Government Printing Office.

U.S. Department of Education. (1981). *Annual report to congress on the implementation of Education for the Handicapped Act.* Washington, DC: Government Printing Office.

U.S. Department of Education. (1993). *Annual report to congress on the implementation of Education for the Handicapped Act.* Washington, DC: Government Printing Office.

Verstegen, D. A. (1994). *Fiscal provisions of the Individuals with Disabilities Education Act: Historical overview.* Palo Alto, CA: American Institutes for Research, Center for Special Education Finance.

EIGHT

Financing Special Education
PROPOSED REFORMS
IN NEW YORK CITY

NORM FRUCHTER

THOMAS B. PARRISH

ROBERT BERNE

As recently as 20 years ago, many students with disabilities were excluded from public education and, when included, were often taught in separate, inadequate, and sometimes inhumane settings. But consistent local organizing, persistent use of the courts, and exposure of the sometimes shameful treatment of children with disabilities led to federal action through laws such as Pub. L. 94-142; court intervention through decisions forcing state and city systems to im-

AUTHORS' NOTE: This chapter is based on *Focus on Learning: A Report on Reorganizing General and Special Education in New York City*, by Fruchter, Berne, Marcus, Alter, and Gottlieb (1995) and a paper that formed an appendix of that report, "Review of Financing Dimensions from Focus on Learning," by Thomas B. Parrish. The authors wish to acknowledge the contributions of Dorothy Siegel, Ross Rubenstein, Diane McGivern, and Carol Ascher.

prove their offerings; and the development of effective district and school-based programs have significantly improved the education of students with special needs. For many, the days of exclusion, callous treatment, and marginal attention are over. In the New York City public schools, for example, almost 13% of the students are classified as disabled and almost 25% of the public school budget is spent on their education.

But for a growing number of critics, this expansion of special education students and costs has triggered warning signals; many charge that special education has become both too costly and too restrictive. Significant expansion of special education registers in many states and districts has focused attention on what is far too often an arbitrary identification system. Failure to define consistent outcome standards for student academic performance in special education placements has generated charges of ineffectiveness in urban, suburban, and rural settings. Throughout the country, the identification, placement, and subsequent educational experience of hundreds of thousands of students labeled as disabled is increasingly being called into question.

A similar focus of reconsideration has spotlighted special education in the New York City schools, long the subject of court monitoring through the landmark Jose P. case first brought in 1979 (see also Zirkel, 1995).[1] As referral rates and costs have risen, stakeholders, providers, and constituents have increasingly questioned whether New York City's special education programs are serving the majority of their students effectively, efficiently, and equitably. There is mounting evidence that the city's special education programs have produced limited outcomes because of these factors:

- Accountability is very limited. There are no useful instructional standards and very little useful data on educational and behavioral outcomes (Board of Education of the City of New York, Office of Information, Reporting and Technology Services, 1997; New York State Education Department, 1997a, 1997b; Office of the Comptroller of the City of New York, 1994).
- Far too many students are placed in separate settings rather than in more appropriate, less restrictive instructional settings defined by state and federal law (Committee on Education and the Law, 1993; U.S. Department of Education, 1989).

- Students of color are overrepresented in special education and particularly overrepresented in separate special classes (Autin, Dentzer, & McNutt, 1994; Board of Education of the City of New York, Division of Special Education, 1990).

- Many students are placed in special education not because of disability but because general education is not meeting their learning needs (Hornbeck & Lehmann, 1991).

- The cost of evaluating, transporting, tracking, reevaluating, mainstreaming, and decertifying students who may not be disabled is siphoning off resources from a resource-starved public education system (Lankford & Wyckoff, 1996).

In response to these pressing problems, the Institute for Education and Social Policy at New York University prepared a report, *Focus on Learning: A Report on Reorganizing General and Special Education in New York City* (Fruchter, Berne, Marcus, Alter, & Gottlieb, 1995), to help guide the (then) Chancellor Ramon Cortines, who had made the improvement of special education one of his top priorities. This chapter is based on that report and a paper prepared as an appendix to that report by Parrish (1995b); we focus on the report's specific finance-related issues that have become the core of current special education reform.

First, we review the major elements of reforms proposed in *Focus on Learning* (Fruchter et al., 1995), particularly the finance implications for elementary and middle schools in New York City.[2] The three main finance recommendations include (a) the creation of an enrichment allocation for each school that merges funds for special and compensatory education, (b) fiscal incentives that encourage schools and school districts to develop appropriate programs in students' home schools, and (c) changes in state funding to both permit and encourage the approach we recommend. Second, we compare the financing dimensions of the *Focus* reforms with similar initiatives in other states. Last, we conclude with a review of the current proposals for special education reform in New York State that drew on our recommendations.

A Proposal for Reform

Focus (Fruchter et al., 1995) concluded that major structural changes are needed to respond more effectively to students experiencing academic or behavioral problems, both in general education and in special education, and particularly those classified as mildly or moderately disabled. We need structural changes to create new school practices that help school staffs respond very differently to the rich diversity of children's learning styles and learning needs. Such new practices have been developed in a small number of New York City's schools; our recommendations encourage the development of new practices in all the City's public schools.[3]

The Ingredients of Reform

We propose a school-based model that restructures schools and classrooms, deploys personnel in new ways, reconceptualizes instruction and assessment, and changes how funds are allocated. Implementing our model would transform our dual system, which currently separates instruction from evaluation and special education students from general education students, into a far more integrated system that better serves the learning needs of all students.

The school-based model invites each school to assess the needs of its more precarious students and to create, with an enrichment allocation consisting of merged special and general education funds, the classroom structure and school organization that best meets all its students' needs. The primary purpose of the enrichment allocation is to ensure that classroom teachers have adequate instructional and nonacademic supports to meet the needs of students with disabilities or students at risk of academic failure. The special education funds to be merged are only those allocated to community school districts (and high schools) for programs for students with mild and moderate disabilities. The general education funds to be merged include compensatory education resources and other supports. We believe that if teaching and learning in general education were significantly restructured, using the enrichment allocation, most students' learning needs could be met without referral to special education and placement in separate settings.

The first step in this reconfiguration is to merge the school-based resources now split into special education and general education allocation streams. General education resources are allocated by formulas driven primarily by student numbers. But special education resources are driven by placements along the continuum of special education services. That is, the amount of funding a student draws is based on his or her special education placement or assignment. In New York State, these placements form a continuum that begins with services provided in the least restrictive setting, the general education classroom. Services can include related services, such as speech and counseling, consultant teachers, or resource rooms. The next, more restrictive level includes special or self-contained classes within a general education setting for all or part of the school day. More restrictive placements involve separate classes within a program cluster or within a school composed solely of self-contained classes. The most restrictive settings involve residential placements or home or hospital placements.

In New York State, unfortunately, funding supports more restrictive placements; the more self-contained and isolated the placement, the more funds that placement generates. In New York City, there are relatively few placements in the general education classroom, the least restrictive level of the continuum. The City's school system places a much higher percentage of children with mild and moderate disabilities in self-contained classes than other school systems, both in New York State and across the nation (Committee on Education and the Law, 1993; U.S. Department of Education, 1989).

Focus (Fruchter et al., 1995) recommends merging the total amount of funding available at the school site, both those funds that support the continuum of special education placements for students with mild and moderate disabilities and those funds allocated for compensatory education and other supplemental supports, for flexible instructional use in meeting all students' needs, with appropriate safeguards to preserve the intent of special education funds.

Allowing special education monies to be blended with other funding streams is consistent with the national reform movement. An example of blended funding has been established under Title I of the Elementary and Secondary Education Act.[4] Schools at which at least 50% of the students are designated as living in poverty are allowed to blend funds from a variety of federal sources to make schoolwide changes for the benefit of all students. In addition, as a part of the reauthorizing legislation for the federal Individuals with Disabilities Education Act (IDEA),[5] federal special education dollars can now be included under the funds to be blended in schoolwide projects. The potential benefits of such blending for special education students are described in a statement issued by the National Association of State Special Education Directors, "Combining funds provided under IDEA and the Elementary and Secondary Education Act's Title I, while maintaining IDEA's procedural safeguards . . . could permit special educators to better participate in the reform process" ("NASDSE," 1994, pp. 3-4)

Under the *Focus* (Fruchter et al., 1995) plan, these merged funds, along with other personnel and financial resources, would comprise an enrichment allocation that each school would use to create a more effective teaching and learning environment for all students, particularly for students with disabilities and students at risk of academic failure. Such restructuring would lead to a system in which each school shapes its instructional environment to best meet all its students' needs, combining resources, including special education funds, that do not follow individual students but meet their needs through a variety of school-based instructional responses.

How Would This Work?

Consider an elementary school that contains 750 students under the current system. Approximately 10% of the school, or 75 students, are categorized as mildly and moderately disabled and they are distributed across four self-contained classes and two resource room pull-out classes. Computing only the cost of teachers and program paraprofessionals and using average teacher salaries, these 75 special education students would generate $320,000 in personnel resources. If the cost of a student in general education is $1,429, then the enrichment allocation is the $320,000 less the $107,000, or $213,000.[6]

The school would receive its formula-driven general education allocation for all its students. But the special education allocation, the $320,000 that would have funded the specific self-contained classes and resource room services, would be provided as a lump sum allocation. If the school, in shaping its instructional plan, decided that the best way to meet the needs of its students with disabilities was to reproduce the pattern of self-contained classes and resource rooms, the school would use all of its allocation to recreate its previous special education configuration. But the school could also choose to use its allocation for different patterns of classroom organization and staff deployment (Mathis, 1996).

All of the school's supplementary allocations, including federal and state compensatory education funds, would be combined with the allocation generated by the special education funding stream to create a comprehensive enrichment allocation focused on the needs of all the school's most precarious students. Thus, funding would continue to address the needs of students with mild and moderate disabilities, but rather than reflexively creating instructional settings outside regular classrooms, funds could be used to enrich mainstream classrooms and to improve the educational environment of all students. The enrichment resources could be used to create flexible groupings, multiage settings, smaller classes for children with particular needs, cooperative learning groups, peer-age and cross-age tutoring, a range of strategies that offer support for classroom teachers and provide small-group or individualized instruction (including the consultant teacher model), counseling assistance for particular behavioral needs, and assistance with speech and language problems.

To ensure that the educational needs of students with disabilities and all other at-risk students are not dismissed, the enrichment allocations would come with a set of stipulations for how they could be used at the school site. One stipulation, for example, would require each school to assess all those students that teachers or parents perceive as potential candidates for future academic or behavioral difficulty, within the context of the school's standards, educational approach, and instructional plan. The current formal assessment process, by comparison, reaches only selected students and involves steps and procedures that may not be appropriate for all children.

To carry out our recommendations effectively, schools, community school districts, and the entire New York City School District need guarantees that their funding will not be decreased because they are meeting their students' needs more successfully by integrating funding and instructional strategies. Therefore, a 5-year waiver that maintains both baseline funding and annual increases (for enrollment increases and inflation) is an essential part of our recommendations. Because particular conditions, such as an increase in student mobility or a sudden influx of immigrants, can sometimes produce an intensification of disability, we recommend that the City School District and the community school districts maintain an emergency reserve fund for allocation to specific schools experiencing legitimate, sharp increases in student need.

To help every school meet student learning needs, we recommend the creation of an instructional support team (IST) in each school. The IST should be composed primarily of classroom and cluster teachers supplemented by supervisors, guidance counselors, clinicians and psychologists working in the school as support staff, as well as related service providers, such as speech teachers and counselors. The IST's prime purpose is to provide informal, rapid-response intervention to help classroom teachers resolve particular instructional or behavioral problems. The IST's priority is to help the classroom teacher develop and implement strategies that reduce or resolve students' learning or behavioral difficulties.

To ensure that ISTs concentrate on helping schools meet their students' learning needs, ISTs will have no power to formally evaluate students or to classify them as disabled. ISTs can refer students to a community district-level multidisciplinary committee on special education (CSE) for formal evaluation, once they decide the school has exhausted its instructional and support efforts. But if district-level CSE evaluation results in student placement in a different school, the referring school will face a fiscal disincentive—it will lose (from its enrichment allocation) the amount of money it costs to educate that student in a new instructional setting, which may well be higher than the cost of educating the student in the home school.

For an example of how this disincentive would work, consider our previously cited elementary school with 75 mild and moderately disabled students and $320,000 in resources as calculated earlier. If a student is referred to a different school where the student's needs would be more effectively met and the annual cost of that program is $6,429, ($5,000 more than the cost of educating the student in general education in the original school), the $5,000 and the $1,429 general education allocation would be deducted from the original school and added to the enrichment allocation in the new school. Incremental transportation costs would also be charged to the sending school.

Formal evaluations would be conducted only by the community district-level CSE teams. For students found to have mild or moderate disabilities, the CSE would recommend placements within the community school district's boundaries or face significant fiscal disincentives similar to those imposed on schools whose students are referred to the district for evaluation and subsequently placed in other district schools. Parents would maintain their right to request a formal evaluation, at any time, without consulting the IST or the school.

Making the school-based model work requires extensive professional development to help teachers recognize and address the needs of students with disabilities; provide opportunities to develop and try out new teaching skills, substantive knowledge, communication skills, and decision-making capacities; and help staff develop the capacity to evaluate how well their school serves its students. Therefore, we recommend significant new investment in school-based professional development.

Once responsibility for decision making, professional development, and instructional planning is lodged at the school site, the issue of educational accountability becomes even more critical. The history of New York City schools' treatment of students with disabilities suggests that we cannot simply give local schools the resources and discretion to reconfigure their instructional organization and assume they will effectively respond to all students' learning needs. Therefore, we recommend the creation of an independent accountability and quality assurance office (AQAO), which would evaluate district and school efforts to phase in the school-based model and review the resulting outcomes for students at risk of school failure and students with disabilities. The AQAO would report to the chancellor and the public about school, district, and systemic instruction and learning outcomes.

The AQAO would also recruit, establish, train, supervise, and support district-level parent advocacy teams in every community school district. These parent advocacy teams would be responsible for ensuring that parents are informed about their due process rights, would provide an informal appeal mechanism for parents or school staff convinced that students' needs were not being adequately met, would help parents access the mediation resources provided by the New York State Education Department, and would function as an early warning system to the AQAO about problematic school or district performance. Teams would include parents, members of public interest or advocacy groups, and professionals outside the school system; all members would be appropriately compensated for their services.

We also recommend major changes in state funding mechanisms because (a) state allocations currently provide significant incentives for school districts to place students in special education and (b) also encourage more restrictive placements in self-contained settings. Current New York State funding formulas encourage the overreferral and overplacement of students into special education because the resources they provide to meet varieties of student need in general education classrooms are far too limited. Funding mechanisms that make placement in special education the major source of additional help promote referral and classification of students as disabled when what many of those students need is more support in general education rather than extraction from it.

New York State funding formulas also create incentives to place students in more restrictive settings because the state's formulas are based on the types of special services students receive and on the amount of time students receive those services. Moreover, the ancillary and indirect costs associated with referral to, assessment by, and placements in special education—evaluation, transportation, supervision, and tracking—increase the cost of each inappropriate referral and placement by thousands of dollars per year per student. These costs rise even more steeply as placements become more restrictive.

It is sometimes argued that such placement-driven systems only generate fiscal incentives when their revenues exceed the cost of the placement required to qualify for them. However, federal and state laws require that special education students receive services appropriate to their needs wherever they are served. Thus, there is no reason to believe that serving students with special needs in a general education classroom with proper levels of support will be any less costly than serving these students in more restrictive special classrooms. When the cost of these alternative settings is the same but the accompanying revenues are much higher for the more restrictive placement, as is true in New York, fiscal incentives for such placements are inherent in the system. In some instances, these incentives will result in placements that are not in the best interests of the special needs children, and they are in violation of the least restrictive environment (LRE) placement provisions of IDEA.

Accordingly, we recommend that the New York State formulas, and particularly the Public Excess Aid formula, be revised so that funding promotes placement in less restrictive settings, creates incentives to educate students in their home or zoned schools, and promotes help to students in general education settings. We examine a set of proposals developed by the New York State Regents that move in this direction in the last section of this chapter.

But before such large-scale changes in state formulas are enacted, implementing our model in New York City requires a broad-based waiver of current state requirements and perhaps changes in legislation as well. Essentially, the State would have to grant New York City a waiver or make changes such as the following:

- Specify a total amount of special education funding, using a baseline fiscal year for the State's Public Excess Cost Aid allocation to the City, and guarantee the provision of that funding, with annual increases, for at least 5 years, insulating the City, community school districts, and individual schools against any decrease in special education registers.
- Allow the funding to be merged with general education funds and other supplementary funding to more effectively meet student needs, with appropriate safeguards to preserve the intent of special education funding.
- Allow merged funding to be used to meet the needs of students with mild and moderate disabilities now placed in self-contained classrooms with a variety of services and supports provided by the continuum of services but predominantly within general education where appropriate.

Our recommendations include a variety of strategies in addition to funding changes to encourage the placement of students with disabilities in close-to-home schools. We believe our recommendations would generate significant efficiency savings through reductions in transportation costs and decreased expenditure on evaluation and placement functions.[7] And we urge that a comprehensive evaluation be instituted, when implementation begins, to assess the effectiveness of the structural changes we recommend.

Last, we argue that continuing to impose budget cuts on general education inevitably results in forcing more students into special education. We believe that expanding the capacity of general education to meet the needs of many students now placed in special education programs for the mildly and moderately disabled can shift significant resources from evaluation, placement, transportation, and tracking to classroom instruction and support. But we cannot expand general education's capacity by merging funds for mildly and moderately disabled students while simultaneously reducing its capacity through budget cuts. Therefore, we believe that, to effectively implement the structural changes we recommend, we must begin to restore funding to New York City schools whose instructional and support capacities have been severely reduced by the budget cutting of the mid-1990s.

A National Context: Issues and Examples[8]

This section places our recommendations in a national context, because this form of comprehensive special education reform is not unique to New York City. School districts, states, and the federal system of special education governance and provision have undergone similar review and in many instances resulted in comparable recommendations.

What is causing this reconsideration of current special education policy across the United States as well as in other developed nations around the world? Based on surveys of special education officials in 50 states (Center for Special Education Finance, 1997) and several dozen presentations and conferences at the state, federal, and international levels over the past several years, this reconsideration seems to be driven by several key factors: questions about funding system incentives and the most appropriate placements for students with disabilities, the costs of those services, and the need for increased decision making and flexibility in the use of funds at the local level.

The issue of most appropriate placement has become contentious because of the emergence of a movement for special education inclusion. The essence of the inclusion claim is that students with disabilities should be granted full rights to be educated with their nondisabled peers. The strongest inclusion advocates argue that all means all, meaning that all students with disabilities should be educated in integrated placements with a diverse mix of other students. Others simply point to the LRE provisions that have been in place since the passage of the federal special education law in 1978. These issues are not unique to the United States, as evidenced by an international conference held in Washington, DC, in which at least a dozen developed countries described their inclusionary goals and progress toward meeting them.

Increasing lawsuits and compliance review findings related to unwarranted segregation in the placement of many special education students have led to a number of questions about how the cost of these placements compare to the provision of less restrictive services. They have also led to the realization that state and federal funding provisions often contain fiscal incentives for increasing the number of students identified for special education and sometimes contain fiscal incentives for attributing more severe disabling conditions to students, or for placing them in more restrictive settings (Parrish, 1995a).

The perception, and sometimes the reality, of increasing special education identification rates and costs raises questions about the degrees of entitlement received by special education students, as compared to all other students, and fuels perceptions that separate services for many discrete categories of students is costly, inefficient, and often not in the best interest of students.

Simultaneously, with increased pressure on schools to be accountable, to have high expectations, and to be able to show results, the general standard of acceptable performance is being raised in school systems throughout the country. As these standards rise, so does the percentage of students unable to meet them and consequently the number of students who are considered in need of some form of special help. All these issues lead to questions of how finite educational resources can best be used to meet the educational needs of all students.

Because the federal government, states, and school districts all allocate funds for special education students to the jurisdictions below them, a common set of issues is confronted at all three levels. Exactly what kinds of program policies should be fostered at these lower levels of jurisdiction, and what kinds of fiscal policies should be created to support them? In addition to issues related to fiscal incentives and disincentives, there are also more traditional sets of school finance criteria to contend with, which relate primarily to the fairness and sufficiency of funds.[9]

What changes in governmental policy have come about in response to these issues? Starting at the federal level, several important policy changes relevant to the New York recommendations are contained in new fiscal provisions of the reauthorized IDEA. The first allows increased flexibility in the use of federal special education funds. Whereas previously these funds could be used only for the direct and exclusive benefit of special education students, changes under the reauthorization allow non-special education students to also derive incidental benefit from their use. Under the new rules, it is permissible for a federally funded special educator to teach a mixed reading class that included a special education student, who was the primary beneficiary of this special instruction, even though general education students also receive incidental benefit from the instruction. This is a smaller but analogous step to the blended funding and service provisions that the *Focus* (Fruchter et al., 1995) report recommended.

A second provision added through the reauthorization is that federal special education funds will eventually no longer be allocated solely on the basis of the number of special education students in a state but rather also on the state's overall school-age population. Similar to the *Focus* (Fruchter et al., 1995) recommendations, the purpose is to remove the fiscal incentive for increased special education identification and to no longer take money away from states who are reducing their special education count. Also included is a hold-harmless provision that does not allow any state to fall below its current level of funding.

To a large extent, the federal government took its cue from several key reform states. Many states have been reviewing their funding formulas to see if they contained fiscal incentives for more restrictive placements. Some of this scrutiny has come as the result of complaints from local school officials that they were losing state funds as they moved to more inclusive placements for their special education students, even though per-student costs had risen or stayed approximately the same.

Another new provision under IDEA, which is in accordance with the *Focus* (Fruchter et al., 1995) recommendations, could affect special education fiscal policy in New York. The reauthorized IDEA required states to demonstrate that if the state special education funding formula distributes assistance to localities based on the type of setting in which a child is served, as in New York, policies and procedures must be in place to ensure that these funding provisions do not result in placements that violate the requirement that children with disabilities be served in the LRE. If such policies are not in place, the state must provide the U.S. Secretary of Education with evidence that it will revise the funding mechanism to ensure that it does not result in restrictive placements.

How and why were fiscal incentives for more restrictive student placements included in state formulas in the first place? One reason is that these allocations were initially developed to relate funding to program cost. Although the principle of linking funding to program cost makes sense, in practice, because the most restrictive placements tend to be the highest costing, many state special education funding formulas inadvertently have created funding incentives for more restrictive placements. Because such formulas were generally designed around a set menu of alternative placement options, general classroom placements with supports for students with disabilities were often excluded from the menu. Thus, in many instances, no funding provisions were in place for fully integrated placements for students with disabilities. Because separate funding provisions for placing students with disabilities in private placements are also sometimes more generous than public school options, they too can create fiscal incentives for more restrictive or isolated placements. For a fuller discussion on removing fiscal incentives for restrictive placements, see Parrish (1995a).

State funding provisions to remove fiscal incentives for certain types of placement are described as *placement neutral*. Other states have taken a step beyond the removal of incentives for certain types of placements to the removal of incentives for further special education identification. The IDEA reauthorization provision described earlier (i.e., to change the basis of special education funding from the number of students identified for special education to the total school-age population of a state) is an example of this type of funding approach.

These funding approaches have come to be called census-based approaches. Their underlying rationale is that variation in the number of students identified for special education is not necessarily a good indication of variation in the true need for these services and that basing funding on the number of special education students in a state, or a district, creates a fiscal incentive for further identification. The degree of impact from such an incentive is not clear. However, conversely, states that have tried to reduce their special education identification rates by serving some special needs students outside of special education have expressed concerns about the fiscal disincentives associated with these policies.

States that have adopted census-based funding approaches include Pennsylvania, Massachusetts, California, and Montana. Vermont has a three-tiered formula, of which this type of census basis is an important component. Similar reform proposals have been developed and are currently being considered in Illinois. But such reforms are clearly not without controversy. One example is the argument by some that census-based systems are unfair precisely because they can allocate equal amounts of special education aid to two districts of the same size, even though one may identify 12% of its population for special education, whereas the other district identifies only 6%.[10]

A related approach to allowing for previously recognized cost variations (based on the number of students identified and perhaps on the type of service received) is to simply freeze district (or school) funding at some current base level. On a statewide basis, this approach was adopted by Massachusetts prior to their new census-based formula and is currently in effect in Utah. At the same time that the cost adjustments in place at the time of the freeze are recognized, districts (or schools) get locked in at this fixed level of reimbursement regardless of the future decisions they make about the identification of students for special education or where they are placed. This approach has the advantage of removing incentives for continuing identification and allows a great deal of flexibility in how special education students are labeled and served, as this funding is no longer tied to specific students, types of placement, or categories of disability.

The *Focus* (Fruchter et al., 1995) recommendation to establish a base amount of revenues for each school and then to hold schools harmless at this level seems closest to the types of base funding approaches with frozen allocations just described. Traditionally, a major point in these systems is not only to reduce allocations for districts if the number of identified students goes down but also to prevent increased allocations if the number of identified students goes up. One problem with this approach is that the base funding amount may prove problematic even in its first year of implementation, if there were inequities in the old system, and could become more problematic with changes in local conditions over time. Because it has no natural self-adjustment mechanism, it will become farther and farther removed from any measure of true student need, and therefore, some adjustment mechanism may be required over time.

What has been the experience of these census-driven-formula states? Vermont offers one example, even though it is not a pure census-based system. In addition to the census-based component, there is a reimbursement component and a third tier that relates to the extraordinary costs that individual districts may face.

Based on a phone survey administered across a sample of district administrators, state policy makers, and special education parents in the state, the overall response to the Vermont system seemed quite positive. The state also realized the expected impact of such a removal of identification incentives—there was a fairly substantial drop in the count of special education students statewide. There were also substantial increases in the numbers of students with disabilities receiving more inclusive, integrated services in their neighborhood schools since the advent of this reform. The State Director of Special Education attributes this at least partly to the change in the funding formula, which removed fiscal disincentives to such inclusive placements; he also points to the years of training necessary to prepare staff both psychologically and logistically for such a transition.[11]

Another lesson learned from Vermont is the importance of follow-up evaluation after decoupling special education funding from a count of special education students. If this revised funding policy leads to a reduction in the number of students identified for special education, there will be questions from the state legislature about why funding for special education needs to be maintained at current levels.

The Vermont reform provided significant additional flexibility in the use of funds, as *Focus* (Fruchter et al., 1995) recommended for New

York City. Although the number of students assigned formal special education labels dropped, the number of students receiving direct services by special education staff actually increased. Thus, similar to the *Focus* recommendations, special education resources were being used in a more flexible and efficient manner to meet the needs of all students and especially students at risk. Evaluation findings showing these results were important in encouraging the state to maintain current levels of support for this program (Vermont Department of Education, 1995).

Perhaps Pennsylvania provides the most powerful example for those interested in implementing the *Focus* (Fruchter et al., 1995) recommendations in New York City schools. Prior to the Pennsylvania reform, costs and special education identification rates were rising at a steady pace, largely because the state had a full reimbursement funding system—it reimbursed districts for basically all that they spent on special education. It was no surprise that this type of blank check led to increased expenditures and referrals in the special education system. Pennsylvania also had a history of decentralization services being provided in special schools run by regional special education units. Similar to the situation in New York, this type of non-locally-based system led to relatively high levels of segregated and remote placements for students with disabilities.[12]

In response, Pennsylvania developed a new funding formula that was quite simple in its orientation but also quite controversial, because it strongly emphasized services at the local level through the redirection of funds away from the providers of regional services. Perhaps the point most important for New York to consider is that Pennsylvania now allocates state special education funds directly to local districts, whereas previously, a substantial proportion of these state funds had gone directly to regionalized service providers. This relatively simple redirection of funds altered the entire decision-making structure because districts could now decide whether to provide services themselves in the home district environment or to purchase services from the regional provider.

This decision became increasingly based on the economics of home versus remote provision and on the most appropriate alternative for each individual child. The result was that many students with special needs returned to their home districts to receive services. Regional operators either had to shut down or change considerably the way they had been doing business. Many of these special district staff members seem to have been hired by local districts, and students with special needs seem to be receiving a less restrictive set of services in their home schooling environments.

Pennsylvania's reform also developed a statewide prereferral system based on ISTs, the same concept at the core of the *Focus* (Fruchter et al., 1995) recommendations described earlier in this chapter. The IST team in Pennsylvania is composed of the referring teacher, the IST teacher, and the school principal. The IST teacher is responsible for leading the IST process at the school and for providing any interim interventions that the team may recommend. This program also calls for the state to provide an intensive year of training for all school staff during the first year of implementation followed by a year of follow-up training. Furthermore, the program is coupled with a state aid system that contains no fiscal incentives for high-cost placements or for identifying a greater number of special education students. Thus, the entire system is designed to provide local districts with the resources, training, and discretion they need to provide a broad array of educational services to students with varying educational needs.

Although Pennsylvania requires that special education funds be spent on special education services, IST services are included in these costs for auditing purposes. The state provided for a 5-year phase-in period to develop IST teams in every school. During the phase-in, participating schools were to receive grants of $30,000 per year to hire an IST teacher, although funds for statewide implementation of ISTs during the phase-in period were not available for all years. Consequently, establishment of ISTs in all schools was uneven.

The state anticipated that the availability of IST services and the fact that state special education aid is not tied to the number of students identified would cause the state's special education counts to drop. Consequently, after 2 years, it was expected that local districts would be able to support the cost of IST teachers through savings from this reduction of direct special education services. This expectation has not been fully realized, and full IST implementation has not occurred as quickly as had been hoped or expected. In addition, although the count of special education students in Pennsylvania has steadied, the expected appreciable decrease in the special education population statewide has thus far not occurred. One reason that the special education counts have not dropped may be that the state still requires that special education funds be spent exclusively on special education students. Thus, flexibility in the use of funds is still limited, and it may still be difficult to get needed remedial services to students outside of special education. However, an evaluation of IST implementation in Pennsylvania found it to be a cost-effective intervention (Hartman & Fay, 1996).

Attempts to incorporate intervention systems where special education aid is directly tied to the number of students identified may face even more formidable implementation hurdles. As special education counts drop in these types of systems, local districts may stand to lose considerable state special education aid. In Oregon, for example, the funding system is based on a single weight, which is applied to all special education students up to a cap of 11%. Because there is no requirement that these funds be spent on special education services, districts have discretion to set up alternative intervention systems, such as ISTs. However, as special education counts drop in these districts, state aid is lost. As a result, phone interviews with local special education directors in Oregon revealed that some of those who had previously incorporated IST-type systems in an attempt to reduce their overall special education counts were now under pressure to get their special education counts back up to the funding ceiling of 11%. Such pressures, however, do not exist in population-based funding systems, such as those found in Pennsylvania, Vermont, Massachusetts, and Montana, because state aid is not dependent on the number of special education students identified. For a discussion and qualitative evaluation of special education finance reform in Oregon, see Montgomery (1995a).

In New York, it is unclear how the prescribed expiration of the 5-year hold-harmless provision specified in the recommendations might affect special education identification patterns. The lesson for New York City may be that the removal of fiscal incentives for the further identification of students may not be sufficient to decrease inappropriate referrals, that this removal must be accompanied by fairly extensive training and the clear establishment of alternative intervention systems for students at risk and that the temporary lifting of fiscal incentives for identification may have little effect if it appears that this is a short-term commitment (e.g., the 5-year hold-harmless period followed by a finance system with incentives to identify).

The New York State
Special Education Finance Formula

Clearly, the *Focus* (Fruchter et al., 1995) recommendations must be made compatible with New York State's special education funding; otherwise, state provisions could limit the added flexibility in the use of special education funds sought by these recommendations or, in an even worse case scenario, the city could lose current levels of state support. District-level reforms that conflict with state regulations and that could result in a loss of local funds will not be likely to succeed over time. Such concern on the part of local districts has provided much of the pressure to reform what have been seen as overly restrictive and inflexible state policies.

Problems with New York State's current special education finance system have been that it has encouraged the overreferral and overplacement of students into special education and has created incentives to place students in more restrictive settings. It has not promoted placement in less restrictive settings and has not created incentives to educate students in their home schools. Short of changing the statewide system, the implementation of *Focus* (Fruchter et al., 1995) recommendations requires that the city request a waiver from the State to guarantee funding over a 5-year period and allow considerable additional flexibility in the use of funds.

In addition, New York State has received pressure from the U.S. Department of Education to change its special education funding system. A number of states have been scrutinized by federal monitors about whether their special education funding formulas contain incentives for more restrictive placements. In the U.S. Office of Special Education Programs Final Monitoring Report (1994), New York was cited based on this issue. In its response, the state refused to agree to any corrective action, because it did not believe that the federal government had authority over such areas. However, since this prior report, federal authority has been enhanced in this area through the reauthorization provisions cited earlier regarding newly placed burdens on states to demonstrate that their special education funding formulas do not promote restrictive placements.

New York State has been working over the past several years to develop alternatives to the current special education funding provisions. Although the power to change the system is held primarily by the State Legislature, the State's Board of Regents has proposed funding reforms consistent with the *Focus* (Fruchter et al., 1995) recommendations described in this chapter, and these are now under review by the Legislature. According to the New York State Education Department (1996, pp. 8-14), the regents have recommended that New York State do the following:

- Provide a 100% increase (from $40 to $81 million) in aid for prevention and support services in general education to strengthen the capacity of school districts to provide support services and other alternatives to students experiencing learning difficulties.

- Determine the count of students with disabilities for special education aid by using a state average incidence rate of disability in school children that varies (increases) with the district's concentration of children living in poverty.

- Implement a transition to the new funding formula by maintaining the current special education funding for 1997-1998, investing dramatically in general education support and preventive services in 1997-1998 and phasing in the new funding system over 4 years beginning with the 1998-1999 year.

- Continue current laws for students with severe disabilities requiring excessive high cost aid in public schools, students with disabilities requiring summer programs, and students with disabilities educated in approved private special education schools.

- Direct the State Education Department to implement an evaluation plan to assess the effects of the new funding system.

- Under the direction of the State Education Department, implement a statewide training effort to provide special and general educators with the skills to educate students with disabilities in the least restrictive environment.

Although it is too soon to know the prospects of these reforms, clearly, they contain many of the elements in the *Focus* (Fruchter et al., 1995) recommendations, and they are consistent with reforms in other states. If implemented, they will contribute to an environment where New York City can move ahead to reform its own system.

The time may be right for New York City, the largest school district in the state and the country, to exercise leadership by encouraging the state to reform its special education funding provisions. Some of the guiding principles presented in this chapter may provide the impetus needed to assist the state in this important area of reform. The possibility of a waiver for New York City might also be considered by the state to help pilot some of these proposals before implementation statewide. There is clear hope for significant reform. In addition to other states, major census-based reform, as proposed for New York State, has been enacted at the federal level and in California within the past year. Pressure also seems to be continuous in many other states. In New York, the regents have proposed a plan that they believe will lead to improved outcomes, and the city schools chancellor has launched a reform initiative consistent with the *Focus* (Fruchter et al., 1995) recommendations. But as always in education reform, the struggle is to turn strong proposals into successful implementation. In New York City and New York State, the battle is far from won.

Notes

1. *Jose P. v. Ambach,* 669 F.2d 865 (2d Cir. 1982), on remand, 587 F. Supp. 1572 (E.D.N.Y. 1984).

2. The elementary and middle schools in New York City are organized into 32 community school districts with some central oversight, whereas the high schools are administered centrally.

3. For examples from New York City schools, see Lieberman, Falk, and Alexander (1994); Ancess (1995); and Falk and Darling-Howard (1993).

4. Elementary and Secondary Education Act, Pub. L. 89-313 (1966).

5. Individuals With Disabilities Education Act, Pub. L. 101-476 (1990).

6. Suppose we have a school with 750 students, 75 of whom have been classified as disabled and placed in the following configuration: 24 students in two classes of 12 with one teacher in each class and $2/3$ of a paraprofessional in each class, 18 students in two classes with one teacher each and one paraprofessional each, and 33 students in two resource rooms with one teacher and one paraprofessional in each. Using average salary for teachers ($40,000) and paraprofessionals ($15,000) the 6 teachers and 5.33 paraprofessionals would generate $320,000. Using a 28:1 ratio in general education and a $40,000 teacher salary, 75 students in general education would generate 75/28 or 2.67 times $40,000 or $107,000. This $320,000 does not include the cost of personnel such as special education guidance counselors, speech teachers, and so on who would be assigned based on IEP requirements.

7. Transportation costs will be reduced with a higher percentage of students attending school closer to home, and we expect that informal assessment will be more cost-effective than the current formal assessment system. In addition, we call for

significant changes in the evaluation, placement, and funding of programs for pre-school and high school children with disabilities.

8. This section of the chapter is based on Parrish (1995b).

9. Although many of the issues to be discussed here will be common to multiple levels of governance, it is also important to note that most of the discussion presented is on research at state and federal levels of governance. For additional discussion of related issues as they pertain more directly to school districts, McLaughlin and Warren (1994) and McLaughlin (1995) are recommended.

10. For a full discussion of some of the pros and cons and other issues related to census-based funding systems, see Parrish and Verstegen (1994).

11. For a discussion and a qualitative evaluation of special education finance reform in Vermont, see Montgomery, 1995b.

12. For a discussion and a qualitative evaluation of special education finance reform in Pennsylvania, see Montgomery and DeSera (1996).

References

Ancess, J. (1995). *An inquiry high school: Learner-centered accountability at the Urban Academy.* New York: National Center for Restructuring Education, Schools and Teaching.

Autin, D. M. T. K., Dentzer, E., & McNutt, B. (1994). *Segregated and second rate: "Special" education in New York.* New York: Advocates for Children of New York.

Board of Education of the City of New York, Division of Special Education. (1990). *Special education students in New York City: A racial/ethnic distribution.* New York: Author.

Board of Education of the City of New York, Office of Information, Reporting and Technology Services. (1997). *Annual School Reports, 1995-96.* New York: Author.

Committee on Education and the Law. (1992, March). Creating fiscal incentives for the inclusion of students with disabilities. *The Record of the Association of the Bar of the City of New York, 47*(2), 230-263.

Falk, B., & Darling-Hammond, L. (1993). *The primary language record at P.S. 261: How assessment transforms teaching and learning.* New York: National Center for Restructuring Education, Schools and Teaching.

Fruchter, N., Berne, R., Marcus, A., Alter, M., & Gottlieb, J. (1995). *Focus on learning: A report on reorganizing general and special education in New York city.* New York: New York University, Institute for Education and Social Policy.

Hartman, W. T., & Fay, T. A. (1996). *Cost-effectiveness of instructional support teams in Pennsylvania* (Policy Paper No. 9). Palo Alto, CA: American Institutes for Research, Center for Special Education Finance.

Hornbeck, D. W., & Lehmann, S. (1991). *Success for each student: A plan to permanently eliminate the special education backlog while improving educational outcomes for all children in New York City.* New York. Unpublished manuscript.

Lankford, H., & Wyckoff, J. (1996). The allocation of resources to special education and regular instruction. In H. F. Ladd (Ed.), *Holding schools accountable.* Washington, DC: Brookings Institution.

Lieberman, A., Falk, B., & Alexander, L. (1994). *A culture in the making: Leadership in learner-centered schools.* New York: National Center for Restructuring Education, Schools and Teaching.

Mathis, J. M. (1996). Cost-effectiveness in teaching and learning. In R. Berne (Ed.), *Study in cost-effectiveness in education: Final report on study group on cost-effectiveness* (pp. 166-167). Albany, NY: New York State Board of Regents.

McLaughlin, M. J. (1995). *Consolidated special education funding and services: A local perspective* (Policy Paper No. 5). Palo Alto, CA: American Institutes for Research, Center for Special Education Finance.

McLaughlin, M. J., & Warren, S. H. (1994). *Resource implications of inclusion: Impressions of special education administrators at selected sites* (Policy Paper No. 1). Palo Alto, CA: American Institutes for Research, Center for Special Education Finance.

Montgomery, D. L. (1995a). *Profile of special education finance reform in Oregon* (State Analysis Series). Palo Alto, CA: American Institutes for Research, Center for Special Education Finance.

Montgomery, D. L.(1995b). *Profile of special education finance reform in Vermont* (State Analysis Series). Palo Alto, CA: American Institutes for Research, Center for Special Education Finance.

Montgomery, D. L., & DeSera, M. (1996). *Profile of special education finance reform in Pennsylvania* (State Analysis Series). Palo Alto, CA: American Institutes for Research, Center for Special Education Finance.

NASDE would link funding for disabled, disadvantaged students (1994, March 9). *Special Education Report, 20*(5), 3-4.

New York State Education Department. (1996). *Cost of high performance: Board of Regents proposal on state aid to school districts.* Albany, NY: Author.

New York State Education Department. (1997a). *A report to the governor and the legislature on the educational status of the state's schools* (submitted February 1997). Albany, NY: Author.

New York State Education Department. (1997b). *New York State school report cards: A focus on academic performance.* Albany, NY: Author.

Office of the Comptroller of the City of New York, Bureau of Audit. (1994). *Audit of the Board of Education's administration of the special education program.* New York: Author.

Parrish, T. B. (1995a). *Fiscal policies in special education: Removing incentives for restrictive placements* (Policy Paper No. 4). Palo Alto, CA: American Institutes for Research, Center for Special Education Finance.

Parrish, T. B. (1995b). *Review of financing dimensions from Focus on Learning.* Palo Alto, CA: American Institutes for Research, Center for Special Education Finance.

Parrish, T. B., O'Reilly, F., Dueñas, I., & Wolman, J. (1997). *State Special Education Finance Systems, 1994-95.* Palo Alto, CA: American Institutes for Research, Center for Special Education Finance.

Parrish, T. B., & Verstegen, D. A. (1994). *Fiscal provision of the Individuals with Disabilities Education Act: Policy issues and alternatives* (Policy Paper No. 3). Palo Alto, CA: American Institutes for Research, Center for Special Education Finance.

U.S. Department of Education, Office of Special Education Programs. (1989). *Compliance monitoring report, 1989 review, New York State Education Department.* Washington, DC: Author.

U.S. Office of Education. (1994, Aug.). U.S. Office of Special Education Programs, Final Monitoring Report: 1993 Review of New York State Education Department's Implemenation of Part B of IDEA. Washington, DC: Author.

Vermont Department of Education. (1995). *Vermont's Act 230 and special education funding and cost study.* Montpelier, VT: Author.

Zirkel, P. A. (1995). *A legal analysis of* Focus on Learning: *Draft report on reorganizing special education in New York City.* Bethlehem, PA: Lehigh University Press.

PART III

TRENDS AND NEW DEVELOPMENTS

NINE

Trends and New Developments in Special Education Funding
WHAT THE STATES REPORT

THOMAS B. PARRISH

JEAN WOLMAN

No one knows exactly how much is being spent on special education in the United States. However, we do know the cost is considerable. The Center for Special Education Finance (CSEF) estimates the cost of special education services for the 1995-1996 school year to be somewhere between $30.9 and $34.8 billion. More precise estimates cannot be derived because current information is not uniformly available.

Congress mandated the provision of special education services in the United States in 1975 under the federal Individuals with Disabilities Education Act (IDEA), which was recently reauthorized under the IDEA Amendments of 1997.[1] However, the federal government has been a relatively minor player in providing support for special education, supplying an estimated 8% of total funds. For the most part, special education fiscal policy is made at the state level. The purpose of this chapter is to present the most current information available on

203

state special education funding policies, state funding reforms, and special education expenditures across the nation.

Types of State
Special Education Funding Formulas

The formulas used by states to distribute funds for special education services are complex and unique. Although a number of frameworks for classifying state special education funding approaches have been suggested over the past two decades, there is much overlap among categories and substantial variation among state funding formulas within categories. State funding formulas are divided into four broad categories to simplify and provide useful distinctions among various funding alternatives and options for funding reform (see Table 9.1).

Weighted

Under a weighted special education funding system, state special education aid is allocated on a per-student basis. The amount of aid is based on the funding weight associated with each student. For example, Oregon applies a single funding weight of 2.0 to all eligible special education students in the state. This means that the amount of state aid for every special education student in a district is twice that received for a general education student in that district. However, most weighting systems provide more funding for those students who are expected to cost more to serve by assigning those students a larger weight. These weight differentials are based on student placement (e.g., pull-out program, special class, private residential), disability category, or some combination of the two.

Flat Grant

Flat-grant funding is based on a fixed funding amount per student. Total state funding available for special education is divided by the special education count for the state to determine the amount of state aid to be received by districts per special education student. A variation to this approach is based on the total number of students in a district rather than the number of special education students. This census-based approach is discussed in greater detail later in this chapter.

Resource Based

Resource-based funding is based on an allocation of specific education resources, such as teachers or classroom units. Unit rates are often derived from prescribed staff-student ratios by disability condition or type of placement. Resource-based formulas include unit and personnel mechanisms in which the distribution of funds is based on payment for specified resources, such as teachers, aides, or equipment.

Percentage Reimbursement

Under a percentage reimbursement system, the amount of state special education aid a district receives is directly based on its expenditure for this program. Districts may be reimbursed for up to 100% of their program expenditures. Usually, there is some basis for determining what costs are and are not allowable, and there may be overall caps on the number of students who can be claimed for funding purposes.

As shown in Table 9.1, almost 40% of the states (18) reported formulas based primarily on pupil weights for the 1994-1995 school year. The remaining states were fairly evenly distributed across flat-grant (10 states), percentage reimbursement (11 states), and resource-based funding (10 states).

Basis of Funding

In addition to formula type, Table 9.1 shows the basis on which the special education funding allocation was made, using the following allocation categories:

TABLE 9.1 State Special Education Funding Systems and Reform, 1994-1995

State	Current Funding Formula	Basis of Allocation	State Special Education Dollars for Target Population Only	Implemented Reform Within the Past 5 Years	Considering Major Reform
Alabama	Flat grant	Special education enrollment	x	x	x
Alaska	Pupil weights[a]	Type of placement			x
Arizona[e]	Pupil weights	Disabling condition			x
Arkansas	Pupil weights	Type of placement	x		x
California	Resource based[b]	Classroom unit	x		x
Colorado	Flat grant[d]	Special education enrollment	x	x	
Connecticut	Percentage reimbursement[c]	Actual expenditures			x
Delaware	Resource based	Classroom unit	x		x
Florida	Pupil weights	Disabling condition			x
Georgia	Pupil weights	Disabling condition	For 90% of funds		x
Hawaii	Pupil weights	Placement and condition			
Idaho	Percentage reimbursement	Actual expenditures	x	x	
Illinois	Resource based	Allowable costs		x	x
Indiana	Pupil weights	Disabling condition			x
Iowa	Pupil weights	Type of placement			x
Kansas	Resource based	Number of special education staff	x		
Kentucky	Pupil weights	Disabling condition		x	
Louisiana	Percentage reimbursement	Actual expenditures	x	x	x
Maine	Percentage reimbursement	Allowable costs	x		x
Maryland	Flat grant	Special education enrollment			x
Massachusetts	Flat grant	Total district enrollment		x	
Michigan	Percentage reimbursement	Allowable costs	x		x
Minnesota	Percentage reimbursement	Actual expenditures	x		x

TABLE 9.1 *Continued*

State	Current Funding Formula	Basis of Allocation	State Special Education Dollars for Target Population Only	Implemented Reform Within the Past 5 Years	Considering Major Reform
Mississippi	Resource based	Number of special education staff	x		
Missouri	Resource based	Number of special education staff	x	x	x
Montana	Flat grant	Total district enrollment		x	
Nebraska	Percentage reimbursement	Allowable costs	x		x
Nevada	Resource based	Classroom unit	x		
New Hampshire	Pupil weights	Type of placement			x
New Jersey	Pupil weights	Placement and condition			
New Mexico	Pupil weights	Services received			x
New York	Pupil weights	Type of placement	x		x
North Carolina	Flat grant	Special education enrollment	x		x
North Dakota	Flat grant	Total district enrollment		x	
Ohio	Resource based	Classroom unit			x
Oklahoma	Pupil weights	Disabling condition			
Oregon	Pupil weights	Special education enrollment		x	
Pennsylvania	Flat grant	Total district enrollment		x	
Rhode Island	Percentage reimbursement	Actual expenditures			x
South Carolina	Pupil weights	Disabling condition	For 85% of funds		
South Dakota	Percentage reimbursement	Allowable costs	x		x
Tennessee	Resource based	Classroom unit			x
Texas	Pupil weights	Type of placement	x	x	
Utah[f]	Pupil weights	Type of placement	x	x	
Vermont[g]	Flat grant	Total district enrollment		x	
Virginia	Resource based	Classroom unit			

(continued)

TABLE 9.1 *Continued*

State	Current Funding Formula	Basis of Allocation	*State Special Education Dollars for Target Population Only*	*Implemented Reform Within the Past 5 Years*	*Considering Major Reform*
Washington	Pupil weights	Special education enrollment	x	x	
West Virginia	Flat grant	Special education enrollment	x		
Wisconsin	Percentage reimbursement	Allowable costs	x		
Wyoming	Percentage reimbursement	Actual expenditures			x

a. Pupil weights: Funding allocated on a per-student basis, with the amount(s) based on a multiple of regular education aid.
b. Resource based: Funding based on allocation of specific education resources (e.g., teachers or classroom units); classroom units are derived from prescribed staff-student ratios by disabling condition or type of placement.
c. Percentage reimbursement: Funding based on a percentage of allowable or actual expenditures.
d. Flat grant: A fixed funding amount per student or per unit.
e. Formula also contains a substantial flat-grant allocation for selected disabling conditions.
f. Formula amounts are now frozen and are based on allocations in prior years.
g. Vermont's special education funding formula also contains a substantial percentage reimbursement component.

Special education enrollment. The number of children identified as eligible for special education services and for which individual education programs (IEPs) are in place is the basis of allocation.

Total district enrollment. Funding is based on the total number of students in the district. A percentage of this total enrollment is assumed to represent the special education population. This type of allocation is referred to as census-based funding.

Type of placement. Student placement (e.g., in a regular education classroom, resource room, special day class, or residential program) is the basis for allocation. The allocation generally increases as a function of some standardized estimate of the cost of the service or placement.

Disability category. The nature of each student's disability (e.g., learning disability, emotional disturbance, profound mental retardation) is the basis for allocation. The allocation generally increases as a function of standardized estimates of the cost of the service required for children within each disability category.

Classroom unit. Districts generate funds based on a number of authorized units. A unit of funding may incorporate part or all of the estimated cost of a teacher or a teacher and an aide.

Actual expenditures. Allocation is based on actual special education expenditures.

Allowable costs. Reimbursement can only be claimed for allowable costs, as defined, reviewed, and approved by the state.

Number of special education staff. Allocation is based on the state numbers of various types of authorized staff (e.g., teachers, aides, therapists).

Services received. Allocation for each child is determined from unit rates associated with the mix and quantity of individual services received (e.g., instruction, therapy, transportation).

Within the context of the basic funding formula, the basis of funding sheds further light on state special education policies and priorities. More precise criteria such as type of placement, classroom unit, number of special education staff, and services received, tend to result in less local flexibility in the procurement and use of resources. They often limit the local provider to prespecified categories of placement, classrooms, staff, and services. More general criteria such as actual expenditures, special education enrollment, or total district enrollment provide more local discretion and flexibility in the identification and placement of special education students. In fact, by using total district enrollment as a basis for funding states are, at least to some degree, choosing to totally de-link funding from student identification and placement.

Census-Based Funding

One emerging trend at the federal and state levels is to use total district enrollment rather than special education counts as the basis for allocating special education funds to school districts. For example, under a state census-based funding system, districts with identical student enrollments receive the same special education aid regardless of the number of students placed in the program, the disabilities of these students, where they are placed, or how they are served.

Proponents of census-based funding believe that it provides maximum discretion to local districts in identification and placement of students with disabilities because it eliminates identification as a basis for funding and severs the link between placement and funding. Other key states are following this trend. In October 1997, California passed legislation establishing a census-based special education funding system,[2] and New York's Governor and Board of Regents have "recommended" the same. Critics, however, point out that such systems simply replace one set of incentives with another (i.e., to identify fewer students for special education services and to place them in lower cost programs). They also argue that census-based funding does not accommodate variability that might exist among school districts based on true student need. Thus far, Massachusetts, Montana, North Dakota, Pennsylvania, and Vermont have implemented census-based funding systems in an attempt to remove fiscal incentives for identifying special education students.

At the federal level, use of census-based funding was hotly debated prior to the 1997 reauthorization of the IDEA. When this lengthy process was finally completed in June 1997, a census-based approach for allocating special education funds was adopted but on a very gradual schedule of implementation.[3]

Criteria for Evaluating
State Special Education Funding Formulas

First delineated by Hartman (1992) and expanded by Parrish (1995), criteria for evaluating special education funding formulas appear in Table 9.2. No single funding formula can easily meet all of these criteria because a focus on one may come at the expense of one or more of the others. For example, increased flexibility may be obtained through diminished accountability, and the establishment of a firm cost basis may jeopardize the reasonableness of the reporting burden. Although each of these criteria will hold value for some constituency, each will have a different priority, depending on state policies.

CSEF asked states to evaluate their special education funding formulas according to these 14 criteria. One major weakness reported across all formula types was the absence of any form of linkage between funding and student outcomes (n = 28)—for example, the incorporation of student results into the accountability system. A second weakness generally reported was a lack of adequate funding (n = 26).

Among the 10 states currently using a flat-grant approach, more than half reported as major strengths that their formula did not encourage overidentification of students for special education, that it was not linked to where students receive services, and that it was understandable. Reported weaknesses from the flat-grant states included that they are not adequately funded, they are not linked to student outcomes, and they are not based on actual costs.

States with pupil weighting systems say that their systems are closely tied to the resource needs of districts in terms of their specific population of students with disabilities. As such, pupil weighting systems are generally held to be equitable. However, depending on the weighting system used, incentives can be created to misclassify students into specific types of placements or into categories of disability that receive higher reimbursement (e.g., more restrictive settings that receive higher weights).

Based on ratings from states using percentage reimbursement funding, these formulas appear to be the least likely to create incentives to misclassify students, because the label assigned a student does not affect funding. Also, these formulas generally do not provide an incentive for a particular type of student placement. However, they can be administratively burdensome and result in difficulties with cost control unless cost ceilings are used or the reimbursable percentage is relatively low.

Among the 10 states using a resource-based formula, over half reported predictability as a strength. In addition, half indicated that

TABLE 9.2 Criteria for Evaluating State Special Education Funding
Formulas

Understandable

The funding system and its underlying policy objectives are understandable by
all concerned parties (legislators, legislative staff, state department personnel,
local administrators, and advocates).

The concepts underlying the formula and the procedures to implement it are
straightforward and "avoid unnecessary complexity."

Equitable

Student equity: Dollars are distributed to ensure comparable program quality
regardless of district assignment.

Wealth equity: Availability of overall funding is not correlated with local wealth.

District-to-district fairness: All districts receive comparable resources for
comparable students.

Adequate

Funding is sufficient for all districts to provide appropriate programs for special
education students.

Predictable

LEAs know allocations in time to plan for local services.

The system produces predictable demands for state funding.

SEA and LEAs can count on stable funding across years.

Flexible

Local agencies are given latitude to deal with unique local conditions in an
appropriate and cost-effective manner.

Changes that affect programs and costs can be incorporated into the funding
system with minimum disruption.

Local agencies are given maximum latitude in use of resources in exchange for
outcome accountability.

Identification neutral

The number of students identified as eligible for special education is not the only,
or primary, basis for determining the amount of special education funding to
be received.

Students do not have to be labeled disabled (or any other label) to receive
services.

Reasonable reporting burden

Costs to maintain the funding system are minimized at both local and state levels.

Data requirements, record keeping, and reporting are kept at reasonable levels.

Fiscal accountability

Conventional accounting procedures are followed to ensure that special
education funds are spent in an authorized manner.

Procedures are included to contain excessive or inappropriate special education
costs.

Cost based

Funding received by districts for the provision of special education programs is
linked to the costs they face in providing these programs.

TABLE 9.2 *Continued*

Cost control
  Patterns of growth in special education costs statewide are stabilized over time.
  Patterns of growth in special education identification rates statewide are
  stabilized over time.

Placement neutral
  District funding for special education is not based on type of educational
  placement.
  District funding for special education is not based on disability label.

Outcome accountability
  State monitoring of local agencies is based on various measures of student
  outcomes.
  A statewide system for demonstrating satisfactory progress for all students in all
  schools is developed.
  Schools showing positive results for students are given maximum program and
  fiscal latitude to continue producing favorable results.

Connection to general education funding
  The special education funding formula should have a clear conceptual link to the
  general education finance system.
  Integration of funding will be likely to lead to integration of services.

Political acceptability
  Implementation avoids any major short-term loss of funds.
  Implementation involves no major disruption of existing services.

SOURCE: Adapted from Hartman (1992) and Parrish (1994).

their formulas have a reasonable reporting burden and provide fiscal accountability. However, more than half of these states reported that their formulas are not equitable; and half indicated that their formulas lacked flexibility in use of resources.

Special Education Finance Reform

To reduce the limitations and maximize the effectiveness of their funding formulas, many states have enacted or are considering special education finance reform. As shown in Table 9.1, 28 states were considering reform as of spring 1995, and 16 states had enacted major reforms within the past 5 years.

Coupled with special education finance reform at the federal level, this degree of change can be viewed as a massive national reform

TABLE 9.3 Major Policy Objectives in States Currently Considering
          Reform

Policy Objective	Total Number (n = 20)	Percentage of States
Equity	15	75
Flexibility in use of resources	12	60
Understandability	10	50
Adequate Funding	9	45
Removal of link to where students receive services	8	40
Linkage to student outcomes	7	35
Fiscal accountability	7	35
Removal of incentive for overidentification	6	30
Reasonable reporting burden	5	25
Predictability	4	20
Basis on actual costs	2	10
Cost control mechanisms	2	10

effort. When asked what issues were driving reform, respondents from 20 states identified more than a dozen factors, as shown in Table 9.3. Cited by at least half of these states were the desire to increase funding equity, provide flexibility in the use of resources, and create formulas that are understandable. It is interesting, however, that about half of the 50 states already have considerable flexibility in the use of special education funds. As shown in Table 9.1, many states do not specifically require that special education dollars be spent on special education students.

State Special Education Expenditures

Comprehensive current data on special education expenditures are lacking. The most recent large-scale study of special education expenditures occurred during the 1985-1986 school year (Moore, Strang, Schwartz, & Braddock, 1988). In addition, the federal government stopped requiring the states to report data on special education expenditures after the 1987-1988 school year. This lack of recent nationally representative data makes it difficult to provide current estimates of the national cost of special education. To address this void, CSEF attempted to obtain more recent expenditure data, surveying states from 1994 to 1996.

In response to CSEF's survey, fewer than half the states were able to report their statewide expenditures on special education. Of the 24 states that were able to report this information, only 13 indicated that they could do so with a "high degree of confidence." Many states do not have education reporting systems that break out expenditures on a programmatic basis. Despite these limitations, the data presented in Table 9.4 are the most current special education expenditure data available by state. The remainder of this chapter compares this information with data from earlier cost studies and federal data collections to provide insight into special education spending trends over time.

The data in Table 9.4 show considerable variability across states in the average special education expenditure per special education student (ranging from $2,758 in Indiana to $8,501 in Connecticut—a ratio of more than 3 to 1). These data also show much variability across states in the local, state, and federal shares of spending. For example, the federal share of expenditures ranged from a low of 4% in Connecticut and Nevada to a high of 17% in Indiana. State support ranged from 23% in Virginia to 94% in Louisiana. The reported local share mirrored this range across the 24 states, from 0% in Louisiana to 69% in Maryland. Half the 24 states reported a state share of 50% or more. Over half of the reporting states were highly confident about their data, 9 states were confident or somewhat confident, whereas 2 states were not confident in the data they reported.

Table 9.5 presents a second view of special education expenditures for all states for the 1987-1988 school year—the last year in which such data were reported by all states. These expenditures are adjusted to 1995-1996 prices based on the Federal Budget Composite Deflator. It is important to note that these data are a decade old and were not considered very accurate by many states at the time they were reported. However, they provide the best and most current data available from all the states.

For each state, two distinct special education expenditures are derived: a) the per-student expenditures in the first column are derived using each state's total special education child count; b) the per-student expenditures in the second column are derived using each

TABLE 9.4 Special Education Expenditures as Reported by States: 1993-1994

State (n = 24)	Total Expenditure	Associated Student Special Education Count	Average Special Education Expenditure per Student	Percentage of Support by Source Federal	State	Local	Confidence in Data
California	$3,070,700,000[a]	550,293[d]	$5,580	5	71	24	SC
Colorado	$260,337,092[a]	76,374[e]	$3,409	9	31	60	HC
Connecticut	$627,331,211	73,792	$8,501	4	37	59	HC
Florida	$1,470,186,078[b]	290,630[d]	$5,059	6	56	38	C
Indiana	$350,430,294[b]	127,079	$2,758	17	63	20	NC
Iowa	$277,700,000[b]	65,039[e]	$4,270	11	70	19	HC
Kansas	$326,106,608[b]	47,489	$6,867	7	54	39	HC
Louisiana	$427,924,416	108,317[e]	$3,951	6	94	0	C
Maine	$145,000,000[b]	30,565	$4,744	8	59	33	HC
Maryland	$757,328,777	95,752	$7,909	5	26	69	HC
Massachusetts	$1,065,523,416	149,431	$7,131	6	30	64	HC
Michigan	$1,334,000,000[b]	188,703[f]	$7,069	6	34	60	HC
Minnesota	$689,656,932[a]	96,542[d]	$7,144	6	70	24	NC
Missouri	$436,778,659	121,419[g]	$3,597	10	30	60	C
Montana	$54,865,132	17,881	$3,068	14	60	26	HC
Nevada	$202,369,114	24,624	$8,218	4	40	56	C
New Mexico	$250,000,000[b]	45,364	$5,511	9	90	1	SC
North Carolina	$344,809,332[c]	142,394	$2,422	15	76	9	HC
North Dakota	$54,560,122	12,180	$4,479	10	31	59	SC
Rhode Island	$147,300,000	25,143	$5,858	5	36	59	HC
South Dakota	$61,618,034	15,208	$4,052	13	49	38	HC
Vermont	$79,155,945	10,131[h]	$7,813	5	39	56	HC
Virginia	$608,692,266	129,498[d]	$4,700	9	23	68	C
Wisconsin	$630,000,000[a]	95,552	$6,593	6	62	32	C
All reporting states	$13,929,607,674	2,581,905	$5,395	7	53	40	—
Highly confident or confident states	$9,514,260,326	1,750,477	$5,435	7	44	49	—

NOTE: States reported for 1993-1994 school year except as designated by a, b, and c; count of students reported by the state associated with the reported total expenditure. Includes age range 3 to 21 except as designated by e through h. HC = highly confident; C = confident; SC = somewhat confident; NC = not confident.
a. 1992-1993
b. 1994-1995
c. 1990-1991
d. Includes age range 0-22
e. Includes age range 0-21
f. Includes age range 0-26
g. Includes age range 3-22
h. Includes age range 5-22

state's total public school enrollment. The first is an indicator of how much is being spent on special education per special education student. The second is a measure of special education expenditures by state irrespective of the number of students identified. For example, whereas the District of Columbia was very high on the first measure ($18,225), it is relatively low on the second ($583) because the percentage of students identified for special education was comparatively low.

When each state's special education expenditure was divided by the total number of special education students in the state, per-student expenditures ranged from $2,272 in Tennessee to $18,225 in the District of Columbia. When the total public school enrollment in each state was used as the denominator, per-student expenditures ranged from $234 in Arkansas to $1,653 in New York.

The data in Table 9.5 also indicated considerable variation in percentages of enrollment in special education, ranging from 3.2% in the District of Columbia to 15.7% in Massachusetts. The table also shows that special education as a percentage of total expenditures ranged from 6.6% (in Arkansas and Montana) to 21.2% (in Illinois) and averaged 12.2% of total Kindergarten through 12th grade expenditures nationwide.

Comparing average expenditures presented in Tables 9.4 and 9.5 raises some questions regarding the relative accuracy of these state expenditure estimates. Table 9.4 shows relatively current special education expenditure data from the 24 states that reported relatively recent data, whereas Table 9.5 shows data reported for 1987-1988 for all states adjusted to 1995-1996 prices. Whereas the average special education expenditures per special education student reported for California across the two tables are quite consistent ($5,580 in Table 9.4 vs. $5,544 in Table 9.5), the estimates for Colorado are not ($3,409 in Table 9.4 vs. $6,171 in Table 9.5). The large discrepancy between these two estimates for Colorado may have resulted from the use of different data across the two years (e.g., different estimates of the count of special education students in the state), or it may suggest a considerable decline in the average special education expenditure per special education student in inflation-adjusted dollars over this time period. Given the imperfect state of available data, these estimates should be used with caution.

TABLE 9.5 Special Education Expenditures per Special Education Student, 1987-1988 (in 1995-1996 prices)

State (n = 50)	Special Education Expenditure			
	Special Education Student	Total Enrollment	As a Percentage of Total K-12 Expenditures	Percentage of Special Education Enrollment
Alabama	$3,334	$433	13.1	13.0
Alaska	$12,620	$1,148	12.5	9.1
Arizona	$4,640	$428	9.5	9.2
Arkansas	$2,345	$234	6.6	10.0
California	$5,544	$503	10.1	9.0
Colorado	$6,171	$525	10.5	8.5
Connecticut	$7,712	$1,144	15.1	14.8
Delaware	$6,047	$691	11.7	11.4
District of Columbia	$18,225	$583	8.0	3.2
Florida	$5,578	$623	12.8	11.2
Georgia	$6,058	$490	12.0	8.1
Hawaii	$9,481	$650	13.8	6.6
Idaho	$3,986	$354	11.0	8.9
Illinois	$8,941	$1,039	21.2	11.6
Indiana	$3,270	$335	7.6	10.3
Iowa	$4,487	$523	10.5	11.6
Kansas	$5,519	$535	11.2	9.7
Kentucky	$3,920	$447	12.8	11.4
Louisiana	$5,173	$420	11.3	8.1
Maine	$3,742	$478	9.4	12.8
Maryland	$5,065	$652	11.1	12.9
Massachusetts	$6,664	$1,045	16.4	15.7
Michigan	$5,464	$512	9.2	9.4
Minnesota	$6,212	$710	13.4	11.4
Mississippi	$2,642	$300	9.7	11.4
Missouri	$3,811	$462	10.5	12.1
Montana	$3,391	$329	6.6	11.7
Nebraska	$3,125	$351	7.4	11.3
Nevada	$8,098	$700	16.5	8.6
New Hampshire	$7,603	$718	13.7	9.4
New Jersey	$3,842	$588	7.6	15.3
New Mexico	$4,969	$535	13.1	10.8
New York	$17,563	$1,653	20.8	9.4
North Carolina	$3,353	$329	8.1	9.8
North Dakota	$4,629	$461	11.1	9.9
Ohio	$8,000	$851	18.4	10.6
Oklahoma	$5,901	$633	17.0	10.7
Oregon	$6,127	$566	10.3	9.2
Pennsylvania	$4,937	$552	9.3	11.2

TABLE 9.5 *(continued)*

State (n = 50)	Special Education Expenditure			
	Special Education Student	Total Enrollment	As a Percentage of Total K-12 Expenditures	Percentage of Special Education Enrollment
Rhode Island	$7,103	$999	15.8	14.1
South Carolina	$2,923	$352	8.7	12.1
South Dakota	$3,410	$374	9.5	11.0
Tennessee	$2,272	$267	7.3	11.8
Texas	$3,532	$327	7.7	9.3
Utah	$2,648	$267	9.0	10.1
Vermont	$6,866	$689	10.9	10.0
Virginia	$4,598	$489	9.8	10.6
Washington	$5,657	$507	10.2	9.0
West Virginia	$3,508	$456	9.9	13.0
Wisconsin	$8,013	$779	14.1	9.7
Wyoming	$6,873	$678	11.1	9.9
U.S. average:	$5,989	$625	12.2	10.7

SOURCE: Table AH1 of the Fourteenth Annual Report to Congress on the Implementation of the Individuals with Disabilities Education Act; Table AA10 of the Twelfth Annual Report to Congress on the Implementation of the Individuals with Disabilities Education Act; the adjustment of 1987-1988 data to 1995-1996 prices is based on the Federal Budget Composite Deflator (NCES, 1996).

Federal, State, and Local Share of Expenditures

Special education is funded through a federal, state, and local partnership. What are the relative shares borne by these three levels of government across the nation, and are these percentage shares shifting over time? Table 9.6 compares the CSEF survey data (Table 9.4) with earlier expenditure information reported by these states. Whereas the combined data indicate that the percentage shares have remained relatively constant over this 11-year period, they also show the local share of special education expenditures to be slowly rising. Data from the "highly confident" states showed the state share as declining in relation to local expenditures. Based on these data, local districts now appear to incur the largest share of special education costs. This may explain the increased concern regarding rising special education costs being expressed by school districts.

TABLE 9.6 Federal, State, and Local Shares of Special Education Spending for Selected Years and Samples of States (by percentage)

	Federal Share	State Share	Local Share
All states			
1982-1983 school year	8.3	53.8	37.9
1987-1988 school year	7.8	56.0	36.2
1993-1994 school year	na	na	na
States responding to CSEF survey			
All responding states (n = 24)			
1982-1983 school year	8.0	54.8	37.2
1987-1988 school year	7.1	57.3	35.6
1993-1994 school year	6.9	52.8	40.3
Somewhat confident to			
highly confident states (n = 22)			
1982-1983 school year	7.7	55.0	37.3
1987-1988 school year	7.0	57.0	36.0
1993-1994 school year	6.7	51.5	41.8
Confident to highly			
confident states (n = 20)			
1982-1983 school year	8.7	50.4	41.0
1987-1988 school year	7.3	50.5	42.3
1993-1994 school year	7.1	44.0	49.0

SOURCE: The 1982-1983 data are from the Individuals with Disabilities Education Act. The 1993-1994 data are from the CSEF Survey on State Special Education Funding Systems, 1994-1995, and the Fourteenth Annual Report to Congress on the Implementation of the Individuals with Disabilities Education Act.

With continued limited public resources and competing demands for other types of public services, states are struggling to provide appropriate educational services to students with disabilities as specified in state and federal law. These pressures have contributed to the high level of fiscal reforms underway in the states. Based on available data, however, it is unclear to what extent the states have been successful in their efforts to control special education costs, as opposed to shifting these costs to local education agencies.

Special Education Enrollment

One basis for estimating changes in the special education expenditure over time is to examine changes in special education enrollment and its relationship to total school enrollment. Tables 9.7 and 9.8 present the changes in total and special education school-age enrollments from 1976-1977 to 1994-1995.

Much of the growth shown in the tables has resulted from more recent and rapidly expanding preschool enrollments. Growth has occurred also through expanding enrollments in the birth-through-age-2 population through the federal Part H program for infants and toddlers—first separately reported for 1987-1988 (U.S. Department of Education, 1997). It is important to note that the overall growth in the special education population is somewhat mitigated by excluding the faster growing preschool and infant programs. On the other hand, future growth in the school-age special education population might be fueled by increasing numbers of young children eligible for services through the Preschool Grants and Infants and Toddlers with Disabilities programs. Continued expansion in the special education population may also be driven by rising numbers of at-risk, school-age children (based on sociodemographic indicators, such as poverty and low-birth-weight infants), and general education reforms, including increased academic standards and rigorous assessments (Parrish, 1996).

As shown in Table 9.7, there has been continual growth in special education enrollments and in the percentage of total school enrollment represented by special education students since the implementation of the IDEA in 1975. It is this steady, uninterrupted growth that may be of greatest concern to policy makers. To express the current situation regarding special education spending in simple terms, an allocation of about one eighth of total school funding (12.2% from Table 9.5) is being used to provide supplemental services for about one tenth of the school-age population (9.77%).

Trends in Special and General Education Expenditures per Pupil

Given rising special education enrollments, it is reasonable to predict that special education expenditures have been rising over time. However, have special education expenditures also been rising on a per-pupil basis? Table 9.9 summarizes the best data available from

TABLE 9.7 Special Education Enrollments in the United States: 1976-1977 Through 1994-1995

| | Population Counts | | | Special Education Counts | | | |
| | Total Resident Population 0-21 | Total Public and Private Enrollment K-12 | Total Public Enrollment Pre-K-12 | Total, 0-21 | By Age Group | | |
Years					0-2[a]	3-5[a]	6-21[a]
76-77	81,962,968	49,484,000	44,338,163	3,691,833			
77-78	81,236,690	48,717,000	43,730,964	3,751,356			
78-79	80,519,163	47,636,000	42,537,021	3,889,061			
79-80	81,025,941	46,645,000	41,573,667	4,005,270			
80-81	80,874,532	46,249,000	41,083,202	4,141,794			
81-82	80,303,955	45,544,000	40,148,373	4,197,972			
82-83	79,583,482	45,166,000	39,540,000	4,254,793			
83-84	78,987,052	44,967,000	39,487,499	4,298,405			
84-85	79,343,915	44,908,000	38,925,000	4,315,094			
85-86	78,582,024	44,979,000	39,349,000	4,316,596			
86-87	78,332,954	45,205,000	39,838,617	4,373,638			
87-88	78,245,423	45,488,000	40,024,244	4,441,418	29,717	335,771	4,075,930
88-89	78,488,526	45,430,000	40,196,263	4,530,909	34,270	360,281	4,136,358
89-90	78,828,518	45,898,000	40,608,342	4,806,403	214,432	381,166	4,210,805
90-91	79,148,525	46,488,000	41,026,499	4,858,095	148,006	389,751	4,320,338
91-92	80,383,000	47,246,000	41,838,871	4,980,654	105,978	415,523	4,459,153
92-93	80,776,385	48,191,000	42,195,454	5,101,589	65,731	449,646	4,586,212
93-94	81,293,686	48,947,000	43,353,428	5,268,297	141,796	488,163	4,736,338
94-95	81,926,587	49,826,000	44,034,416	5,555,685	165,253	524,458	4,865,974

SOURCE: Most of the data in this table are from the U.S. Department of Education (e.g., 1990, 1992, 1997), Office of Special Education Programs Data Analysis System, except for the public and private school enrollment counts for 1987-1988 to 1994-1995, which are from the National Center for Education Statistics (NCES; 1996).

a. Data are unavailable for the years 1976-1977 through 1986-1987.
b. Figures for ages 0-2 are for the Federal Part H program. Prior to 1987-1988, data were not available by age group for the Chapter 1 of ESEA (SOP) program.

TABLE 9.8 Special Education Enrollments in the United States:
1976-1977 Through 1994-1995

Years	Total Compared to Resident Population (by percentage)	Total Compared to Public and Private Enrollment (by percentage)	Total Compared to Public Enrollment[a] (by percentage)	Ages 6 to 21 Compared to Total Public and Private Enrollment[a]	Ages 6 to 21 Compared to Public Enrollment
76-77	4.50	7.40	8.33		
77-78	4.62	7.70	8.58		
78-79	4.83	8.16	9.14		
79-80	4.94	8.59	9.63		
80-81	5.12	8.96	10.08		
81-82	5.23	9.22	10.46		
82-83	5.35	9.42	10.76		
83-84	5.44	9.56	10.89		
84-85	5.44	9.61	11.09		
85-86	5.49	9.60	10.97		
86-87	5.58	9.68	10.98		
87-88	5.68	9.76	11.10	8.96	10.18
88-89	5.77	9.97	11.27	9.10	10.29
89-90	6.10	10.47	11.84	9.17	10.37
90-91	6.14	10.46	11.84	9.30	10.53
91-92	6.20	10.54	11.90	9.44	10.66
92-93	6.32	10.59	12.09	9.52	10.87
93-94	6.60	10.96	12.38	9.68	10.92
94-95	6.78	11.15	12.62	9.77	11.05

a. Data are unavailable for the years from 1976-1977 through 1986-1987.

various sources that can be used as a basis for comparing special to general education expenditures per pupil across the nation. All of the expenditures shown in this table are presented in terms of constant 1989-1990 dollars.

The first block of data in the table estimates special education expenditures from three national cost studies, using data collected during the 1968-1969, 1977-1978, and 1985-1986 school years. These data suggest that the average special education expenditure per special education student, adjusted for inflation, expanded during this period at an average rate of 4.1% a year. In addition, by dividing this overall period into two separate time segments based on the timing of the three studies, growth in the average expenditure per pupil appears to be considerably higher (6.9% per year) for the earlier time

TABLE 9.9 Changes in Special and General Education Expenditures
per Pupil Over Time (expressed in 1989-1990 dollars)[a]

Year	Expenditures	Average Annual Percentage Change	
		By Time Segment	Overall Time Period
Average expenditures			
per special education student			
Based on national cost studies,			
excluding general education cost[b]			
1968-1969	$2,103		
1977-1978	$3,820	6.9%	
1985-1986	$4,153	1.1%	4.1%
Based on national data,			
excluding general education costs[c]			
1983-1984	$3,862		
1986-1987	$4,546		5.6%
Average expenditures			
per general education student			
Based on national cost studies,			
excluding special education costs[b]			
1968-1969	$2,288		
1977-1978	$3,270	4.1%	
1985-1986	$3,247	(0.1%)	2.1%
Based on national data,			
including special education costs[d]			
1983-1984	$3,963		
1986-1987	$4,538		4.6%

a. The adjustment of data to 1989-1990 prices is based on the Federal Composite Deflator.
b. Kakalik, Furry, Thomas, & Carney (1981); Moore et al. (1988); Rossmiller, Hale, & Frohreich (1970).
c. State-reported data published in annual reports to Congress (U.S. Department of Education, 1991, and various prior years).
d. U.S. Department of Education (1992, 1995).

period (1968-1969 to 1977-19178) than for the later period (1977-1978 to 1985-1986) when the annual rate of growth was 1.1%.

Another source for examining changes in special education expenditures over time is national data obtained from the State Expenditure Survey, which was conducted for the years 1983-1984 through 1986-1987 and used to derive estimates of the special education expenditure per special education student for that period of time. These data suggest an average rate of growth in the expenditure per special education student of 5.6% per year, as shown in Table 9.8. Based on these various estimates, it appears that the average change in special education expenditures per pupil over this period of time has been between 4.1% and 5.6% per year.

The lower part of Table 9.8 shows two comparable measures of the change in general education expenditures per pupil over time. The first set of estimates is derived from the same three studies described earlier. Because an important purpose of these studies was to compare special to general education, expenditures on special education were carefully extracted from the general education estimates. This is important because it allows expenditures on special education versus general education to be compared in isolation from one another. As with the special education expenditures, the average expenditure per general education student changes at a faster rate during the time period between the first and second studies than between the second and third (4.1% vs. 0.1%).

A second set of data that can be used to compare the relative rate of growth in the average general versus special education expenditure per pupil comes from the national State Expenditures Survey. These data hold an advantage over those from the national studies in that they are based on actual reported expenditures nationwide, rather than on the results of three separate studies with different samples of districts and data collection methods. On the other hand, they are less appropriate for comparing special to general education expenditures because the general education totals do not exclude special education. That is, the general education expenditure is derived by dividing the total education expenditure, including special education, by total students. Thus, if the special education expenditure per student is rising at a faster rate than that for general education, as the data in Table 9.8 suggest, this measure of the rise in the general education expenditure will be somewhat overstated. The rate of growth in expenditures per special education student shown for this time period is 5.6%, compared to a 4.6% change in overall expenditures per student.

In summary, two bases for comparing growth in special education expenditures per special education student in relation to general education expenditures are presented in Table 9.8. Both bases of comparison have relative strengths and weaknesses, and neither provides a definitive answer to whether the special education expenditure per special education student is rising faster than for general education. However, both sets of indicators point to faster growth in the special education sector. On the basis of national cost studies, it appears that the average annual rate of growth in the special education expenditure per special education student is about twice that for general education (4.1% to 2.1% per year). On the basis of national data for the period 1983-1984 to 1986-1987, it appears that the annual growth differential is about 20% (5.6% to 4.6% per year). Based on these findings, it seems reasonable to estimate that the special education expenditure per student is growing at a faster rate than comparable general education expenditures and that this rate differential per year is somewhere between 20% and 100%.

Conclusion

What do the data presented in this chapter suggest? Are special education enrollments and costs rising at a sufficiently fast level across the states to justify the significant concerns being expressed by educators and policy makers? Are special education costs absorbing an excessive portion of our public investment in education? As an article in CSEF's Fall 1996 newsletter suggests, "the absence of recent, accurate, and comparable cost data may exacerbate the perception that special education expenditures are encroaching upon general education resources," and make it difficult "to clarify the magnitude, causes, and implications of [special education's] growth" (Wolman & Parrish, 1996).

Nevertheless, as this chapter suggests, the special education population has been growing at a significantly faster rate than the general education population. Add to this the prediction that the general education population will grow by over 10% over the next 10 years and the observation that special education expenditures per student have been growing at a faster rate than general education expenditures, and it is not hard to imagine considerable strain on special education budgets over the next decade (Parrish, 1996). Given the apparent shifts from state to local funding, this added stress may be especially hard for local districts to bear.

At the same time that the need for future programs and services is predicted to escalate appreciably, the demand for services already may be outstripping the availability of resources in some states. These trends suggest that a crossroad in special education policy may be upon us or quickly approaching. The fairly substantial policy changes included in the recently reauthorized IDEA appear to support this conclusion. Current state interest in restructuring education is likely to continue to build and will focus on efforts to increase the effectiveness of, as well as to contain expenditures on, programs for children with disabilities. If services are restructured, choices must be made about what changes should occur and what programs and services should be affected.

One critical question that confronts the development of future fiscal policy in special education is whether funding should retain its purely categorical nature. Reform advocates are questioning the efficiency of the multiple administrative and service structures needed by categorical programs and are calling for increased flexibility through the blending of funds to best meet the special needs of all students.[4]

Some changes have already occurred: Under Title I of the revised Elementary and Secondary Education Act (ESEA),[5] high poverty schools are allowed to blend funds from a variety of federal sources to make schoolwide changes for the benefit of all students. Similarly, under the IDEA Amendments of 1997 (Pub. L. 105-17), local education agencies may use IDEA funds to carry out a schoolwide Title I program (under section 1114 of ESEA of 1965).

In addition, traditional accounting measures that have primarily focused on procedural requirements and on limitations on the allowable use of funds may be forced to give way to more meaningful forms of program and school-based accountability measures based on student performance. The development of such results-based accountability systems may well be among the most critical components in the design of future special education finance policy.

Notes

1. Individuals with Disabilities Education Act, Pub. L. No. 94-142 (1990).

2. Poochigian and Davis Special Education Reform Act of 1997 (California Assembly Bill 602, Chapter 854).

3. Federal funding under the IDEA has been based on a flat-grant system in which federal aid to states is based on each state's number of children with disabilities who are receiving special education programs and services, up to 12% of a state's school-age population. Under the IDEA Amendments of 1997 (Pub. L. No. 105-17), funding will continue to be based on the same child-count formula until appropriations reach approximately $4.9 billion. At this point, a new formula based on total student enrollment (85%) and poverty (15%) will apply to new monies in excess of the appropriation for the prior fiscal year, subject to certain limitations.

4. For a discussion of issues related to this type of blending at the federal and local levels, see CSEF Policy Papers 5 and 6: Verstegen (1995) and McLaughlin (1995). Also, see Parrish (1997) for a more in-depth discussion of state special education finance reform issues.

5. Elementary and Secondary Education Act, Pub. L. No. 89-750 (1966).

References

Hartman, W. T. (1992). State funding models for special education. *Remedial and Special Education, 13*(6), 47-58.

Kakalik, J. S., Furry, W. S., Thomas, M. A., & Carney, M. F. (1981). *The cost of special education* (A Rand Note). Santa Monica, CA: RAND.

McLaughlin, M. J. (1995). *Consolidated special education funding and services: A local perspective* (Policy Paper No. 5). Palo Alto, CA: American Institutes for Research, Center for Special Education Finance.

Moore, M.T., Strang, E. W., Schwartz, M., & Braddock, M. (1988). *Patterns in special education service delivery and cost.* Washington, DC: Decision Resources Cooperation.

National Center for Education Statistics. (1996). *Digest of education statistics 1996.* Washington, DC: U.S. Department of Education, Office of Educational Research and Improvement.

Parrish, T. B. (1994). *Fiscal issues in special education: Removing incentives for restrictive placements.* Palo Alto, CA: CSEF.

Parrish, T. B. (1995). *Criteria for effective special education funding formulas* (Policy Abstract). Palo Alto, CA: American Institutes for Research, Center for Special Education Finance.

Parrish, T. B. (1996). *Special education finance: Past, present, and future* (Policy Paper No. 8). Palo Alto, CA: American Institutes for Research, Center for Special Education Finance.

Parrish, T. B. (1997). *Special education finance* (Special Education in an Era of School Reform Series). Washington, DC: Federal Resource Center.

Parrish, T. B., O'Reilly, F., Dueñas, I. E., & Wolman, J. (1997). *State special education finance systems, 1994-95.* Palo Alto, CA: American Institutes for Research, Center for Special Education Finance.

Rossmiller, R. A., Hale, J. A., & Frohreich, L. E. (1970). *Educational programs for exceptional children: Resource configuration and costs.* Madison, WI: National Educational Finance Project, Department of Educational Administration, University of Wisconsin.

U.S. Department of Education. (1990). *Twelfth annual report to Congress on the implementation of The Individuals with Disabilities Education Act.* Washington, DC: Office of Special Education Programs.

U.S. Department of Education. (1992a). *Fourteenth annual report to Congress on the implementation of The Individuals with Disabilities Education Act.* Washington, DC: Office of Special Education Programs.

U.S. Department of Education. (1992b). *Historical trends: State education facts.* Washington, DC: National Center for Education Statistics.

U.S. Department of Education. (1995). *Projections of education statistics to 2005.* Washington, DC: National Center for Education Statistics.

U.S. Department of Education. (1997). *Nineteenth annual report to Congress on the implementation of The Individuals with Disabilities Education Act.* Washington, DC: Office of Special Education Programs.

Verstegen, D. A. (1995). *Consolidated special education funding and services: A federal perspective* (Policy Paper No. 6). Palo Alto, CA: American Institutes for Research, Center for Special Education Finance.

Wolman, J. A., & Parrish, T. B. (1996). *Escalating special education costs: Reality or myth? The CSEF Resource.* Palo Alto, CA: American Institutes for Research, Center for Special Education Finance.

Trends and New Developments in Special Education Finance Litigation

DEBORAH A. VERSTEGEN

The courts have long been involved in the area of special education. As early as 1971 in the *PARC v. Commonwealth* decision in Pennsylvania, the practice of excluding mentally challenged children from public schools was struck down as unconstitutional.[1] This ruling was later extended to all children with disabilities in *Mills v. Board of Education of District of Columbia* (1972).[2] The primary focus of the case was the district court's decision that lack of funds was no excuse for the lack of programs and services for children with disabilities. These two cases opened the door to the provision of a free and appropriate education for children with disabilities, a right that would subsequently be enshrined in law and in federal statute under the Individuals With Disabilities Education Act (IDEA), previously named the Education for All Handicapped Children Act.[3]

The judicial branch of government has also been instrumental in determining the meaning and requirements associated with state and federal legislation in special education. Court decisions have interpreted regulatory or statutory language, such as requirements for an

AUTHOR'S NOTE: Reprinted with permission from the *Journal of Education Finance* 23(3), 277-308.

TABLE 10.1 The New Wave of School Finance Litigation (Activity Since 1989): States in Which the School Finance System Has Been Ruled Unconstitutional by the State's Highest Court

Alaska	*Matanuska-Susitna Borough Sch. Dist. v. State*, 931 P.2d 391 (1997).
Illinois	*Committee for Educational Rights v. Edgar*, 672 N.E.2d 1178 (1996).
Kansas	*Unified School District 229 et al. v. State*, 885 P.2d 1170 (1994).
Maine	*School Admin. Dist. No. 1 et al. v. Commissioner*, 659 A.2d 854 (1994).
Minnesota	*Skeen v. State*, 505 N.W.2d 299 (1993).
North Dakota	*Bismark Public School #1 v. State*, 511N.W.2d 247 (1994).
Oregon	*Coalition For Equitable School Funding v. State*, 811 P.2d 116 (1991).
Rhode Island	*Pawtucket v. Sundlan*, 662 A.2d 40 (1995).
Virginia	*Scott v. Commonwealth*, 443 S.E.2d 138 (1994).
Wisconsin	*Kukor v. Grover*, 436 N.W.2d 568 (1989).

SOURCE: D. Verstegen, University of Virginia.
a. Majority (3) ruled in favor of the plaintiffs but North Dakota requires four justices to declare a statutory law unconstitutional. Nebraska supreme court upheld the dismissal of an appeal because the case did not state a cause of action, but there was no ruling on the constitutionality of the school finance system.

"appropriate education,"[4] "mainstreaming" (Huefner, 1994), the "least restrictive environment" (Osborne & Dimattia, 1994), a "continuum of services," or due process procedures (e.g., Kubicek, 1994). In addition, the courts have determined legitimate cost requirements imposed on states and localities consistent with the requirements of federal and state statute for a free and appropriate education for children with disabilities in the least restrictive environment.[5]

Recently, the courts have addressed a new aspect of special education related to the constitutionality of the state special education finance system. These judicial decisions have been part of the broader set of school finance decisions recently emerging from state high courts. Just since 1989, 21 supreme courts have ruled on the constitutionality of the education finance system. In 10 states, the finance system was upheld (see Table 10.1). In 10 states, it was invalidated (see Table 10.2). Currently, litigation is active in a majority of states, and concern over the threat of a possible court challenge affects most of the remaining states.

Court decisions in school finance emerging since 1989 have been referred to as the *third wave* or *new wave* of school finance litigation.

TABLE 10.2 The New Wave of School Finance Litigation (Activity Since 1989): States in Which the School Finance System Has Been Ruled Unconstitutional by the State's Highest Court

Arizona[a]	*Roosevelt Elem. School Dist. v. Bishop*, 877 P.2d 806 (1994).
Kentucky	*Rose v. Council for Better Education*, 790 S.W.2d 186 (1989).
Massachusetts	*McDuffy v. Sec'y of the Exec. of Education*, 615 N.E.2d 516 (1993).
Montana	*Helena Elementary School District No.1 v. State*, 769 P.2d 684 (1989). Modified in *Helena Elementary School D. 1 v. State*, 784 P.2d 412 (1990) (delaying effective date of decision).
New Jersey	*Abbott v. Burke*, 575 A2d 359 (1985); *Abbott v. Burke*, 575 A.2d 359 (1990); *Abbott v. Burke*, 643 A.2d 575 (1994); *Abbott v. Burke*, 693 A.2d 417 (1997).
Ohio	*DeRolph v. State*, 677 N.E. 733 (1997).
Tennessee	*Tennessee Small School Systems v. McWherter*, 851 S.W. 2d 139 (1993).
Texas	*Edgewood Indep. School Dist. v. Kirby*, 777 S.W.2d 391 (1989); *Edgewood Indep. School Dist. v. Kirby*, 804 S.W.2d 491 (1991); *Edgewood Indep. School Dist. v. Meno*, 893 S.W.2d 450 (1995).
Vermont	*Brigham v. State*, 692 A.2d 384 (1997).
Wyoming	*Campbell Co. School Dist. v. State*, 907 P.2d 1238 (1995).

SOURCE: D. Verstegen, University of Virginia.
a. Arizona had the capital outlay provisions of the finance system found unconstitutional; Alabama's high court stayed the lower court's remedy decision.

Although overlaps and caveats are present, over time, judicial activity related to the constitutionality of state finance systems has occurred in three waves (Thro, 1990). During the first wave of school finance litigation, occurring between 1960 and 1972, plaintiffs alleged school finance disparities constituted violations of the equal protection clause of the United States Constitution. During the second wave of activity, from 1972 to 1988, claims were based on equity guarantees in state constitutions, state education articles, or both. In the new wave of school finance litigation beginning in 1989, plaintiffs have generally alleged violations of the state constitution based on direct application of the education article, and issues of adequacy have accompanied traditional equity arguments (Verstegen, 1994; Verstegen & Whitney, 1997). This opens the door for judicial reform of state finance systems because a decision that turns on the plain meaning of the education article is restricted to the educational arena; it does not have the broad reach of fundamentality or suspect class holdings—which have the potential of affecting virtually all other functional areas included in state constitutions.

The new wave of school finance litigation has propelled school finance reform to the top of state policy agendas. It is forcing states to reexamine all the issues concerning educational equity that they have previously dealt with, but there are important new directions, as well. Recent court rulings have not only incorporated a new approach, basing their claims on the concept of educational adequacy rather than relying solely on the ideal of finance equity. They have also called for systemic, not additive, change and have included challenges to the constitutionality of specific provisions of the finance system, including those for capital outlay; rural, small, and urban schools; and programs for children with special needs, including children with disabilities.

The research discussed in this article addresses the high court decisions emerging during the third wave of school finance litigation as related to children with special needs. Although nearly every recent judicial opinion has addressed the high costs associated with the provision of education for students and districts with special needs, three recent state supreme court decisions—in Alabama,[6] Wyoming,[7] and Ohio[8]—addressed not only the constitutionality of the general school finance system but also whether the special education finance system passed constitutional muster. These state systems for financing programs for children receiving special education and related services included both population-based funding systems and pupil-weighted systems. They addressed both equity and adequacy issues.

What have these state high courts ruled concerning state special education finance systems? Did certain types of formula meet the scrutiny of the courts? Do extra funds provided for students with special needs contribute to unjustified funding disparities among school systems within a state, or are these additional funds necessary and required under the law? Do inadequately funded special education programs and services encroach on regular education funds, and if so, is this unconstitutional? These questions are discussed in this chapter. First, state finance decisions addressing special education are analyzed by state. Then, overall themes related to special-needs students across these states are discussed, and emerging issues are highlighted.

Because the provision and governance of education is a state responsibility under the U.S. Constitution, state high court decisions apply only to the state where the decision has been rendered. However, these judicial opinions provide a broad set of important considerations for other states as they face court challenges or seek to avoid them altogether. They also are useful to the majority of states seeking to modify their special education finance systems in an effort to make them more equitable and adequate while providing incentives for localities to meet the full intent of the law: the provision of a free and appropriate education for children with disabilities in the least restrictive setting.

Alabama: Inequity and Inadequacy

The Alabama Coalition for Equity Inc. v. Hunt;
Harper v. Hunt (1993)[9]

In a sweeping lower court decision in Alabama,[10] later affirmed by the Supreme Court on remedy,[11] the court struck down the entire education system, finding that education was a fundamental right and citing an inequitable and grossly inadequate funding system as infringing on that right. The court referred to testimony indicating the grim conditions in Alabama's schools: children who had to carry bottled water to school because the drinking water was contaminated; schools without textbooks; children attending unsafe and deteriorating schools; and schools infested with termites, fire ants, and rats. In some schools, curricula failed to meet minimum state standards, and no provisions were made for students seeking an advanced program (required for admission to a university) or for children who were gifted and talented or eligible for a special education.

The Alabama Court addressed the state special education funding system directly. The court noted that "state officials have forthrightly acknowledged the stark disparities in the opportunities provided to disabled children of the State that are directly attributable to the wealth of the school system these students attend" (Coalition, 1993, at 124). These inequities continued in spite of state laws requiring appropriate instruction and special services for all children with disabilities as well as federal law, which places the ultimate responsibility for special education on the state.[12]

Appropriate Education

Experts for the subclass of children with disabilities represented by John Doe argued that children with disabilities did not receive an appropriate or adequate education.[13] Moreover, they alleged that disparities in educational programs for children with disabilities were related to the wealth of the school system a child attended, curtailing their equal educational opportunities under the law.[14] It is important that the court boldly stated that "this disparity is as meaningful and substantial as the differential treatment of children in regular education programs."[15]

The court reviewed testimony from Dr. Snell, an expert witness, who defined an appropriate education as a specified level of quality in education[16] that included at least seven components: (a) inclusion (the education of children with disabilities with their nondisabled chronological peers); (b) program support (resources needed to support special education statewide), (c) curriculum (the educational goals and objectives in each child's IEP), (d) instruction (the methods used to teach the curriculum), (e) peer support (encouragement and opportunities to socialize with nondisabled peers), (f) preparation for adult life, and (g) collaborative teaming (opportunities, formal and informal, for special education teachers to meet with regular education teachers concerning each child's program and needs).[17]

In addition, Dr. Snell instructed the court, an appropriate education must be designed to benefit a child with disabilities through individualized programs and services tailored to meet the needs of the child. For the child to benefit, related services, such as speech and transportation, must be provided. Moreover, the measure of success of a special education program was the outcome for that particular child.[18] However, several deficiencies were found in Alabama schools, including the "complete absence of meaningful transition programs," the lack of individualized instruction, and teacher in-service and development programs that were "so poor that teachers do not know enough to ask for help."[19]

Dr. Rostetter,[20] also accepted by the court as an expert witness, found that deficiencies in program support (the second of Dr. Snell's components) prevented children with disabilities from receiving an appropriate education in Alabama. He found that program support was the basis for the implementation of the other six factors necessary for the provision of an appropriate education for children with disabilities. Program support consisted of (a) policy development and implementation, (b) staff and program development, (c) resources (human and financial), and (d) monitoring and evaluation. Although the state provided guidelines to localities that addressed these areas, testimony indicated that they were not implemented. Notably, the court found that resource deficiencies consisted of a "critical shortage of teachers and support staff"[21] and poorly trained teachers.

Mr. Blackwell, another expert witness, spoke to the severity of the problem by stating that "some school systems cannot offer programs for children with certain disabilities because they do not have anyone trained or certified to teach those special education areas."[22] Moreover, local authorities "are unable to provide the staff and program development needed to ensure even minimum standards in instruction for children with disabilities in Alabama . . . [and] money often restricts the availability of these services."[23]

The court agreed, holding that the lack of human and financial resources resulted in an "inappropriate education" for many of the state's children with disabilities and "contravenes the state's own plan" for administration and operation of special education programs.[24]

Deficiencies were also found in the fourth component of program support: monitoring and evaluation. Although the state was required to ensure that all localities were providing a free and appropriate education to all children with disabilities and was required to withhold funds from school systems that were not in compliance, testimony indicated that "the state is reluctant to take away funds from local systems because lack of money is often already part of the reason school systems are not providing an appropriate education."[25] In addition, the lack of an effective state monitoring system resulted in an inability to identify and resolve potential problems for children with disabilities and in statistics of disproportionality related to race and disability eligibility. For example, in predominantly black school districts, 51.77% of children with disabilities were identified as educable mentally retarded, whereas in predominantly white school districts, only 16.32% of exceptional children were so identified.

The court reasoned that although there were no state court cases interpreting the term "appropriate" in this context, federal cases constructing this word have been adopted by the state. Through the receipt of aid under the Education for All Handicapped Children Act as amended, recipients were required to provide an appropriate education to children with disabilities, and state regulations mirrored the language of federal law. Thus it said, "the Court cannot construe the Alabama statutory and regulatory language differently from the federal meaning without ignoring the clear intent of the Alabama legislature to benefit from federal aid to special education."[26] Using the Rowley standard articulated by the U.S. Supreme Court to define an appropriate education,[27] the state court found that Alabama failed to meet the test. Relying on expert testimony, the court noted that some school districts did not offer certain programs to children with disabilities because there were no qualified staff to teach some students. Moreover, the problems were statewide because the state could not give school systems the support needed to hire, train, and retain qualified staff.

The court also found that the total-enrollment method of funding special education was "irrational and arbitrary in violation of the due process clause of the Alabama Constitution and has no relationship to the public interest in appropriately educating students with disabilities."[28] The state constitution's due process clause required that the statute or law in question should be reasonable and bear a substantial relationship to the public need.

Special Education Finance System

Since 1972, the State of Alabama has funded special education through the total-enrollment method. Using this method, a school system received money earmarked for the education of children with disabilities based on the school district's total enrollment, including the enrollment of disabled and nondisabled children. According to the

Court, this resulted in school systems "with *larger* percentages of special education students receiving *less* money per pupil than school districts with fewer special education students."[29] As long as the percentages of special education students varied from system to system, the court found, the total-enrollment method would result in inequities. School districts with high percentages of children with disabilities received less funding per pupil than districts with relatively lower percentages. Thus, "the total enrollment method is not based on the needs of special education students and does not take into account the number or the cost of educating those children."[30]

The court also reviewed a proposal for a weighted funding system[31] and addressed the question: would a weighted child-count funding system be preferable to an enrollment-based system? It noted that the Alabama State Board of Education voted to change the method of distributing funds for special education to a weighted child-count method to be phased in over the following two years. Under this system, funding would be based on (a) the number of special education children in each school system and (b) the setting in which exceptional children were educated. Children who spent the largest part of the day in restrictive settings would receive more funds (have a higher weight); children in less restrictive settings would receive less funding (have a lower weight). Although the court found that it "is undisputed that the effect of [a change to a weighted student system] will be to inject some degree of equity into the funding distribution for children with disabilities," it failed to fully endorse such a system.[32]

The court said that a weighted funding system would still be inadequate because state aid would provide only 70% of the funding needed for special education. State administration, staffing, monitoring, and teacher training would remain inadequate and, "for less affluent systems, inequitable."[33] Moreover, according to the court, such a system would not meet the full intent of the law because under a weighted child-count system of funding,

> basing revenues on more restrictive placements may encourage school systems to isolate children with disabilities from non-disabled schoolchildren. . . . Therefore the court is not prepared to find that the inequities in the total enrollment method of

distributing funds have been remedied by the change to the weighted child count method.[34]

Final Holding: Unconstitutional

The subclass representing children with disabilities therefore asserted two claims unique to children with disabilities that were upheld by the court: (a) Exceptional children and youth are deprived of their statutory right to an appropriate education and special education services and (b) the Alabama system of funding for special education is irrational and violates the due process clause of the Alabama Constitution.[35] The court found the system for financing the general education system in Alabama was unconstitutional and that "Alabama cannot at present offer an appropriate education to . . . [children with disabilities] because of deficiencies in program support," also overturning the special education financing system.[36] The court emphasized that children with disabilities had the same constitutional right to an equitable and adequate education as did other children in the state.[37]

Therefore, it was ordered and decreed

that Alabama school-age children, including children with disabilities, have and enjoy a constitutional right to attend school in a liberal system of public schools, established, organized and maintained by the state, which shall provide all such school children with substantially equitable and adequate educational opportunities.[38]

Wyoming: Inequity, Inadequacy, and Encroachment

Campbell County School District v. State (1995)[39]

In a recent high court decision in Wyoming, issues related to special education were reviewed by the court, including the equity and adequacy of the special education finance system and the encroachment of special education funding on funding for students in general education programs. The Wyoming court held that the education finance system was unconstitutional, including provisions related to special education funding.

As background, in 1980, the Wyoming Supreme Court, in *Washakie v. Herschler,*[40] found that education was a fundamental right and that the school finance system was unconstitutional because wide disparities in funding among school districts failed to afford equal protection to school children in the state. The court held that "funding disparity results in educational opportunity disparity," stating that until financial equality was reached, there was no hope of achieving "equality of quality" schooling for all children across the state.[41]

In the 1995 decision, the Wyoming high court reviewed legislative action subsequent to the Washakie ruling. It noted that the legislature, in response to that decision, implemented what was considered at the time to be a transitional system of funding and had issued several findings on the finance system, including the need to include cost differentials in a newly designed system. The court quoted Wyoming session laws of 1983 that stated,

> Issues of equitable funding in Wyoming involve more than measurements of differences in funding per student between school districts and a corresponding attempt to lessen the disparity unless consideration is given to factors such as increased costs of education in rural districts, equality of programs in rural districts, extraordinary requirements for funds in impacted school districts due to an influx of students and special needs of students.[42]

Therefore, the court found, the Washakie ruling required the legislature to take into consideration various balancing factors and devise a state formula that weighted the calculation to compensate for the special needs of children and other legitimate educational cost differentials. It provided allowances for such variances among individuals, groups, and local conditions but held that these factors must not be arbitrary but be legitimate and based on research and studies.[43]

However, the temporary funding system became permanent, and attempts to include cost differentials in the system that recognized the excess cost requirements—for children with special needs (such as children with disabilities) and school districts with uncontrollably higher costs (such as rural and urban districts)—were unsuccessful.[44] After over a decade of operation, in 1992, the so-called temporary finance system was again challenged in court.

Equity and Cost Differentials

Challengers alleged the "evil was once again disparate spending" caused by arbitrary and irrational factors in the distribution system[45] that had no relation to "educational costs" and that "educational dollars must be based on need related to the quality of education."[46] That is, "wealth-based and not cost-justified" disparities were unconstitutional under Washakie's requirement of "equality of financing in order to achieve equality of quality."[47] Furthermore, challengers alleged that post-Washakie changes to the finance system had exacerbated disparities. Thus, whereas the "triggering issue" in Washakie was wealth-based disparities, the 1995 decision extended that decision beyond wealth-based disparity to other causes of disparity, such as failure to fund adequately district costs related to size, facilities, and student needs, including the needs of students with disabilities.

The district court ruled that the challengers bore the burden of proving that the disparities were not cost justified (later reversed by the high court), but they did not have to demonstrate that unjustified disparities caused harm to educational opportunity; "harm was presumed."[48] Witnesses for both plaintiffs and defendants agreed that the cost of education varied according to student characteristics and other factors, such as the costs of utilities, transportation, and classified and certified personnel, but the distribution formula made no adjustment on the basis of such factors.[49] It was also agreed that one district's increased costs should not be compensated while another's were ignored. In essence, the court held that excess costs related to justifiable special needs must be compensated equitably across all school districts in the state.

Adequacy, Equity, and Encroachment

Adequacy issues were also raised in the decision and were related to the encroachment of the special education finance system on funding for children in general education. The high court noted that superintendents of challenger districts provided evidence that their actual costs exceeded the operating revenue provided through the finance system because the funding plan made no adjustment for varying educational costs. Superintendents also

> provided evidence of deficiencies caused by less than full reimbursement of transportation and special education expenditures. The deficiencies are made up from the revenue meant for education of the general student population . . . . [C]ombined deficiencies result in insufficient revenue which can be devoted to average students who comprise the majority of students. The actual number of classrooms and staff and the amount of support needed to educate those students are [therefore] inadequate.[50]

Representatives of large districts testified that in addition to suffering "deficient funding" caused by the failure of the state to pay for the actual costs of special district and student needs, they "suffered from cost pressures generated by school population growth and student characteristics."[51]

Throughout the high court decision, it was pointed out that studies must provide evidence that all differences in funding were cost justified and that these differences cannot be arbitrary or determined without research support. Justifiable differences, it was held, can include differences in costs resulting from size, such as small and large districts; in transportation costs; and in student needs, such as special education costs and the costs of educating at-risk students. Moreover, the court held, the goal of the system for all children, or educational success, must be defined as graduating from high school equipped for a role as a citizen, participant in the political system, and competitor both intellectually and economically.[52]

The court found that education was a fundamental right; it, therefore, reviewed the system using the highest standard of review, strict scrutiny, "to determine whether the evil of financial disparity, from whatever unjustifiable cause, has been exorcized from the Wyoming educational system."[53] It focused on three aspects of the state formula that allowed differential revenue for school districts. First, recapture provisions had permitted districts to keep 109% of a base funding amount if their locally raised revenues from an optional mills levy were above that amount.[54] Although the additional 9% of funds were defended as being the result of social costs incurred in areas where mineral extraction occurred, the court noted that no study justified these disparities. This optional mills levy,[55] permitted under statute, was found to be "totally dependent upon the local wealth of individual school districts," which bore no relationship to the expense of educating students in any particular community.[56]

Second, capital outlay provisions limited funds to 10% of assessed value of real property, but poor school systems could not raise enough for even a single school building because they had low assessed valuations. This resulted in facility differences across the state and unmet needs for poor districts, an area later related to unmet facility needs for children with disabilities.

Third, the overall mechanism for funding schools, which was based on the number of classrooms units needed to operate a school and supported at $92,331 per classroom unit, also "failed to provide any specificity in identifying costs."[57] Associated provisions benefiting small schools because they cost more, whereas large schools benefited from economies of scale, "were revealed as assumptions without basis in study or empirical data."[58]

In striking down the state finance system, the high court in Wyoming found unpersuasive the state's defense that disparities were a result of local control and stated that

> In view that an educational system is a function of state control, it would be paradoxical to permit disparity because of local control . . . . There cannot be both state and local control in establishing a constitutional education system.[59]

Addressing the costs of educating students with special needs directly, the Wyoming court held that a "proper education today requires that broad categories of students' needs must be addressed with appropriate education programs" and resources because children with impaired readiness to learn do not have the same equal opportunity for a quality education as do those children not affected by personal or social ills simply because they do not have the same starting point in learning. A legislatively created finance system that distributes dollars without regard for the need to level the playing field does not provide an equal opportunity for a quality education. Having no losers in the system requires there be no shrinking pie but a pie of the size needed. Once education need is determined, the pie must be large enough to fund that need.[60] A child's "impaired readiness to learn" according to the court, was affected by "social ills, learning deficiencies and the system itself which forces them into large classes or large schools" (Campbell at 1278) because of inequitable funding and lack of adequate support for facilities.

Final Holding

The Wyoming Supreme Court issued a decision in 1995 finding the school finance system unconstitutional under provisions of the Wyoming Constitution, including provisions related to special education funding.

The court instructed the legislature to design the best educational system, determine the cost, and fund it. Aspects of the best or quality education system include not only small class sizes and low student-computer ratios but also "ample appropriate provision for at-risk students, special problem students and talented students."[61] In a ringing conclusion, the high court held that

Because education is one of the state's most important functions, lack of financial resources will not be an acceptable reason for failure to provide the best educational system. All other financial considerations must yield until education is funded.[62]

It is important that this included providing adequate and equitable educational programs and services to children with disabilities based on research studies of associated costs.

Ohio: Inequity, Inadequacy, and Inaccessibility

DeRolph v. State (1997)[63]

In Ohio, the supreme court decision followed a trial court ruling that declared the finance system for general and special education inadequate, unequal, and unconstitutional.[64] Stating that "the State must bridge the gap which separates our present educational system from education excellence," and quoting from an anonymously written poem entitled, *The Bridge Builder*,[65] the trial court pointed out that "every day education becomes more and more important, and the connection between education and the rights guaranteed [by the education article] becomes greater and greater." Thus, it held that education was a fundamental right and that "the deprivation of that right operates as a substantial deterrent to the public's future economic well-being."[66]

An Adequate Education

In finding the system unconstitutional, the lower court called for an adequate education for all children. An adequate system of education must have as its goal to provide each and every child with at least the following competencies and inputs:[67] (a) sufficient oral and written communication skills to enable students to function socially and economically in Ohio and globally; (b) sufficient mathematics and scientific skills to function as a contributing citizen to the economy of Ohio and globally; (c) sufficient knowledge of economic, social, and political systems, generally, and of the history, policies, and social structure of Ohio and the nation (to) enable the student to make informed choices; (d) sufficient understanding of governmental processes and of basic civic institutions to enable the student to understand and contribute to the issues that affect his or her community, state, and nation; (e) sufficient self-knowledge and knowledge of the principles of health and mental hygiene to enable the student to monitor and contribute to his or her own physical and mental well-being; (f) sufficient understanding of the arts to enable each student to appreciate his or her cultural and historical heritage and the cultural heritages of others; (g) sufficient training or preparation for advanced training in academic or vocational skills, and sufficient guidance, to enable each child to choose and pursue life intelligently; (h) sufficient levels of academic or vocational skills to enable public school students to favorably compete academically or in the job market with their counterparts in Ohio, in surrounding states, across the nation, and throughout the world; (i) sufficient support and guidance so that every student feels a sense of self-worth and ability to achieve and so that every student is encouraged to live up to his or her full potential; (j) sufficient facilities, equipment, supplies, and instruction to enable both female and male students to compete equally within their own schools as well as schools across Ohio and worldwide in both academic and extracurricular activities; (k) sufficient monitoring by the General Assembly to ensure that this State's common schools are being operated without there being mismanagement, waste, or misuse of funds; and (l) sufficient facilities for each school district across the State that are adequate for instruction, safe, sanitary, and conducive to providing a proper education as outlined by the stated criteria.

In part, this definition of an adequate education was also cited by the lower court in Alabama and the Kentucky and Massachusetts high court decisions on the constitutionality of the education finance system. However, the Ohio court added the third competency and items i through l. Thus, the concept of adequacy was expanded by the court to include a dual focus consisting of outcomes and inputs.

Inequity and Special Education Finance

According to Ohio's lower court, all students, including children with disabilities, were entitled to adequate special education programs and services. However, the court pointed out that many exceptional children and youth were excluded from special education programs and services altogether, because of fiscal constraints. It highlighted this issue in its lengthy opinion, which held that

Probably the saddest set of facts regarding the special education of our State's students involves the identification of students as being in need of special education. [In some districts,] students tend to not be identified as handicapped until they have failed two or three grades. To do so earlier would require districts to provide more programs which typically would not be funded by the state. The education system harms those who need it most. Instead of this system being receptive to the needs of our handicapped children, school districts are forced to delay identification of these students for financial reasons.[68]

Testimony indicated that because the costs of special education are mandatory, to provide programs and services for children with disabilities, school districts were "forced to rely on their general fund money more and more in recent years to fund the required [special education programs] that are mandated but unfunded by the state."[69] That is, if the local costs for special education exceeded state and federal funding, they were paid for from the school district's general fund budget. Moreover, the greater the payment from the general fund, the fewer the funds that were available for regular education. Financing special education, therefore, was a critical issue as costs swelled and the special education budget captured increasingly larger shares of the general education budget.

Inequities in programs and services for children with disabilities in poor versus wealthy school districts were linked to the way in which Ohio allocated school funds. Testimony cited in the opinion revealed that under the school funding system, the amount of money that supported Ohio schools bore no relationship to the actual cost of educating a student. As related to special and vocational education, experts testified that providing a uniform amount of state funding to all districts for special education programs and services, "represent[ed] a flaw in the system of school funding, because they work[ed] against the equalization effect of the formula."[70] Moreover, the state did not pay the full cost of special education. "In fact, children in funded handicapped 'units' are not included in the state basic aid formula."[71]

Ohio's schools were funded through a foundation program—this provided a guaranteed amount of money (a minimum) for each student from a combination of state and local funds. This amount of money was further adjusted by the "cost of doing business" that assumed higher costs in cities than in rural areas. The grand total was then split between the state and locality based on the total taxable value of real and tangible personal property in the district (times a certain percentage).

The finance system then took special factors into account, such as categorical programs for vocational and special education and transportation. However, no adjustment was made for local ability to pay for education—rich and poor districts were funded alike:

> Thus, funds for handicapped students, for instance, whose education costs are substantially higher (due to state mandates of small class size and because of related extra services) are disbursed in a flat amount per unit (see R.C. 3317.05). If the actual cost exceeds the funds received, wealthier districts are in a better position to make up the difference.[72]

The state of Ohio provided finances for the support of special education programs and services through a unit-funding method. This provided additional assistance to school districts according to a formula that took into account salary schedule, retirement and fringe benefits, and a fixed amount for all other expenses. The problem was that the formula was not fully funded. For example, in fiscal year 1993, the number of unfunded special education units operated by Ohio school districts without state reimbursement climbed to 847 units. In addition, although the state required a supervisory unit if a district operated 20 special education units, supervisory units had not been funded in 5 years. Moreover, so-called experimental units comprised well over one third of all classroom units operating in the state. Using this approach, students were permitted to be taught by teachers who were not certified to teach special education. The number of experimental units grew from 300 in FY92 and FY93 to 3,800 units in FY94. Finally, unit funding did not provide assistance for making facilities accessible to children with disabilities, no state funds were provided to meet the requirement for transitional services, and only half of the eligible preschool population was being served.[73]

Inequities also persisted in special education programs and services, and programs and services for children with disabilities failed to meet statutory requirements. For example, over a 3-year period, more affluent districts in Ohio spent, on average, $8,651 for special education pupils, whereas the average per pupil expenditure in less affluent districts was $4,318. However, special education expenditures represented a larger percentage of total school district expenditures for the poor districts (20.81%) than for the wealthy (10.81%).

School Facilities

The lower court poignantly commented on the dire state of Ohio's facilities, explaining that, "This court saw grown men and women cry as they explained the conditions and situations in which some of the youth of this State are educated.[74] Testimony from a school board member indicated that "his animals were housed better than his district's school children—at least they were dry and warm."[75]

Like the lower court opinion, a substantial part of the supreme court decision addressed the appalling condition of Ohio's school facilities, including accommodations for children with disabilities. Citing the "dirty, depressing" conditions of the schools young children attended, the high court also reviewed evidence of the unsafe conditions that existed in the schools. For example, in one school district, 300 students were hospitalized because carbon monoxide leaked out of heaters and furnaces. Asbestos was present in 68.6% of Ohio's school buildings and a scant 30% had adequate fire alarm systems and exterior doors. There were leaking roofs, outdated sewage systems that caused raw sewage to flow onto the baseball field, and arsenic in the drinking water of certain schools. In other schools, cockroaches crawled on the restroom floors and plaster was falling off of the walls.

It is important to note that for children with disabilities, the high court took issue with their lack of access to schooling and noted that only 20% of the buildings had satisfactory handicapped access. For example,

> Deering Elementary is not handicapped accessible. The library is a former storage area located in the basement. Handicapped students have to be carried there and to other locations in the building. One handicapped third-grader at Deering had never

been to the school library because it was inaccessible to someone in a wheelchair.[76]

Final Holding

The high court struck down the finance system as unconstitutional and instructed the General Assembly to "create an entirely new school financing system."[77] This included a new funding scheme for general education, school facilities, and categorical programs, such as vocational and special education. Given the severity of the problem, the court pointed out that "the importance of the case cannot be overestimated.... practically every Ohioan will be affected ... [F]or the 1.8 million children involved [including children with disabilities], this case is about the opportunity to compete and succeed."[78]

It is interesting that in invalidating the finance plan, the high court overturned a previous 1979 decision that upheld the funding system, *Cincinnati School District Board of Education v. Walter,*[79] stating that the scheme had changed in the interim, and even defense witness testimony indicated that it was "immoral and inequitable."[80] The high court rejected as unfounded any suggestion that the problems presented by the case should be left to the General Assembly to resolve, stating, "This case involves questions of public or great general interest over which this court has jurisdiction. We will not dodge our responsibility.... [T]o do so is unthinkable."[81]

Discussion and Highlights of Court Decisions Related to Special Education Finance

State high court decisions emerging during the third wave of school finance litigation have struck out in bold new directions. Just since 1989, high courts in 21 states have issued rulings on the constitutionality of their school finance systems. These decisions represent a turning point from earlier judicial decisions in many respects (Verstegen, 1994). These court cases have added issues of adequacy to the usual challenges based on inequalities between wealthy and poor districts within a state. In addition, many state high courts have recently reviewed the state finance system with attention to specific aspects of the scheme as it relates to special needs—such as the needs of urban and rural school districts and children receiving special education and related services. Of the 10 high court decisions rendered since 1989 in which finance systems have been invalidated, 3 have included a challenge not just to the general education finance system but also to the special education finance system. In each of these cases, the special education funding system has been found to be unconstitutional.

In Alabama, the court defined an appropriate education and considered whether it was available to all children with disabilities across the state, regardless of whether they were being educated in poor or wealthy areas. The court held that children with disabilities suffered the same discrimination based on local wealth as did children in the general education system. Lack of funding circumscribed the ability of some districts to attract qualified teachers or to offer programs for children with disabilities. Funds were not available to train teachers in these areas, provide transition services, or offer individualized instruction. Lack of funding curtailed the availability of an appropriate education for children and youth with disabilities.

The Alabama court also reviewed the mechanism for distributing state aid for special education—an enrollment formula—and found it violated the equal protection clause of the state constitution. This was so because as numbers of special education students identified in a school district increased, funding per child decreased.

However, it is important to note that the court did not uniformly endorse the major finance alternative to population-based formulas for exceptional children and youth: weighted student systems. Although these formulas were considered more equitable, the court took the opportunity to say that weighted pupil systems could work against the full intent of the law by providing fiscal incentives for more restrictive placements for children receiving special education and related services.

The Alabama decision raised several issues for states grappling with how best to finance a free and appropriate education for all children with disabilities: What is the future of total-enrollment-based funding formulas? Will other state high courts find them similarly unacceptable? If so, what alternatives exist to these methods of funding? As stated, the court reviewed both enrollment funding and th major alternative method of funding special education—weighted pupil programs—but was unable to fully endorse either method as equitable, adequate, and providing incentives for the provision of a free and appropriate education in the least restrictive setting. This indicates that new models of state support for financing programs and services for children with special needs are necessary, although the vision of what they may be and how they may provide incentives for meeting the full intent of the law has not yet crystallized. Thus, this decision portends the need for a new special education finance—one that meets the needs of children and youth in schools and classrooms, provides incentives for educating exceptional children and youth in the least restrictive settings, and meets their individual needs in the most appropriate fashion.

Unlike the Alabama decision, issues emerging from the Wyoming court case that affect special education financing developed along a different line of reasoning. The Wyoming court reviewed and struck down the general education finance system in part because it neither included research-based cost differentials that recognized the real costs of providing schooling in small and urban districts nor recognized the justifiable costs of financing schooling for children in special education or other categorical programs. This omission and the lack of sufficient support for special education resulted in the encroachment of special education costs on general program funds and caused both the general and special education finance systems to be found inadequate, inequitable, and unconstitutional.

This ruling is important for several reasons. First, it suggests that states are responsible for determining and supporting the excess costs of education for districts and students with special needs, including children with disabilities. Second, it recognizes that financing special education and general education are inextricably intertwined. This is so because when special education is inadequately financed, it encroaches on revenues for general education to cover its mandatory expenses. Last, the decision points out the need for research on the costs of special education and other needs-based factors that are ⸱timate and require additional funds and holds that these costs be linked to state funding provisions and supported by the state. Wyoming decision also raises several questions. First, must the ar the full share of special education costs? A necessary corol-ᵢs question is: can the costs of special education be shared by the state with local school districts? The court decision suggests that both state and local funds may be used to pay for the high costs associated with special education programs and services. However, such cost sharing must be provided through an equitable funding system that is conditioned on local wealth. Other options to state-local financing, such as full state funding, may also be acceptable. If state-local cost sharing based on an equitable finance plan is the preferred alternative, chief issues include how these shares might best be determined and the level of services that should be funded. Altogether, these specific policy questions have not been addressed by the courts. However, the Wyoming court called for cost studies to guide legislative decision making and said that the legislature must devise the best system, cost it out, and fund it. According to the court, all other financial considerations must yield until education is funded.

Turning to the last case reviewed, Ohio, issues related to special education finance focused on equity and adequacy, but facilities concerns were also prominently featured. As in the Alabama and Wyoming opinions, the inequitable and inadequate finance system was struck down as unconstitutional, and the court also addressed several specific funding provisions, including special education, and found them unconstitutional as well.

The Ohio finance system provided additional funding for special education programs and services but failed to fully fund mandated state services. Moreover, state aid was disbursed to local school districts without regard to their ability to pay for education. When funds were insufficient, wealthy districts could easily make up the difference, but poor districts could not, due to low property tax bases. This resulted in differences in funds available for special education across the state and an inequitable special education finance system based on whether or not a child was born in a wealthy or poor school district. This decision indicates that when funding is provided from state and local sources, state funding must be conditioned on local wealth and it must be adequate, thereby providing sufficient funds to meet state mandates and requirements.

The court also devoted a substantial amount of attention to the poor state of school facilities in Ohio. Testimony revealed that 80% of the buildings were not accessible to children with disabilities and that many school buildings were not only deteriorating and dirty bu unhealthy and unsafe—not only for children with disabilities but f all children. This indicates that school buildings still restrict the realization of a free and appropriate education for children with disabilities and must be taken into account in state finance systems, most of which do not provide direct aid for capital outlay much less the funds necessary for the excess costs needed to equip school buildings with specific features to provide equal opportunities to learn for children with disabilities.

In sum, the paramount issues in all of these cases for children with disabilities centered on the equity and adequacy of the state school finance system. Courts in Alabama, Wyoming, and Ohio held that disparities in funding for children with disabilities that were linked to the wealth of the school district were unconstitutional. Inequitable funding led to differences in the quality and equality of programs and services for children similarly circumscribed. Inadequate funding for special education restricted the availability of a free and appropriate education for exceptional children and youth. Inadequate funding led to the encroachment of special education financing on general education support and reduced funding available for all children. Inadequate and inequitable support for special education across the state resulted in a financing system conditioned on local—not state—wealth, as required under the law, and abridged equal opportunities for children with disabilities across the state.

Thus, these courts invalidated features of finance systems that resulted in the inequitable and inadequate support of schooling for children with disabilities and prevented them from receiving an appropriate education and having access to safe schools and needed programs and services. Taken as a whole, the recent state high court decisions addressing the constitutionality of the special education finance system suggest that inequitable and inadequate special education finance systems across the states are vulnerable to future court challenges because they curtail the availability of a free and appropriate education for children with disabilities and restrict equal educational opportunities. Moreover, these high court decisions suggest that developing new systems of financing facilities as well as programs and services for children with disabilities aimed at meeting the intent of the law should be a top priority on state policy agendas.

broad parameters of a new special education finance system suggested by the rulings. First, the new system must be cost that is, the costs of providing an appropriate education must be determined through research studies; they must be legitimate and justifiable. Second, the real costs of the provision of special education and related services must be incorporated in the state finance system and supported by the state, either through full state assumption or state-local cost sharing. If the funding of special education and related services is shared with localities, then state aid must be equitable— that is, conditioned on local ability to pay for education. Third, the provision of special education and related services must be uniform across the state, regardless of whether a child is born in a more or less affluent area. Last, facilities must be safe, healthy, and accessible to all children, including children with disabilities. In addition, these costs are a state, not a local, responsibility.

At the heart of the intersection between general education finance litigation and special education finance litigation are two important possibilities for the future. First, as this analysis reveals, the focus of general case law related to school finance litigation can be applied successfully to special education finance systems. Where this has occurred, in each case financing for special education has been found to be inadequate, inequitable, or both—and state high courts have held that special education finance systems were unconstitutional under their respective state constitutions. Second, though not yet contemplated, is the possibility of applying the long and enduring set of special education case law to general education systems, including the meaning of the right to a free and appropriate education for children with disabilities. It is important that courts in Alabama and Wyoming as well as 13 other states (A. Hickrod, as cited in Alexander & Salmon, 1995, pp. 42-43) have held that education was a right for all children— not just children with disabilities. Might special education case law provide important legal reasoning and precedent to courts as they seek to interpret this right to an education for all children?

Ultimately, the new wave of school finance litigation may finally provide the means to achieve the fair and adequate funding of educational programs and services for all children with disabilities in America's public schools—an elusive goal but one that was enshrined into law and statute in the 1970s through judicial decisions and codified into statute with the passage of the landmark IDEA (previously called the Education for All Handicapped Children Act). Moreover, the success of the plaintiffs in the recent court cases indicates the continued viability of a legal strategy for realizing the rights of children, including children with disabilities, to equal and adequate educational opportunities in America's schools across the country.

Notes

1. *Pennsylvania Association for Retarded Children v. Commonwealth of Pennsylvania*, 334 F. Supp. 1257 (E. D. Pa. 1971).

2. *Mills v. Board of Education of District of Columbia*, 348 F. Supp. 866 (D.C. DC 1972).

3. Individuals With Disabilities Education Act, Pub. L. 91-230.

4. See, for example, *Board of Education of the Hendrick Hudson Central School District, Westchester County et al. v. Rowley*, 3 EHLR 553: 656.

5. *Liscio v. Woodland Hills School District*, 734 F. Supp. 689 (Pa. 1989); *Barnett v. Fairfax County Board of Education*, 927 F.2d 146 (4th Cir., 1991); *Roncker v. Walter*, 700 F.2d 1058 (6th Cir., 1983).

6. 624 So.2d 107 (Ala. 1993) Opinion of the Justices. For *Alabama Coalition for Equity et al. v. Hunt*, CIV. A. Nos. CV-90-883-R, *Harper v. Hunt* CV-91-0117.

7. 907 P.2d 1238 (Wyo. 1995).

8. *DeRolph v. State*, 677N.E.2d 733 (Ohio 1997). Note: Pages referred to throughout are from slip opinion, March 24, 1997.

9. Opinion of the Justices, 624 So.2d 107 (Ala. 1993). *Coalition for Equity et al. v. Hunt*, CIV.A. Nos. CV-90-883-R, *Harper v. Hunt* CV-91-0117.

10. Opinion at 165 (Ala. 1993).

11. Opinion at 107 (Ala. 1993).

12. Opinion at 124 (Ala. 1993).

13. Opinion at 141 (Ala. 1993).

14. Opinion at 142 (Ala. 1993).

15. Opinion at 142 (Ala. 1993).

16. Opinion at 162 (Ala. 1993). The court remarked that "no reported state court cases interpreting the term 'appropriate' in this context, the sub-class argues that federal cases constructing this word have been adopted by the state" and the "Court agrees."

17. Opinion at 142 (Ala. 1993).

18. Opinion at 142 (Ala. 1993).

19. Opinion at 142 (Ala. 1993).

20. Dr. Rostetter was responsible at the United States Department of Education for reviewing and monitoring states to ensure compliance with federal special education laws from 1976-1986.

21. Opinion at 143 (Ala. 1993).

22. Opinion at 143 (Ala. 1993).

23. Opinion at 143 (Ala. 1993).

24. Opinion at 143 (Ala. 1993).

25. Opinion at 143 (Ala. 1993).

26. Opinion at 163 (Ala. 1993).

27. *Hendrick Hudson District Board of Education v. Rowley*, 458 U.S. 172 (1982). According to the court, an appropriate education, as defined in Pub. L. 94-142 as amended, is satisfied according to the court, when the State provides personalized instruction with sufficient support services to permit the child with a disability to benefit educationally

from that instruction. Such instruction and services must be provided at public expense, must meet the State's educational standards, must approximate grade levels used in the State's regular education, and must comport with the child's IEP. If the child is being educated in regular classrooms, the IEP should be reasonably calculated to enable the child to achieve passing marks and advance from grade to grade. The State is not required to maximize the potential of each child with a disability commensurate with the opportunity provided children without disabilities.

28. Opinion at 164 (Ala. 1993).

29. Opinion at 125 (Ala. 1993).

30. Opinion at 125 (Ala. 1993).

31. Weighted funding systems provide funds according to "weights" which represent the excess costs of providing programs and services (e.g., to children with disabilities). For example, if a child in a learning disability (LD) program costs 50% more to educate than a child in a general education program, the LD child would be counted as 1.5, indicating they should receive general education funding (the level of 1.0 in the system) plus an additional 50% (a weight of 0.5).

32. Opinion at 126 (Ala. 1993).

33. Opinion at 126 (Ala. 1993).

34. Opinion at 126 (Ala. 1993).

35. Opinion at 162 (Ala. 1993).

36. Opinion at 143 (Ala. 1993).

37. Opinion at 162 (Ala. 1993).

38. Opinion at 165 (Ala. 1993).

39. Supra, *Campbell* 907 P.2d 1238 (Wyo. 1995).

40. *Washakie Co. Sch. Dist. No. One v. Herschler* 606 P.2d 310 (Wyo. 1980).

41. Supra, *Campbell* at 1238.

42. *Campbell* at 1247 (cited from 1983 Wyo. Session Laws, Ch. 136, p. 399-400, Wyo.)

43. *Campbell* at 1269 (Wyo. 1983).

44. *Campbell* at 1248 (Wyo. 1983).

45. These include the divisor, the municipal divisor and the classroom unit value (CRU), *Campbell* at 1263 (Wyo. 1995).

46. *Campbell* at 1263 (Wyo. 1995).

47. *Campbell* at 1250 (Wyo. 1995).

48. *Campbell* at 1252 (Wyo. 1995).

49. *Campbell* at 1252 (Wyo. 1995).

50. *Campbell* at 1252 (Wyo. 1995).

51. *Campbell* at 1252 (Wyo. 1995).

52. *Campbell* at 1278 (Wyo. 1995).

53. *Campbell* at 1266 (Wyo. 1995).

54. Provisions that require local school districts to return local revenue in excess of a state guaranteed amount of funding, raised from state and local revenues. The guaranteed amount is referred to as the "foundation" amount of funding.

55. Additional locally imposed property taxes.

56. *Campbell* at 1269 (Wyo. 1995).

57. *Campbell* at 1266 (Wyo. 1995).

58. *Campbell* at 1266 (Wyo. 1995).

59. *Campbell* at 1269 (Wyo. 1995).

60. *Campbell* at 1278 (Wyo. 1995).

61. *Campbell* at 1279 (Wyo. 1995).

62. *Campbell* at 1279 (Wyo. 1995).
63. Supra, DeRolph.
64. Trial Court, Opinion—*DeRolph et al. v. Ohio*, Case No. 22043, Findings of Fact, Conclusions of Law, Order and Memorandum, at 463.
65. *DeRolph* at 464 (Ohio, 1997).
66. *DeRolph* at 463 ff. (Ohio, 1997).
67. *DeRolph*. The competencies were also cited in the supreme court decisions in Kentucky and Massachusetts. The Ohio court added competency 3 (d) and 9 through 12 (i-l), three of which address inputs, including supplies, equipment, and facilities.
68. *DeRolph* at 472 (Ohio, 1997).
69. *DeRolph* at 15 (Ohio, 1997).
70. *DeRolph* at 16 (Ohio, 1997).
71. *DeRolph* at 471 (Ohio, 1997).
72. *DeRolph* at 365 (Ohio, 1997).
73. *DeRolph* at 473 (Ohio, 1997).
74. *DeRolph* at 474 (Ohio, 1997).
75. *DeRolph* at 28 (Ohio, 1997).
76. *DeRolph*, p. 16 (Ohio, 1997).
77. *DeRolph* at 40-Remedy (Ohio, 1997).
78. *DeRolph* at 11 (Ohio, 1997).
79. 58 Ohio St.2d 368, 12 O.O.3d 327, 390 N.E.2d 813.
80. Supra, DeRolph.
81. *DeRolph* at 11-12 (Ohio, 1997).

References

Alexander, K., & Salmon, R. G. (1995). *Public school finance*. Boston: Allyn & Bacon.

Huefner, D. S. (1994, February). The mainstreaming cases: Tensions and trends for school administrators. *Educational Administration Quarterly, 30*(1), 27-55.

Kubicek, F. C. (1994, Spring). Special education reform in light of select state and federal court decisions. *Journal of Special Education, 28*(1), 27-43.

Osborne, A. G., & Dimattia, P. (1994, September). The IDEA's least restrictive environment mandate: Legal implications. *Exceptional Children, 61*(1), 6-14.

Thro, W. E. (1990). The third wave: The impact of the Montana, Kentucky and Texas decisions on the future of public school finance reform litigation. *Journal of Law and Education, 19*(2), 219-250.

Verstegen, D. A. (1994, November). The New Wave of School Finance Litigation. *Phi Delta Kappan, 76*(3), 243-250.

Verstegen, D. A., & Whitney, T. (1997). From courthouses to schoolhouses: Emerging judicial theories of adequacy and equity. *Educational Policy, 11*(3), 330-352.

American Education Finance Association Board of Directors, 1997-1998

Index

CORWIN PRESS

The Corwin Press logo—a raven striding across an open book—represents the happy union of courage and learning. We are a professional-level publisher of books and journals for K–12 educators, and we are committed to creating and providing resources that embody these qualities. Corwin's motto is "Success for All Learners."